JC YS WITH A CAMERA

Corby Steelworks, February 1982

TED READING

UNDER MY STAIRS BOOKS

First published 2018

ISBN 978-1-900467-54-4

Produced by Finial Publishing on behalf of Under My Stairs Books

Printed by Henry Ling Ltd, The Dorset Press, Dorchester, Dorset, DT1 1HD

Cast includes - not in any particular order of appearance

Pre war Kodak 620 metal box camera. 120 film 1961
Kodak 44A 127 film 1961
Kodak Retinette 1A 35mm 1961/62
Fed 2 35mm 1962/63
Mamiyaflex C20 TLR 120 film 1963/64
Zenith SLR 35mm 1964
Minolta SR1 SLR 35mm 1964 - 66
Iris's old plastic Halina 127 film 1967 - 69
Kodak Retinette 1B 35mm 1970 - 1977
Reid 35mm 1977
Pentax K1000 SLR 35mm 1977-1980
Minolta Autocord TLR 120 film 1978
Mamiyaflex C220 TLR 120 film 1979
Pentax KX SLR 35mm 1980-2008

The author acknowledges his elderly Acer Lap Top, his right index finger and the photo editing app Picasa. Save for the removal of imperfections and damage all film stock is as scanned, save a few images where I have deleted some very boring people.

The Stars of the 1979 film 'Hanover Street' Blackbush August 1978

INTRODUCTION & ACKNOWLEDGEMENTS

This being my fourth book it is, I hope, something of a companion to my previous efforts. The first two books were titled 'Point & Shoot' which summed up my photographic skills, such as they were in the 1960s. The third book 'Diesels, Depots & Oildrums' moved on to British Rails 'blue' period taking in diesel depots, workshops and much else. Looking back that was a desperate time photographing in those bland corporate days which was a pity as there was much of interest in the motive power of the day. It is only in recent years as the 'blue' fades into history people have become nostalgic about it. 'Journeys with a Camera' hopefully gives a little background to both the 1960s where I have adopted something of a autobiographical account through to the1980s where I hope to have caught a much wider slice of our railway and industrial past. Never did I think that any of my picture taking would a book make such thoughts came much later. 'Journeys...' revolves around what I was able to photograph, the pleasure being in taking the photograph. However one subject that I failed to record till later in life was to wander down to the sea, the sea and the lonely sky. Well around docks actually. So I am happy to be able to dip into what I call 'The Collection' a large mass of negatives and transparencies that have since been acquired at auctions. That the photographers are no longer with us is not in doubt and I derive some satisfaction that some of their work has appeared in print so to speak. As regards the written word I must acknowledge the help given to me by many people to many to mention and the use of good old fashioned books as well as that Lap Top thing, without which there would be no book. On the railway front a great deal of thanks go to Mike Woodhouse not only for use of his photographic collection but also for his intimate working knowledge of British Rail. As regards to my young days with the motorbikes and such like thanks go to Clive Featherstone, Peter Askey, John Durrant and Clive Wall for access to their photographic collections. My thanks go again to John Villers my publisher and to Iris the other half of 'Under My Stairs Books'. It was pure chance that we met John on a German railway adventure and chance again we got talking about book publishing. I seem to remember he only volunteered to publish the one book, I can only thank him for taking on another three. He is without doubt a man with the technology at his finger tips. Iris on the other hand has accountancy at her finger tips and by this book has now long become accustomed to me living under the stairs. When it comes to the finance Iris actually is 'Under My Stairs Books' and without her everything would descend into chaos.

Mike Woodhouse, Exmouth August 2017

Iris Reading, Paddington September 2015

Drama on the Warsaw to Berlin express.

Iris sees the funny side of Ted just mentioning to John, his publisher, about doing another book.

Early Days and memories of trains...........

As a young sprog my family lived in Shepherds Bush, West London and my Dad being self employed at the time had his workshop in nearby Chiswick. My Mother would take me over there from time to time and I have vague memories of railway level crossing gates. But no trains. On later research this line turned out to be a little used branch running from Hammersmith to Chiswick and had closed to passengers years previously. Whether my Mother realised this I do not know but it would explain the lack of trains.

At around the age of four, which would be in the late 1940's, we moved out to Greenford, Middlesex and here mother had more luck taking me to wave at passing London Transport Underground trains. Much to our delight, drivers and passengers would wave back. Mother was obviously preparing me for something.

We certainly didn't have a car and holidays were limited to one week a year which generally meant Brighton with older brother Reg, Mum, and Aunt Cis. Days out would also be enjoyed with the occasional excursion by train. On one such day out Aunt Cis bravely took the pair of us to Southend which meant Fenchurch Street station and Midland Region 2-6-4 tanks. With no pencil and paper Auntie promised me she would remember all the train numbers. Well, she didn't. What Aunt Cis was good at was for ever cleaning little boys dirty faces with her handkerchef, ...Yes, Aunt Cis firmly believed in spit and polish.

Another day out was from Greenford's little used Western Region station to the Isle of Wight for a coach trip around the Island. The coach was, according to brother Reg, a Southern Vectis Bedford OB. The highlight of the trip was being stopped by the only traffic lights on the Island, or so our driver told us. Now little things like that stay in your mind. Railway memories were confined to watching a Class O2 0-4-4T *Freshwater* pulling its red coaches along Ryde pier and a streamlined 'Merchant Navy' at the mainland dockside station. This, I presume, would have been Portsmouth, but sadly I have no idea.

The author with his Mum at Brighton in the 1950s.

Other highlights that I recall in this period was the Festival of Britain in 1951, the other being the 1953 Coronation which I had to sit and watch on our telly, a brown Bakelite box with a nine inch screen and a giant magnifying glass set up in front. I would have preferred to watch Roy Rogers and Trigger.

Greenford seemed to consist of endless well groomed 1930s semi detached houses with gardens. In those days 1930s suburbia could be posh. No cars, and you could play games in the streets. And poke your nose into dirty old pig bins. They were an early form of communal food recycling. On one occasion Dad mistakenly threw the Sunday joint into a pig bin ... when Mum went looking to cook it Dad realised what he'd done then had to retrieve it. Not pleasant, but then that joint would last all week.

Visiting my Uncles and Aunts were to be avoided at all costs other than Uncle Ted and Aunt Hilda. Living in East Finchley that meant for us a bus ride up the North Circular Road passing over the Iron Bridge at Neasden. This crossed not only the London Transport running lines but also the old Great Central main line out of Marylebone. Extensive goods yards were to be found on the left side of the North Circular whilst Neasden's locomotive shed could be seen set some distance back on the opposite side of the road.

Steam locomotives, forever a mystery to me, would be lined up in the shed yards, a permanent pall of smoke always hanging over the whole site. Neasden even had two coaling plants. Occasionally passenger trains would be seen rattling past pulled by Metropolitan Line Metro-Vick Bo-Bo electric locomotives. Not that I knew what they were at the time.

London and its trams

If visiting relatives wasn't bad enough, brother Reg and myself would be regularly dragged out on shopping expeditions up to London with Mum and Aunt Cis. I doubt we were really wanted, Dad obviously sloping off elsewhere.

Of the shops I remember little other than Gamages, a huge departmental store, which had a massive model railway on display. What also stays in my mind was the hustle and bustle of London, waiting in bus queues, boarded up bombsites and London's Underground trains, buses and trams. Truth to tell I can't actually recall seeing London's trams, more travelling on them. I think I thought them very old compared to buses. They had hard seats and you suffered a considerable amount of banging and jolting. But most strikingly of all ... they had no steering wheels! At my young age this struck me as odd. Any connection between this and the rail tracks that the trams ran on obviously passed me by. You can see here that I wasn't going to be grammar school material.

But what really attracted me about those trams was the rail tracks set in the road running all over the place with all manner of points and crossings etc.

Young I might have been but obviously a railway enthusiast in the making.

Dad takes us to Swindon Works. August 1954

Swindon Works August 1954.

It is pure chance that we visited Swindon Works in August 1954 when Roy Rossiter, my future brother-in-law also visited the Works. This trip had been organised by Roy's school and they were accompanied by a photographer from the local paper, The Middlesex County Times. Roy's photographs only came to light whilst sorting out his effects following his death. I simply love this photograph taken in the foundry for two reasons: firstly the boy standing just above the pouring ladle who is without a tie. Now what sort of mother would send her son on a trip without a tie? Unbelievable. Secondly is the lad on the extreme left with the creases in his trousers - his mother must have had the flat-iron on them!. With pen and note book at the ready his enthusiasm knows no bounds - perhaps they were casting number plates that day? My future brother-law-law stands in the back row third along from the foundryman.

(Trinity Mirror Southern)

This was to be a real highlight with Dad taking brother Reg and I to one of the regular Wednesday open days at Swindon Works. An express train journey from Paddington had me showing distinct signs of paranoia as the train roared past what would have been Reading loco sheds. All those train numbers lost to me for all time. I almost cried. From then on I dashed madly across the carriage hanging my head out of the windows determined not to miss any more train numbers till I succumbed to coal smuts in both eyes. Thank God Aunt Cis wasn't with us, she would have run out of spit and handkerchefs.

Over the passing years the tour itself has dimmed but I'm left with the impression they seemed to take you everywhere around the Works except where there were any steam locomotives. We actually lost track of the tour in the foundry. Dad being a pattern maker by trade was forever talking to the foundry men. The Foundry Manager, I think, had to rescue us to rejoin the party.

At some stage we reached 'A' Shop. My memory fails me other than the broad gauge loco *North Star* stuck up on a plinth and new build BR Standard No.77019 with the cab attached but no boiler. Poking its nose into 'A' Shop was No. 667 a little South Wales tanker. What I do remember most of all were many wire meshed wooden framed tucker boxes with one containing nothing more than a lump of smelly mouldy cheese.

Why I should remember that I do not know, but it's odd the things that stay in your mind. I think I probably felt sorry for the uneaten cheese. Well I was only nine.

Of the return journey I remember nothing other than a little tanky No.5815 shunting around Swindon station.

The tour didn't 'do' the dump so I came home disappointed and Dad came home with a headache. I don't think he was used to spending a whole day with his children.

Trainspotting, short trousers, bottles of pop and the flicks.

By the mid 1950s trainspotting with my school chum Clive Featherstone, aka Buster, occupied our tender ten years or so. We would take ourselves off to London and its mainline railway terminals where stepping up from the Underground you would be welcomed by the echos of whistles and loco exhausts reverberating around the massive train shed roofs.

Otherwise a cycle ride down to Southall would bring you to an old iron footbridge which spanned the main running lines out of Paddington. This footbridge had a spur to the loco sheds and there you were safe. Earlier spotting excursions to Jacobs Ladder footbridge at West Ealing would have the local 'Teds' throwing your ABCs and notebooks onto the tracks below.

The author (left) with Buster, Shelley Close, Greenford, c.1956.

But London's terminal stations offered you variety be it watching a maroon 'Coronation' Class Pacific *Sir William Stanier* pulling out of old Euston station or streamlined green 'A4' Pacifics lined up at the buffer stops at Kings Cross.

Over the road at St. Pancras, other than a couple of 'Jubilees' precious little ever seemed to happen other than losing all my biros over a locomotive footplate when an obliging engine crew offered me a go on the shovel.

Waterloo seemed to have the largest arrivals/departures board ever seen which forever clattered away to itself. Being Southern Region all rolling stock was green other than the odd exotic chocolate and cream Pullman car which seemed to complement every express train, be it steam or electric.

Other notable memories of that period include a 'Dukedog' 4-4-0 shunting old wooden wagons up by Southall gasworks and a quick glance of one of the last surviving 'Star' Class 4-6-0s passing by. Buster always reckoned he once saw an ROD 2-8-0 at Southall, if he did I missed it because that's something I would remember.

Of the 'new' traction I recall gas turbine locomotive No.18000 tucked away in the recesses of Platform 11 at Paddington and stylish Great Western railcars in maroon, green, and blood and custard running under the footbridge at Southall to and from the loco shed.

Those were indeed the days of short trousers, 'S' belts, bottles of pop and jam sandwiches. In those days we wandered where we pleased, subject to the limitations of our pocket money. So a couple of bob wouldn't get you far. But it would get you into the Flicks, by which I mean the pictures.

HMS Ajax and The Battle of the River Plate. The film that is.

On going to the Flicks one memorable film that sticks in my mind was 'The Battle of the River Plate'. As a young lad I loved war films and this one was a naval epic. But not only was this a war film, but a war film in colour and with real warships.

Around the age of ten or so Buster and I were quite knowledgeable about warships, much time being spent in Ealing Reference Library swotting over nearly every edition of 'Janes Fighting Ships' ever published. Even the Great War.

The film, released in 1956, recorded the events that occurred in the South Atlantic during the opening months of the Second World War.

The film had us transfixed, the dastardly Germans had the *Admiral Graf Spee*, a modern pocket battleship, albeit in the guise of an American cruiser and the good old Brits had three cruisers, *HMS Exeter*, and two sister ships *HMS Ajax* and *Achilles*. The latter warship actually reprised its role for the film. For the other two warships *HMS Jamaica* and *HMS Sheffield* stood in for the *Exeter* and *Ajax*. Both these ships had also seen action in the Second World War. They were the real thing.

Many, many years later this film was to surface in my conscience. Whilst checking through innumerable strips of negatives in what I refer to as 'The Collection'. I came across a 35mm negative of a British light cruiser. On scanning it turned out to be one of the Leander Class cruisers which totalled five ships which included the *Ajax* and *Achilles*. Of the five, one was sunk during the war, one, the *Achilles* was transferred to the Indian navy following the war and the other three *Leander*, *Orion*, and *Ajax* were all scrapped by the late 1940s.

Which one was mine ?

Hours were spent sorting through 35mm film strips to reassemble the film in frame number order and many more hours deliberating over the locations. It soon fell into place, we had two chaps taking a motorcycling holiday long long ago. The only clue came from a single negative of a trawler in harbour. It's registration was PZ. Penzance. A Cornish holiday. With the help of Google Maps locations were confirmed including one of Falmouth Docks. Our cruiser was none other than *HMS Ajax* herself, now out of commission moored in the River Fal waiting the scrap man.. A well documented event.

Our young chaps I reckoned were taking their Cornish holiday in around 1947/48. One of them was in the RAF. But as for 35mm film. That was unusual….

A sad sight. *HMS Ajax* laid up in the Fal estuary, 1947/48. Broken up by Cashmoors, Newport 1949.
(The collection)

Boys will be boys..................

Whilst Buster and I were a scruffy pair, we were not rough if you get my drift, but it has to be said that a little bit of mischief was not beyond us. Nicking pastries and cakes from the rear of the local bakers was good fun till the day the baker got wise to us and chased us half across Greenford.

Whilst possessing the usual array of small arms from pea shooters and catapults we progressed through the ranks to air pistols and knives. Even 'flick' knives. However we didn't go in for carving up cinema seats and that sort of thing. School desks were fair game though. Down some of Greenford's tougher streets it was not uncommon to find air rifles and shotguns left propped up in various corners. Even 'souvenirs' from the Second World War were par for the course.

By our early teens in the late 1950s our pocket money had increased as had the length of our trousers. Buster and I had matured into competent 'shed bashers', skilled in the art of evasion and ingenuity, more so with Buster a natural leader of men, well me anyway.

At the age of fourteen I would apply for shed permits in my best adult handwriting. A motley band of lads would then be rounded up and we would try our luck. Explaining away the absence of a suitable adult got us into Camden where at least I copped Standard Class Pacific *Duke of Gloucester*, whilst the railway police at Kings Cross threw us out permit and all. One of our band, more vocal than the rest of us, declared the railways were nationalised and belonged to the people. So, said the irate copper "Go down to head office, that being Northern House along from Kings Cross station and explain yourselves". So oft we all marched. They threw us out as well, our orator still clutching my ill gotten permit in his hand... defeated.

........and some boys could be hooligans.

Hooliganism was, as always, about, and this did extend to trainspotters. On one occasion, 1959 it was, I found myself doing Swindon Works with some of Buster's older mates. Buster himself was unable to go on this little jaunt which was a pity because we saw his last 'King' working an up train through Bath. However Buster's mates were something else, they eventually managed to push a trolley off the end of one of Swindon's platforms. If that wasn't bad enough whilst travelling onto Bristol better entertainment was to be had by hurling light bulbs from carriage windows. Not that I got involved, not me ... well perhaps only the one. However light bulbs aside, we only had enough money for a single ticket so the return journey was to be made ... with a platform ticket. To me Bristol was at the other end of the world, but its three loco sheds were a temptation not to be missed. One thing for certain, I would never have attempted it on my own.

The famous (sometimes claimed)100mph record breaking 4-4-0 *City of Truro* was residing at the rear of Bristol Bath Road shed while Barrow Road, a rather cramped square built roundhouse, held a fascinating assortment of elderly steam locomotives. These included former Midland Railway Class 2P 4-4-0s Nos.40501 & 40537, a Class 1F half cab tank loco No.41879, a Somerset & Dorset 7F 2-8-0 No.53810 but, best of all, were the two little Pugs, Nos.51217 & 51221 they being little 0-4-0 saddle tanks of the former Lancashire & Yorkshire Rly. Rare 'cops' for me, very rare 'cops' indeed.

With little money we walked back to Temple Meads station, purchased our platform tickets then to be told the best thing to do was to split up. As a 13 year old I was on my own and now in a right funk so took refuge in the toilet. Lucky for me the return trip in the carriage toilet went in record time for those were the early days of diesel hydraulic traction. With utter relief on returning to Swindon station crowds of railwaymen and others gathering round the 'Warship' class diesel loco. Seemed we had been travelling at speeds in excess of 100mph but with me in a sweat hiding in toilet I'd not noticed the speed and was just thankful to get back, but hells bells.......I'd done the ton ... on a train.

Relating this story some years later to fellow motorcyclists no one believed me that I first did the ton on a train. But it was true enough although I sort of missed out on the trainspotting bit. Might have mentioned the light bulbs though.

Push Bikes and Red Buses

For us youngsters our most prized possession was our push bikes. Otherwise known as 'treadleys'. Buster had a lightweight job built up from parts with a Reynolds 531 tubed frame, fixed wheel and two large plastic drinking bottles attached to his drop handlebars. His Mother, bless her, had a ginger beer plant and made loads of the stuff. Whilst we were cycling along one day one of the bottle corks flew out and hit him square in the eye shortly followed by the other which managed to hit him in the other. Direct hits on both counts. After that Buster lost the taste for ginger beer.

A type T single-decker photographed at Greenford on the 211 route to Ealing Broadway, c.1950s. *(Michael H C Baker)*

I drooled endlessly over brand new Claud Butler and Dawes bikes in our local cycle shop. At around fifteen pounds and fitted with drop handlebars and ten speeds they didn't come cheap. Dad wasn't impressed and eventually provided me with a sturdy gents maroon Rudge complete with Sturmy Archer three speed gearing, full chain guard and rod brakes. And steel mudguards. It weighed a ton. No doubt he thought this a proper bike for a young lad, I thought it more suited to old men, cloth caps and bicycle clips. And coppers.

Some years later, the 211 service to Ealing Broadway is now using RF type single-decker buses, again photographed at Greenford. *(Author's collection)*

I actually attempted cycling around London's loco sheds on it. Herculean efforts were required to pedal the monstrous thing along. It could be argued that it was built for comfort, speed was never a factor with the Rudge. One epic was with school chum Mike Woodhouse. Why I volunteered for this I cannot fathom because it soon became apparent that Mike being a keen cyclist took London in his stride. I certainly didn't. Then I fancy one Sunday afternoon Buster was bored and coerced me into another cycling experience to South London's loco sheds of Nine Elms and Stewarts Lane. It was 1960 and whilst Nine Elms was as busy as ever it still held scores of run down steam locos Many were dumped out in the shed yards following the electrification of the Kent coast main lines. Unknown to me it would be the last time I would see a lot of those old dears in steam … if at all.

Stewarts Lane on the other hand still had the vestiges of a main line shed, well just, and still a bugger to get in so whilst picking up our bikes round the back we managed to get thrown out. Well better that than being thrown out trying to get in. So all that remained was to pedal the Rudge home, every sodding mile back round the South Circular Road. Secretly I was glad when some bugger nicked the thing.

Other than our push bikes, getting about meant either walking or public transport. We did a lot of walking in those days. But we grew up with London Transport's red double decker RT buses which took you everywhere you wanted to go. As well as the RTs, Greenford still

Greenford to Ealing Broadway push-pull service. c.1950s. *(Dewi Williams)*

End of steam.
The new order diesel railcar at South Greenford Halt, 1962. *(Mike Woodhouse)*

played host to the old cut away cab single decker Type T's. These old dears took us to school but were eventually replaced by the more modern RF single deckers. The bus fare was a ha'penny in old money, or nothing if you could dodge the conductor which was, for us school kids, considered fair game.

Greenford station was served by both British Railways and London Transport's Underground. A local push pull service worked to Ealing Broadway. Many hours would be spent on school sport days lazing on the grass idly watching a 14XX 0-4-2T tank drifting past high on the embankment by Perivale Park pulling its two maroon auto coaches suitably named *Wren* and *Thrush*. The service was dieselised in 1958.

London Transport's Underground service was the Central Line with its red 1920s clerestory roofed period stock that could whisk you away into Central London in a fug of cigarette smoke. At night you could lie in bed listening to steam locos shunting wagons in Greenford's railway yards with freight trains working through or, if the wind was in the right direction, the ton up lads on big British motorbikes winding up along the Western Avenue till finally fading away at speed past Northolt aerodrome.

Hang up the washing on the Siegfried line

Well not quite. The picture dates to the late 1960s and captures my place of employ namely the British Bath Works, Greenford, West London. It could be said that we were not the best of neighbours and whilst some residents just accepted the factory for what it was others took umbrage to the noise and dirt. Some, newly taking up residence alongside the factory would be oblivious to what lurked at the bottom of their gardens, then created merry hell when they finally did. Bring on the washing. By stirring up the local press to highlight some of the problems living next door to what they claimed was the factory from hell they hoped to get us closed down. The local press duly obliged not that it had any effect. True enough the company did eventually take some measure to come to terms with the local residents but it would be a change in the way we lived that eventually silenced the British Bath Works.

Summer Holidays

Holidays for us was usually a one week affair at Brighton, and always at Mrs Mac Donald, No 9 Grafton Street. Corn flakes for breakfast before she chucked you out for the day, wind or shine. Year in, year out we went to Brighton. We did go to Ramsgate one year. By train. 1948 so the holiday snaps tell me. Another year, 1956, we went to Leysdown on the Isle of Sheppey.

Don't remember much of the Ramsgate holiday other than vague recollections of Victoria station, steam engines and a rusty wreck of an old war time fighter on the beach. Seemingly ignored by all and sundry.

The Leysdown holiday turned out to be novel , a week in a holiday camp. We had never done that before. I think it came cheap as I'd never had a holiday in a garden shed before. The shed even had a name, 'Malaya'. However the garden sheds were luxury compared to the caravans situated further down the field. These wretched things were the motliest collection ever seen, mostly jacked up on blocks having long lost their wheels. Further down in the long grass a few ancient wooden gypsy caravans struggled on, some even fitted with crude wooden extensions on stilts. A couple of girls had one the same week as us, Dad referring to them as the 'Lushbods'

Meanwhile the camp in the next field was the proper job with gaily painted wooded chalets and neatly trimmed grass. Poor old mum never lived it down. One bonus was a totally intact but derelict air field along the sea front which we could explore. The sentry box stood empty and silent, we just wandered in past the closed barrier.

The Brighton High Speed Trials c. 1960. Photographs courtesy Alan Hummerstone. Taken with his Halina 35mm camera. As can be seen at that time twin lanes were used and the course length was 1km.

For Brighton we occasionally travelled down by train, green electric units, again from Victoria station but usually it was by road from Greenford Broadway. Coaches would line up in the early morning opposite the War Memorial, Valiant were bright red, Venture were yellow and Southdown were green. Such would be our disappointment if our coach would be the one with the cut away cab, which meant she would be some old tub.

Brighton's sea front in those days boasted paddle steamer trips from Palace Pier.

I thought our paddle boat was named *The Brighton Belle* but sadly not, according to the Lap Top it was sunk at Dunkirk. Then we had Volks Electric Railway which ran for a mile along the coast to Black Rock. The cars were of beautifully polished wood and on their journey along actually passed through the car sheds situated mid way along the line.

Another highlight at Brighton was the High Speed Trials held along the sea front which as a young lad I witnessed on more than one occasion. Best remembered were big beautiful Bentleys in British racing green and motorcycles with silver aluminium full fairings. These would tear down Madera Drive along the front towards Black Rock. It was there that you could get up close and mingle amongst the cars and bikes. To my young eyes a remarkable sight.

At the other end of the scale there was even a working windmill up on the downs.

Sometime in the mid 1950s an open top bus ride over to nearby Newhaven would find remnants of the last war much in evidence. Rows of rusting half submerged landing craft and derelict wooden MTBs or Air Sea Rescue boats were littered along the banks of the River Ouse as we walked along a path down to the sea.

By 1959 I finally escaped Mum and Aunt Cis to spend my week up on the railway station. Bunking into the loco shed without Buster certainly tested my resolve. But I actually managed it … the once. Beautiful Class 'L' 4-4-0s were stored alongside the loco shed but now sadly out of use, their chimneys sacked over, others I was told were rumoured to be stored in the Works.

Brighton station was busy that sunny summer with a great variety of old pre-grouping Southern types still around including the old Brighton Works shunter, a Class 'A1X' Terrier tank repainted in original LB&SCRly livery.

I even took myself off on the old push and pull train to Horsham, a Class 'H' tank and two old wooden carriages. With the Horsham shed Foreman eyeing me up from his office my resolve wilted and I failed to look for alternative ways in. Buster would have been appalled.

Something the whole family shared in was witnessing 'P' Class tank loco No.31556 shunting at Shoreham Harbour. Observed from the open top deck of a yellow Brighton bus whilst passing by the docks, No.31556 would then become a 'train' number the family would never let me forget.

Further trainspotting adventures

Further travels in 1959 included an excursion with Terry Bennet, another school chum, into Southern territory. The East Kent electrification scheme was now well under way and as our gleaming new EMU pulled out of Charing Cross I actually remember feeling scruffy and somewhat out of place with the bright and breezy bucket and spade brigade. Ladies wore bright print dresses while chaps sported open neck white shirts and gray flannel trousers. No ties.

Perhaps getting on the wrong train might have had something to do with it as our train flew past our destination of Gillingham and then Faversham finally stopping at somewhere called Whitstable & Tankerton. Just where was that?. Anyway a friendly porter put us on a return stopper but we missed out Faversham as the shed was empty and on bunking into Gillingham we got thrown out with only three locos on shed.

Travelling on to Tonbridge via Strood and Paddock Wood proved interesting enough. From Strood our modern day traction went only as far as Maidstone West when we changed to an antiquated steam train. A venerable Class 'H' 0-4-4 tank then continued onto Paddock Wood puffing through the beautiful sunny Kent countryside with a pair of elderly wooden coaches in tow. We, I fancy, were the only passengers. Onwards to Tonbridge I cannot recall but by compensation for the day's lack of steam Tonbridge shed was busy enough and as a bonus held a decrepit Class 'O1' 0-6-0 No.31258, easily recognised by its outside framed tender. Further excitement was to come for taking us onwards to Redhill we were pulled by a Class 'L' 4-4-0, whilst on finally passing Redhill shed we noted several 'Schools' Class locos in the yards. Sadly we had run out of time to pay a visit.

The following year, 1960, I found myself again heading into Southern territory only this time heading

Day trip to the south east with Terry Bennet, Summer 1959.
Top: Class 'H' No.31517 at Maidsone West which pulled us to Paddock Wood.
Middle: Class 'Q1' No.33037 on Tonbridge loco shed.
Bottom: Class 'O1' No.31258 on Tonbridge shed, photographed by Mike Woodhouse the following year.

A day out to Bournemouth, June 1960. Mr. Ferathersone on his 650cc Ariel Huntmaster sidecar outfit on which he took us down to Bournemouth and Eastleigh.

down Bournemouth way riding pillion to Buster's Dad on his motorcycle combination. To Buster and I this meant only one thing, Eastleigh and Bournemouth loco sheds. Buster had been relegated to the sidecar with Mum as I was too tall to squeeze in the back. This was the first time I'd been on a motorcycle and clung on to Buster's Dad for grim death. I doubt he realised it.

Buster's Dad was a motorcycle enthusiast and within a few years I was to develop that condition myself. It was not unknown for him to swap engines at the drop of a hat whipping out a 500cc single to drop in the 650cc twin if he felt the occasion warranted it.

It was a warm sunny June day and of Bournemouth loco I remember little other than it was very busy with Pacific classes and the shed yard displayed a large sign requesting engine crews to keep their charges quite. Fat chance.

Eastleigh shed was by comparison extremely spacious but totally dead. Perhaps Sundays at Eastleigh were quiet days. Lines of locos, mainly Southern classes, were out of steam at the rear of the depot including many on the scrap line which ran alongside the perimeter fence by Eastleigh airfield. From where, I might add, the prototype Spitfire first flew some twenty four years previous. Included in the scrap line that day were several withdrawn class 'T9' 4-4-0s, still graceful locomotives despite their now care-worn condition.

As Buster's Dad would no doubt occupy himself doing a plug chop or adjusting chains or some such thing, Buster's Mum would be waiting so we though it better to bunk around the shed with me shouting out the numbers and Buster scribbling them down. Trouble was although I could see the locos alright it was the numbers I had a problem with. Buster couldn't believe it declaring I must be as blind as a bat.

It has to be said that I was becoming aware of a rapid defiency in the eye ball department. Something not to own up to as I gravitated from the rear of the classroom, my natural habitat, to the front.

'Lord Nelson' class No.30860 *Lord Hawke*, photographed the following year outside Eastleigh loco shed with my Kodak 44A box camera.

So my remaining school days were then spent in dread of eyesight tests and that fate worse than death, being prescribed NHS spectacles. The fact that I couldn't read the blackboard didn't do much for my education but better that than suffer the serious physiological damage of being branded 'four eyes' by my peers. Then to cap it all, having managed to dodge all the eye sight tests that school could throw at me, I fell foul at my first company eye test so was reduced to the dreaded National Health spectacles anyway. But the up side was that the world became a lot clearer, especially when riding the bike and I could actually see through a camera viewfinder. Well it does help. And with the likes of Buddy Holly and Michael Caine now making glasses fashionable with their thick black rimmed frames nobody called you 'four eyes' any more.

Moped mania

Make mine a moped

Top: This Raleigh moped was not mine but lives on at the Launceston Steam Museum.
Middle: A touch of speed, John Durrant on Paul's NSU Quickly. Man and moped in perfect harmony.
Lower: The quest for speed, Paul's NSU Quickly with handlebars upside down racing style.

That the motorbike would come my way was inevitable. It's 1961, and now being a working lad, any interest I once had in buses evaporated when having to use them on a daily basis. No wonder two wheels looked attractive, no more waiting in queues for crowded buses for me. That's when they turned up that is.

With Buster already roaring around on a 650cc BSA Super Rocket my introduction to two wheels was far more modest, a hand-me-down moped care of older brother Reg. With pedals to get it started I thought that if the thing broke down I could pedal it home till the day it did … and no you can't.

Manufactured by Raleigh of push bike fame, it was both gray in colour and appeal, coming fully equipped with matching plastic leg shields, full screen and two large pannier bags.

Getting it going required some physical effort. By furiously pedalling along, the engine, all 49cc of it, would fire up producing clouds of billowing blue smoke as you went on your way.

An extremely practical but totally unstylish PVC two piece riding suit which went under the name of the 'Black Prince' came with it. Wellington boots, thick white woollen navy socks and a silver crash helmet fitted with the then revolutionary spinning turbo visor completed the outfit.

I looked anything but a black prince. A complete nerd would be nearer the mark.

The Black Prince was finally disposed of when my Dad's old fur lined sheepskin coat came my way. I thought it had a bit of dash. Totally useless for motorcycling as the wind blew straight through it and when it came on to rain … As for the revolutionary spinning turbo visor, well that eventually spun off one day never to be seen again.

Motorcycling came to school chum Peter Askey with some difficulty. Overcoming considerable parental opposition Peter eventually settled for a little blue 125cc Honda Benly. She was one of the early Japanese breed of motorcycles imported into the country with a pressed steel 'monocoque' frame and forks a square headlight and indicators etc.

Talk about a laugh nobody could take these tin plate Japanese bikes seriously. However the little Honda had a turn of speed that would put a British machine of double the capacity to shame.

And brakes to match.

Then the inevitable happened. Perhaps by word of mouth, I forget, other lads on all manner of

It's 1962 and Paul Wells and John Durrant pose on Geoff Ward's duel seat NSU 50cc Quickly at Feltham loco shed. If the poor dear had to cope with these two for any length of time she would soon be reduced to a very slow Quickly.

Ah, the old Turbo Visor, something else best forgotten. *(Courtesy John Durrant)*

bikes appeared on the scene, several still being shed bashers such as us. Life took on a new dimension, you could say we were now a gang. We became 'The Rabble'.

We rode a motley collection of machines. Whilst I had just progressed from my Raleigh moped to a 250cc Zundapp Trophy Peter Askey had his hard-won 125cc Honda Benly. The rest of the gang rode an assortment of machines. With Geoff Ward and Paul Wells still on their NSU mopeds they found themselves desperately flat out everywhere we went, Paul was even reduced to turning his handlebars upside down racing style in a desperate last bid for more speed. Whilst the mopeds could managed 35mph or so John Durrant rode a stylish red 50cc Honda which was no moped and could touch 50mph while Clifford Dart alias 'Deem' rode a traditionally British BSA Bantam. With Peter and John on four stroke Hondas the rest of us rode two strokes which back then required lubricating oil to be physically added to the fuel tank. With the ever present fear of two stroke engine seizure one worked on the basis that too much oil was preferable to too little which resulted in a blue haze following us everywhere we went. Motley bikes they may have been but we all had aspirations for more powerful machines which by coincidence occurred along with the decline in steam, and our interest in it.

With John acquiring his 50cc Honda his old NSU Quickly moped was quickly reduced to becoming our local 'off road' dump bike. Its final fate was to be chucked into the cut as was its eventual replacement Paul's 197cc Francis Barnet which he now had no use for. Caught speeding on it didn't warrant a driving ban but a little matter of no MOT, no road tax and no insurance didn't help matters. Greenford's dump was a long disused and heavily overgrown mountain of Londons old rubbish which skirted the Grand Union canal along with a vast area of waste land which once provided hutted accommodation for local war workers. By the 1960s it had became one vast playground for the young and not so young to get up to all manner of fun and mischief. The dump was also home to Greenford's wildlife which teemed with slow worms and adders many of which once captured went home in a jam jar. Today (2017) it's a vast housing estate so no more slow worms, adders or off road motorbikes.

Journeys with a camera - a beginning.

Early experiences 'under the stairs'

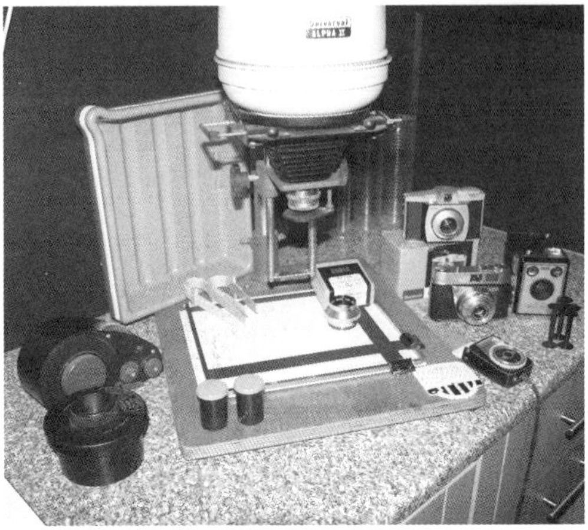

Typical 1960s photographic kit, mostly my own.

Photography was not a part of my family's everyday life. Taking pictures was viewed as some form of mystic art and accompanied with a degree of uncertainty as to whether the pictures would come out or not. Our family camera was an elderly primitive metal Kodak box brownie. Loading film into it was a trial in itself. With only eight exposures it was not surprising that it only appeared on holidays. My parents couldn't really be bothered with it.

Then one sunny Sunday in December 1960 my life was to be turned upside down when Buster up's and does the impossible and turns up on a cycle ride over to Feltham loco shed... with a camera. A modern shapely plastic job care of his Mum and Dad.

Busters pictures, proudly distributed around class 4B, were impressive as not only did they all come out but I featured in about half of them. I'd hardly ever seen myself in photographs before. The thought of taking my own pictures had never entered my head but it wasn't long before I had Dad loading the families box brownie with film and I was soon on my way to Old Oak Common to have a crack at this railway photography business. Waiting impatiently for a week whilst Boots the Chemist processed the film the result was beyond all my expectations. All my eight pictures came out. I thought them incredibly good.

A camera-less author, top, posing in front of Class 'G16' No.30494 at Feltham loco shed in December 1960, whilst the lower picture shows the author some four years later at Old oak Common, armed to the teeth with both 35mm and roll film cameras.

A few months later I was left a little money which was burning a hole in my pocket so I rushed out and bought a swish modern plastic Kodak 44A camera similar to Busters. On proudly showing this to school chum Peter

Askey I could see he wasn't overly impressed. And he was two years younger than me. What would he know?.

But Peter's Dad Frank would, he being a keen amateur photographer. Shaking his head on presenting it to him sort of gave me a clue. It came as a box set including a flash. That didn't help either. The chap at the photography shop said it was the ideal camera for me as I handed over the money. He obviously held me in low esteem. Dear old Frank was right, it did little to improve my photography and what little it did do was only with the help of the sun.

Eventually under Franks guidance Peter and I learnt the mysteries of the dark room be that loading films under the stairs or printing pictures in the suitably 'blacked out' kitchen.

With steam in rapid decline taking endless close up photographs of locomotives became an obsession and a 'point & shoot' philosophy evolved which virtually overshadowed all else. Peter realised much sooner than I the importance of capturing steam's last fling on the main line. Any lack of artistic creativity and an inability to capture steam in its environment never stunted our desire for better cameras. For that I thank hire purchase.

By the time the 'New Approach' to railway photography came into vogue we were well away with the motorbikes.

Box camera snaps.
First photographic efforts taken by myself with the family's old pre-war 620 Box Brownie, Old Oak Common, January 1961.

Left: The author and Peter Askey photographing a London-bound train hauled by No.5026 *Criccieth Castle* north of Oxford, May 1963. This picture was taken by Peter's Dad, Frank and originates from a heavily degraded colour transparency.

Below: My resulting picture.

Fratton Loco shed - an enigma. 1962 - 64

Fratton loco shed closed in 1959. Well it certainly ceased to exist in my Ian Allan ABCs. And that, as far as I was concerned, was that. That is until a shed bash down Eastleigh way in October 1961. This excursion had been organised by myself, permits included, to catch the last remaining withdrawn Class 'T9' 4-4-0s. I had missed them at Exmouth Junction loco shed some months before and wanted to catch up with them at Eastleigh prior to scrapping. Only I failed. They had been hauled over to Eastleigh from Exmouth Junction during the summer and spent, unusually, only a matter of weeks on 'scrap row' at the rear of the loco shed prior to scrapping. Just my luck.

Class 'M7' No.30245 (w/d 11/62), 26th July 1964.

Class 'Q' No.30538 (w/d 7/63), 26th July 1964.

Class '0298' No.30587 (w/d 12/62), 26th July 1964.

Anyway whilst wandering round Eastleigh shed we got into conversation with some local lads and the subject of Fratton loco shed came up.

To our surprise they reliably informed us that whilst I had thought the shed long closed it was anything but with the Hayling Island branch 'A1X' Terrier tanks permanently stabled there. As we already had Southampton Docks and Salisbury in our sights, we gave Fratton a miss but on our next run down Eastleigh way in February 1962 we paid Fratton a visit. The shed was a single square built roundhouse which had suffered badly in the Second World War and for one thing lacked anything in the way of smoke troughs. This was just as well as the majority of the fifteen steam loco's 'on shed' were out in the yards and included three of the little 'A1X' Terrier tanks. Surprisingly tucked away inside the shed were two locomotives, 'King Arthur' No.30777 and a 'L1' No.31757, both having been withdrawn in late 1961. In fact the 'King Arthur' had been on the scrap line at Eastleigh back in October 1961. We came to the conclusion that they had been placed there in store for possible preservation, sadly no pictures were possible inside since it was nearly dusk by the time we arrived.

Paging forward some fifty plus years, on researching for this article I was surprised to find when delving through back issues of the 'Railway Observer' the first reference to preserved locomotives in storage at Fratton was on the 11th February 1962. Then I remembered it was I who had actually sent off the report to the 'RO' in the first place.

Any preservation plans for No.31757 were sadly to fail as, whilst she was still there in May 1962, she had been scrapped at Eastleigh by early 1963, being the last of the class to go.

Our next visit to Fratton was in April 1963, eleven locos were in steam out in the yards with a single 'A1X' Terrier tank residing inside the roundhouse. Their tenure at Fratton was coming to an end as the Hayling Island branch would close at year's end. Stored around the turntable were now withdrawn locos 'M7' No.30245, 'King Arthur' No.30777, 'Lord Nelson' No.30850, two 'Schools' Nos.30925/26, 'Z' class No 30952 and 'U' class No.31610. Both the 'King Arthur' and 'Lord Nelson' had been separated from their tenders which were stored on a separate road. By July 1963 two Class '0298s' Nos.30586/7 had joined the others around the turntable, although by August 1963 both 30586 and 31610 were back at Eastleigh for scrapping.

'Lord Nelson' class No.30850 (w/d 8/62) and 'King Arthur' class No.30777 (w/d 10/61), 14th April 1963.

'Schools' class No.30926 (w/d 12/62) 26th July 1964.

'Z' class No.30952 (w/d 11/62) 26th July 1964.

January 1964 saw 'T9' Nos.120(30120) and 'Q' Class No.30538, both withdrawn the previous July, joining what was now something of an impressive collection of Southern Railway locomotives at Fratton. Sixteen other locos were out in the yards, nine in steam, the others all out of use. By the 26th July the 'King Arthur' and the 'Lord Nelson' had moved out into the yards having now been reunited with their tenders.

However Fratton's tenure as a museum store was soon to come to an end, as during September 1964 firstly Nos.30245, 30587, and 30850 were towed away to Stratford Works to be shortly followed by 120, 30777, and 30925, leaving only Nos.30538, 30926 and 30952.

By 1965 No.30926 had found her way back to Eastleigh and eventually preservation across the pond in America only to return to the UK many years later. Nos.30538 and 30952 were not to be so lucky. No.30538 had been scrapped by the end of 1964 whilst the attempt to preserve No.30952 had failed and it was scrapped in January 1965 the last of the class to survive.

Stabling of steam locomotives continued throughout 1964/65 with occasional use into 1966, by which time the shed was now roofless.

Fratton loco actually closed in 1967 and was demolished two years later. Whilst much of this article comes from our own records, a note of thanks goes to the RCTS magazine 'The Railway Observer' which has proved to be invaluable.

Three Snaps at Stratford April 1962

Works shunters. Class J69 Nos. 45 & 44.

Class B12 No. 61572.

Class J15 No. 65457.

Coming across just three pictures taken at Stratford in early 1962 and scratching my head wondering why only three on checking my albums soon revealed negatives numbered 34, 35, & 36. I had run out of film. All photographers regret missed opportunities and this was one of mine. But greater than not having any more films was failing to record anything on the Eastern region when I still just had a chance to do so. Everything I photographed in the dying days of steam during the 1960s was on the Western Region with a smattering of Southern. This was not the case when Buster and I started shed bashing around London in the late 1950s as we paid our respects to all the Eastern Region sheds Stratford included. On arriving at LT's Stratford Central Line station, the tube train would have climbed rapidly out of its tunnel before shooting into the daylight and good clean fresh air. My gaze would then always go northwards across the main BR running lines into the far distance and look down upon a divergence of railway lines with a huddle of old railway buildings in-between including the rear of the Works corrugated tin loco shed. Stretching away in one direction would always be a line or so of dead rusting steam locomotives their numbers too far to be seen. Many of these locos would have lost their coupling rods while others were tenderless or even lacked their boilers. All would be withdrawn, some actually in the process of being dismantled. Back on my platform I could only stand transfixed and stare with utter frustration not only because their numbers eluded me but that the unseen loco sheds and all else did as well. Meanwhile Buster had sized up the situation. Stepping down to the little used Low Level station we literally walked off the end of the platform through the adjacent tunnel under the main running lines above. With that line up of withdrawn steam locomotives ever closer we sidled up to the nearby junction signal box and on looking up and not seeing the signal man made our dash across the running lines and kept on running till we made the security of that old tin clad loco shed. At that point you knew you were in, all you had to do then was stay in. For two 14 year old boys this was pure Commando stuff. Several visits were made to Stratford through 1959 and 1960 and in that time despite a new diesel depot being built on part of the steam shed site something in the region of 400 steam locomotives would easily be seen. Back to April 1962 on what would be my last unofficial visit to Stratford my companion on this occasion was Peter Askey and presumably we made our usual way in. The top picture features the old tin clad Works shed whilst the lower two pictures were taken in the dispersed yards whilst making our way to the loco shed proper. On this visit Stratford loco sheds and yards had thinned out dramatically with only 55 steam loco's present the largest classes being represented by nine B1s, eleven L1 tanks and eight J15s. Diesels numbered seventy one. Stratford closed to steam the following year.

End of the 'Kings' - a trainspotter's reflection. 1962-64

Greenford, West London was situated in Western Region territory of British Railways, the descendants of the Great Western Railway, otherwise known as God's Wonderful Railway. For young trainspotters such as us this was important. It meant we were Great Western enthusiasts. This would be compulsory. Therefore its steam engines were the finest ever built. So for that reason the 'King' class locos were the finest express locomotives ever. Over the years we had certainly seen plenty of them either at Paddington or in action passing Southall and Greenford heading express trains West or up to the Midlands.

'King' class No.6000 *King George V* at Old Oak Common loco shed, August 1962.

On taking up shed bashing with Buster, Old Oak Common became another second home and we had soon copped the lot. After that you took them for granted.

On a Home Counties Railway Club overnight trip to Liverpool during the winter of 1960 we were pulled by a 'King' from a cold misty Paddington station as far as Wolverhampton Low Level station. Here in the early hours of the morning we changed motive power for a 'Castle', but so blasé had I become I failed to show any interest in the locos concerned. Why bother, I'd copped all my 'Kings' and 'Castles'. Of interest, the return working from Liverpool Lime Street was by a maroon 'Princess' which eventually got us back to Euston at three o'clock on a Monday morning. With no such things as mobile phones and few people owning a landline telephone, by the time I arrived home my mother was about to report me missing to the police.

Even on starting to take my own pictures I was never concerned in capturing the 'Kings' on film. With an old metal Kodak box camera and eight exposures per film, and dependant on the sun, you had to be right choosey as to what you photographed. Anyway the 'Kings' would be around for ever. Wouldn't they?

But things were to change rapidly. I should have taken heed, January 1962, saw two beautiful 'Princess' Class Pacifics dumped outside Willesden roundhouse with chimneys sacked over and plates removed.

'King' class No.6028 *King George Vi* at Old Oak Common loco shed, July 1962.

No.6014 *King Henry VII* passing Greenford station, August 1962.

‘King’ class No.6011 *King James I* at Old Oak Common loco shed, September 1962.

A visit to Swindon Works in 14th February 1962 found Nos.6011 and 6018 in 'A' Shop with No.6012 outside in the yard. Unbeknown to me at the time these were to be amongst the last 'Kings' to receive a classified repair at Swindon Works. A further visit on 11th March found, for the first time, no 'Kings' being overhauled in Works with only No.6006 outside in the yard alongside the main line. That it had been withdrawn in February I did not realise till later. The real portent for the future was seeing, for the first time, a 'Castle' on the dump. She was No.5069. Both of these locomotives did not linger although the 'Castle's' boiler returned to Works for re-use. Within a few months the summer of 1962 was upon us and we would see the start of mass withdrawals of the 'Kings'. I was to be caught napping.

'King' class No.6006 *King George I*, Swindon Works March 1962.

June 1962 saw British Railways Standard 2-6-4 tank locomotives being placed in temporary store at Old Oak Common from Plaistow. By 22nd July these had been joined by a single line of nine GW types stored out in the shed yards along by the coaling plant. These included 'Kings' Nos.6020 and 6029, both withdrawn that month and both initially retaining their name and number plates. By the 12th August they had been joined out in the yard by a recently withdrawn No.6009 with Nos.6025 and 6028 and 'Castle' No.7020 being stored in the former Western Pullman/carriage sheds. These locos I was reliably informed had been placed in store to cover diesel failures through the summer timetable. For that reason they all retained their name and number plates.

A few weeks later, 26th August, another visit to Swindon Works confirmed it was nearly all up for the GW express locomotives. Whilst three 'Castles' were 'in Works', outside presented a different story with long lines of recently withdrawn locos including eight 'Castles' and two 'Kings', Nos.6023/24. These two had recently arrived from storage at Cardiff Canton and still retained their name and number plates. On the dump were Nos.6004/8/13 and these lasted a few more months being cut up during October and November 1962.

A visit to Wolverhampton (Stafford Road) on the 23rd September found recently withdrawn 'Kings' Nos.6001/2/7 on shed and Nos.6012/14/15/17/22 stored out in the yard alongside one of the loco shed's perimeter walls. Although their chimneys were sacked over they all retained their name and number plates. None of these 'Kings' would ever see Swindon again, being scrapped by Cox & Danks at Oldbury throughout 1963.

On that same day No.6027 was out of steam and in need of some repairs at Banbury whilst No.6016 was stored at Leamington Spa. Both locomotives were withdrawn that month and also found their way to Cox and Danks scrap yards at Oldbury.

One week later, on the 29th September, Old Oak Common's dump had increased to twenty eight locomotives including 'Kings' Nos.6010//20/21/29 and eight 'Castles' stored alongside the coalier with Nos.6009/19/26 and two 'Castles' alongside the Grand Union Canal. Nos.6025 & 6028 remained in the former Pullman/carriage sheds although they were never required to cover diesel failures. However 'Castle' No.7020 did return to revenue earning service. Many of the stored 'Kings' at Old Oak Common could now be referred to as dumped although they were still fully coaled up. Whilst Nos.6025 & 6028 still retained their name and number plates all the others had had their plates removed, save Nos.6009/19 which retained their smoke box number plates. Perhaps they were found impossible to shift. However in the meantime No.6010 had suffered a further indignity in having lost its copper capped chimney, believed to have been stolen.

Following the September withdrawals only Nos.6000/5/11/18/25 remained 'on the books' and these were all withdrawn in November/December 1962. I can only recall seeing Nos.6000/5/11 in steam at Old Oak Common through this period. No.6025 was still stored along with No.6028 in the former Pullman/carriage sheds, but even she, No.6025, had departed for Swindon by the 24th November 1962.

Two more visits were made to Swindon in 1962, on the 11th November and the 16th December. Nos.6008/13/23/24/26 were noted on the dump in November with No.6013 being cut up that month and Nos.6023/24 having departed for a South Wales scrap yard leaving only Noa.6008/26 by December. Interestingly, No.6008 still retained its nameplates. By that December visit the recently withdrawn No.6000 itself was languishing in the locomotive shed.

'King' class No.6000 *King George V* residing in Swindon loco shed, December 1962.

On the 2nd December 1962 No.6011, withdrawn that month, was noted stored at Didcot.

Of interest to me was that No.6025 had departed Old Oak Common by the 24th November but was not present on my visit to Swindon Works on the 16th December 1962. However she was recorded by the 'Railway Observer' magazine as being at Swindon on the triangle on the 27th January 1963. In the interim period either she had stopped of *en route* or I had failed to recorded her on the 16th December.

Throughout 1963 Old Oak Common's locomotive dump remained steady at 25 to 30 locos with stored locos also now being scattered around inside the shed itself. On the 19th January 1963 Nos.6005/10/20/28 were resident, with No.6020 going by June, No.6010 by October and No.6005 by December, leaving No.6028 as the lone survivor into 1964 now languishing outside the former Pullman sheds.

Swindon Works was visited twice in 1963, on the 26th May and the 22nd September. The May visit produced No.6000 inside 'A' Shop stripped of name and number plates with a further four 'Kings' outside in the Works yard including Nos.6025 & 6026 parked up as a tender-less pair, but likewise stripped of plates whilst Nos.6011 & 6018 still retained their full regalia.

Perhaps as a act of defiance No.6018 which had recently worked the 28th April SLS Special was lined up along the main line resplendent with her name and number plates, save the smoke box plate, her buffer beam bearing the inscription 'No 6018' in Great Western style.

For passing travellers gazing out of their train carriage windows the spring of 1963 would have been the last time at least two 'Kings' would be seen fully dressed outside Swindon's 'A' Shop.

By September No.6000 had joined Nos.6011/25/26 outside in the yard, No.6018 having just been cut up. No.6011 had by now lost its name and number plates. No 'Kings' were on the dump on either visit. Swindon cut up No.6026 in November 1963 with No.6011 going in January 1964.

Following this visit and reading about problems with No.6000 I wondered, as did others, whether

The last 'King' in the London area.
'King' class No.6028 (w/d 11/62) dumped at the rear of Southall loco shed.
The tender bears the legend 'Balls to Beeching'. March 1964.

No.6000 and 6018 had swapped identities.

With closure of Old Oak Common to steam now imminent, the bulk of the stored locomotives had been cleared and by the 26th January 1964 only six remained. 'King' No 6028 and the majority of the other locos had by then been towed to Southall forming a large dump at the rear of the loco shed. She was still present on 7th June but had gone with all but two of the other locos by 26th July 1964, being the last 'King' to survive in the London area. She was finally cut up in August of that year by private contractors in South Wales. Meanwhile my last record of stored steam at Old Oak was on the 11th April 1964 with Nos.4701, 5060/70, 5919, 7009/15/27 being present but they also were soon on their way to Southall.

Swindon Works was visited again on the 2nd February 1964 the only 'Kings' being present were Nos.6000 and 6025 in the Works yard, with No.6010 on the dump. No.6025 was cut up in May 1964.

Two more visits to Swindon Works were made in 1964, on 5th July and 8th November, and produced only the sorry site of No.6010 on the dump. She had been withdrawn in June 1962 and had survived some two and a half years before finally being cut up in February 1965. Perhaps someone didn't want her to go.

Whilst proof reading this article my chum Mike Woodhouse took a somewhat academic approach and recorded all the 'King's that I had noted down. Seemingly all of them … except one No.6003 it seems. This I failed to appreciate, I had obviously not come across this particular locomotive so had better add that she was withdrawn in June 1962 and was scrapped at Swindon a few months later.

The last of the 'Kings' to be scrapped, No.6010 (w/d 6/62) on Swindon Works dump, November 1964, and a sorry sight she looks.

'King' class Nos.6021 and 6020 (both w/d 7/62), Old Oak Common, September 1962. *(P Askey)*

Withdrawn 'Kings' stored out of use.

Top: No.6017 *King Edward IV* (w/d 7/62) on Wolverhampton Srafford Road loco shed, September 1962. Lower: Nos.6026 and 6019 (both w/d 9/62) at Old Oak Common loco shed, September 1962.

1962 - The end of the 'Kings'

'King' class locomotives Nos.6024 and 6023, having recently arrived on the West Pond site at Barry Island, March 1963.

Excursions to Barry Dump 1962-1964

Woodham Bros was an old established company working in the scrap business at Barry Docks. They initially became involved in railway work scrapping wagons but commenced taking on locomotives in 1959, initially from Swindon Works. These locos were scrapped fairly quickly on a site near to Barry locomotive works and the Docks pumping house. As the number of redundant steam locos increased, storage commenced from 1961 onwards utilising the former West Pond site which had been infilled following the Second World War.

Barry Docks opened between 1889 and 1898, and prior to the Great War was the UK's largest exporter of coal with over one hundred miles of sidings feeding forty five rail connected hydraulic hoists for tipping coal direct from rail wagons into waiting ships below.

Class 45XX No.4561 and other former GW types complete with cabside numberplates, March 1963.

My own introduction to Barry goes back to the 14th October 1962 during a rather tortuous train spotting trip to South Wales with one 'Ban the Bomb Bob'. In those days Barry Dump wasn't the great attraction that it would later become, you didn't go to South Wales for Barry Dump as it was just another loco dump amongst many that were springing up in the 1960s.

Bob and I had met up at Old Oak Common a few months previous to this South Wales epic. Bob was a character, politically motivated, an idealist, a rebel in a Donkey jacket and steel toe capped boots. Not at first glance what a trainspotter should look like. Bob also believed in free transport for the masses, he didn't 'do' public transport so he hitch hiked everywhere he went.

As an aside 'Ban the Bomb Bob' was to come up in conversation many years later whilst talking to a chum about cameras that I had owned. Having once purchased a brand new Russian Fed 2 camera my chum having had a long career in the MOD informed me that back in the 1960s the Russians took particular interest in people purchasing their goods especially cameras. They would through their agencies employ low grade operatives to check out if such purchasers had Communist leanings. That I had met up with Bob a few months after buying the Fed 2 made me think. Was 'Ban the Bomb Bob' a low grade Communist operative checking me out for left wing tendencies. He was, without doubt, an active left winger … but an informer?. Sadly he would have little to inform about me. But interesting don't you think?

Anyway getting back to the plot, following an early morning start Bob and I arrived at Gloucester and its loco sheds some twelve hours later, by which time I reckoned we must have walked most of the way. Being near to the railway station my feet kindly informed me that they had had enough so we travelled onwards to Cardiff by train, a 41XX Prairie tank if I remember correctly. Somewhat exhausted we kipped down in one of Cardiff General station's waiting rooms. Bob already knew that if you held a valid ticket the station staff couldn't chuck you out so we had purchased tickets up to Cardiff Radyr. But that didn't stop the police waking you up every hour. By about one o'clock in the morning and getting a bit fed up, we walked round to Canton shed to find it half demolished. A pannier tank No.5749 was in light steam with chains attached being used as a wrecking loco.

'Western' class diesels were stabled in the carriage sheds. Back at the station waiting room and unable to sleep we caught the first early morning train up to Radyr. This comprised of a 56XX tank and two carriages, the guards van holding half a dozen pigs. We woke the Radyr Shed Foreman, permit in hand, who much to his credit loaned us a railway lamp to jot down the loco numbers in the yard. After more adventures 'on the road' and, much to Bob's approval, we wormed our way into Caerphilly Works and evaded the Cardiff Dock police to bunk into East Dock shed. We finally arrived at Barry on a dull miserable Sunday afternoon. A short walk from the loco shed bought you to an area of flat infilled land known as the West Pond site which stretched from the oil terminus near to Number One Dock to the Barry Island railway viaduct. Twenty eight ex-Great Western tank locomotives occupied a few of the many sidings there, the locomotives themselves being generally in good order with many still retaining their cast number plates.

Due to the contraction of the railway industry at that time Woodham's put the scrapping of locomotives to one side, concentrating on wagons of which there seemed an inexhaustible supply.

The prospect of hitch hiking back home on a Sunday evening was too much for me.

After a long tiring day on Saturday and very little sleep I was done for ... so I went home by train curling up in the corner of a compartment and sleeping most of the way home. Bob on the other hand hitch hiked all the way back home.

Top: Barry dump, West Pond area. Bottom: The High Ground site. Both June 1964

As a weekend it had had its moments, taking in some 400 steam locos at nine loco sheds as well as Barry dump and Caerphilly Works. But many 'photographic opportunities' were missed, such as the demolition of Cardiff Canton loco shed due to the lateness of the year and the vagaries of hitch hiking. With three loco sheds visited in total darkness and others at dusk. I finally realised that I was now more interested in taking pictures of locos than taking their numbers. And to cap it all some months later I lost most of the negatives.

Some six months later on the 2nd/3rd March 1963 I returned to Barry on a sunny weekend shed bash with an organised party doing the South Wales sheds. At least this time I had the luxury of rail and coach travel. And a night in a B&B. As far as the dump was concerned just three locomotives had joined the ranks, another tanky and to my surprise two 'Kings' Nos.6023/24 which had only recently arrived.

'Jubilee' class No.45690 resides alongside the former Barry Railway locomotive works. June 1964.

However by the time of my next visit to South Wales on the 21st June 1964 things had changed. Woodham's had acquired many more steam locos and these were now to be found not only in the West Pond site but also around the former Barry Railway Locomotive Works, the docks pump house and No 1 Dock itself.

The Locomotive Works had closed in 1959 but had continued with wagon repairs until final closure in 1963.

Not only had the Great Western locomotive numbers rapidly increased they had been joined by five Southern Moguls, an S&D 2-8-0 and a Midland 'Jubilee', some of the latter examples being lined up alongside the now closed Wagon Works.

Shortly after this visit the former Works were demolished.

This trip was accomplished on my motorbike, travelling overnight to South Wales enjoying a beautiful sun rise riding the twisty road down from Gloucester through Chepstow and onto Newport and Cardiff.

Following Barry and bunking into Cardiff and Newport loco sheds by day's end I was tired and convinced that on the journey back I actually fell asleep on the bike whilst following a tanker. Riding as pillion was Colin who worked in Kelvin studios, Greenford's local photographers. Colin had relatives up the South Wales valleys and as he was keen to briefly see them so he came along for the ride. But taking Colin was not a good idea as he had never been on a solo motorbike in his life. He knew nothing of 'going with the bike' into corners so initially he caused me some hairy wobbles. Anyway he soon learnt but I never told him of my sleeping episode on the return ride.

Barry Railway locomotive works following demolition.
'Jubilee' class No.45690 remains in the same position. (*P Askey*).

And as for Barry Docks, whilst hundreds of steam locomotives were rescued from Woodham's yard none of the hydraulic coal hoists, the reason for Barry Docks existence, were deemed worthy of preservation.

Longhedge Works, Battersea, May 1963

Longhedge Locomotive and Carriage Works was opened by the London, Chatham & Dover Railway in the early 1860s, the nearby locomotive sheds opening at the same time. The Works were expanded over the following twenty five years becoming a very tight site, criss-crossed by railway viaducts and bordered by existing roads and railways alike. The northern part of site undertook locomotive work and the southern part concentrated on carriages, whilst the running sheds, which were considerably rebuilt in the 1880s, were situated to the east of the Works. The whole site inherited its name from a former farm on the site.

The London, Chatham & Dover amalgamated with the South Eastern in 1899 to form the South East & Chatham Railway. Longhedge Works was then wound down in favour of the former SERly Works at Ashford, Kent, locomotive construction ceasing at Longhedge in 1904 and heavy repairs in 1911. The Pullman Company then took over the carriage works till the late 1920s when they moved to Preston Park, Brighton whilst the locomotive works continued with light engine repairs. With the closure of the nearby Battersea Park loco shed in the early 1930s all of its allocation was transferred to Longhedge which from then on became known as Stewarts Lane. The old carriage works on the southern side of the site were then partially cleared and over the years redeveloped and extended as EMU carriage sheds the depot remaining in active use today. The locomotive works were to suffer a different fate with engine repairs eventually ceasing at some time the old buildings then falling into disuse. It is possible that some parts of the old works were rented out for commercial use. By the time of my photographs the works were long out of use some of the buildings remaining in a derelict state since suffering bomb damage during the Second World War. These old locomotive works always struck me as being somewhat grim, even institutional, although having something of an Italianise quality to them. That they survived relatively intact for so long after falling into disuse is surprising, however the site was finally cleared for redevelopment at the beginning of the 21st century. The whole works site was originally encompassed by a ten foot high brick wall with, as I recall, only two gatehoused entrances. Not good for trainspotters. Sections of this wall still remain today especially around the EMU carriage sheds which still retain some of the original works buildings.

Stewarts Lane MPD in May 1963.
Top: Entrance from St. Andrews Street and Dickens Street.
Middle: Stewarts Lane MPD near to closure.
Lower: The famous depository that formed Stewarts Lane's northern boundary.

Stewart Lane's turntable, July 1963

This was located some distance from the loco shed in a far corner of the old Longhedge Works. Worth including this picture as I have never seen any of the turntable let alone any of it in use. The dilapidated building to the left of the turntable was Longhedge House former residence of the Works Manager and, I understand, was demolished shortly after this picture was taken.

Stewarts Lane. July 1963 & November 1961

In immaculate condition Battle of Britain Class Pacific No.34088 *213 Squadron* resides out of steam inside Stewarts Lane loco shed on the 5th July 1963 having recently worked a Derby Day royal train. Whilst allocated to Nine Elms shed Stewarts Lane had the reputation for turning out locos in tip-top condition when the circumstances demanded it. Why she was still on shed I don't know but this would be the last time a Southern Pacific would grace Stewarts Lane, this really was the end of an era. Taken in a near empty loco shed during November 1961 Class C No 31317, lower picture, resides in light steam. She would be withdrawn a few months later. Surprisingly that old shed wall as seen in the picture still stands today although nothing else of the old steam shed does the site having long gone the way of an aggregate plant.

Longhedge Works. July 1963

The long closed Longhedge Works was something generally ignored by trainspotters on Club trips they having little time for distractions. Those having managed to bunk in would consider themselves lucky to have got as far as the loco shed itself. So the old loco Works separated as they were from the noisy loco shed by great railway viaducts was something of a quiet and deserted backwater and therefore generally ignored. The adjacent Longhedge carriage works remained intact having long been adapted for electric traction. The former loco fitting shop, top picture, was a long narrow building that ran lengthwise to the other Works buildings including the loco erecting shop, lower picture. The Works yard is its usual deserted self save for a Wickham engineers' inspection trolley No.DS53. The former loco works site was finally cleared for redevelopment in 2009 the erecting shop being one of the last buildings to be demolished.

Neasden coaler.
I meet my Nemeses, and other adventures

Neasden loco shed had closed in 1962 and by the autumn of the following year I was led to believe that the site was being cleared. So on the spur of the moment I jumped on the old bike to have a last look and take some pictures. The 'old bike' was a second hand single-cylinder two-stroke 250cc German made Zundapp. To me she had an extremely good turn of speed bearing in mind my previous bike was little more than a moped.

So with youthful inexperience I would tear about on it and reckoned she would touch 90mph with me flat on the tank. Well that's what the speedo said.

At work most of my fellow apprentices neither believed me or my bike's speedo, but what would they know of German technology? These were the people that invented rockets, proper ones that is, one of which had demolished my Dad's parents house. Well we can't all be perfect can we.

Anyway, to get to Neasden I took off, eventually riding up the dual carriageway North Circular Road in a carefree sort of mood wearing little more than jeans, shirt and jumper.

Eventually I came across Neasden loco shed which was situated just south of the Iron Bridge which crossed the main line out of Marylebone station. However the loco shed being on the opposite side of the road a little detour was called for by going over the bridge and then eventually coming back on yourself.

The Iron Bridge had long been a challenge to the local 'ton up' lads because immediately following the bridge and heading North the road turned into a tight left hander then swept round into a fast right hander.

Whilst riding along on this particular day and on approaching the bridge the red mist came down and I found myself running the Iron Bridge flat out. I didn't plan it, it just happened. The only thing I did manage correctly that day was to line the bike up approaching the bridge. That saved me from a lot of grief. Taking all the road and cutting the first inner apex on the left worked well but after that I haven't a clue what happened. All I know is I survived. My feet weren't even on the footrests as I swept out of the right hander with the old bike's wheels almost up the kerb. I just hung on to the handlebars.

As I straightened the bike up I knew I'd been damn lucky but what the hell I'd done it even if I had nearly 'shit a brick' in the process. Being young, exuberance soon takes over, but even so on retracing my way back down the North Circular to the Iron Bridge my speed was determined more by discretion than valour. Turning off into a side road I eventually took to a cinder path which led to the now closed loco shed.

The yards had already been partially cleared with a new coal concentration depot occupying part of the site. The old shed itself was a sea of total dereliction. You could hardly credit it. Every pane of glass was shattered.

This took me back to a few years earlier when wandering into the recently closed Mitre Bridge electric depot at Willesden, West London. There, another sea of total dereliction had met my eyes.

It was a large airy depot with a high roof and on that day held many withdrawn L&NWRly 'Oerlikon' electric units. Everything was vandalised. Everything was smashed. Even the glass in the roof hadn't escaped. The place was as quiet as a tomb. save me crunching on a sea of broken glass. I got out quick.

But back to Neasden. Its 1930s mechanical coaler, now totally trackless, still stood and the thought came to me what an incredible photograph could be taken from its top. So without a thought I charged up the rusty metal ladder. Being before the days of Health & Safety there were no safety hoops or anything like that. By not looking down I got to the top all right, no problem there, it was only when I neared the end of the ladder and my head popped over the top that fear set in. I couldn't take any pictures … because I couldn't take my hands of the ladder. Believe me, even looking across the top of the coaler was not an option. I was very near to panic, only now I had all the time in the world to saviour it. So shaking like a leaf and keeping my eyes firmly shut I slowly descended the ladder.

If post traumatic stress had been invented in 1963 I would have had it. Even now thinking about it gives me the shivers.

The following week was to be my eating of the humble pie. Milking the Iron Bridge episode for all it was worth, even my fellow apprentices though I was really pushing my luck. Even spinning a yarn. That the bike could do 90 was bad enough, but actually taking the Iron Bridge at 90, well I ask you. Foolishly I stood my ground and demanded satisfaction. This caused a stir and my challenge was soon accepted. Thankfully nobody wanted a re-run over the Iron Bridge but within days I was running flat out through the nearby Hanger Lane underpass on the Western Avenue with a 650cc BSA Super Rocket up my arse. My claimed 90mph took a hammering, 70 to 75mph absolute tops.

There was some solace as a few of the older chaps thought this turn of speed for a 250 quite acceptable, but I was deflated. Totally.

Bloody German technology ... no wonder they lost the sodding war.

Ivatt 4MT No.43047, ex-Works in Swindon Works yard, July 1964.

Foreigners at Swindon Works. 1964

Ivatt 4MT No.43015 alongside Swindon loco shed coaling plant, February 1964. *(P Askey)*

Stanier 5MT 2-6-0 No.42983, rolling chassis outside Swindon Works A Shop, February 1964.

Stanier 5MT 2-6-0 No.42961 Swindon Works yard, July 1864.

During1963 steam locomotive work at Horwich Works was run down in favour of multiple units, carriages etc. May 1964 was to see the last steam locomotive going through Works, any future work being transferred away to Western and Southern Region Works.

At the time I was unaware of this, so finding 'foreign' locomotives on Swindon Works during my first visit in 1964 came as something of a surprise. That the 'Kings' had gone was bad enough but to find these Midland jobbies about the place was indeed the final straw. Worse was to follow as all steam locomotive repairs would cease by year's end, the Midland incursion being short lived indeed.

My first trip to Swindon in 1964 was on 2nd February and on the loco shed we found Ivatt 4MT 2-6-0 No.43015 dumped behind the coaling plant. The triangle held two more Ivatts, Nos.43070 and 43132 whilst 'A' Shop held Stanier 5MT 2-6-0 No.42954 and Ivatt No.43002, with the frames of Stanier No.42983 outside in the Works yard. Oddly enough another foreigner, was on the dump, Midland 4F No.44411 (w/d10/63).

Some five months later on 5th July, 'A' Shop still held Stanier No.42954 which had been joined by classmate No.42978 and two Ivatts Nos.43074 and 43120. Out in the Works yard were Staniers Nos.42945 and 42953, and Ivatts Nos.43001/90 and 43137, whilst around the turntable was Stanier No.42961 and Ivatt No.43047 having been recently outshopped.

My last trip to Swindon in 1964 was on 8th November and steam locomotive repairs were rapidly winding down. 'A' Shop held Stanier Nos.42945 and 42975 and Ivatts Nos.43001/5/12/112/137. Also on 'A' Shop that day were a 'Grange', 'Modified Hall', and a Standard Class 9F with another 'Modified Hall', a Standard Class 5MT and five pannier tanks out in the yard. Greater surprises were to be found in 'C' Shop which contained two Eastern Region 'V2' 2-6-2s Nos.60922 and 60945 (both w/d 7/64) in the process of being cut up with fellow sister locos Nos.60809/12/942 (w/d 7/64 & 5/64) out on the dump, with 18 former GWRly types and another foreigner a Midland 4F No.43940 (w/d 10/64).

Ivatt 4MT No.43001 parked up outside the boiler and Stationary engine shop, July 1964.

Class 4F No. 43940 on Swindon Works dump, November 1964.

Class V2 No.60942 on Swindon Works dump with C Shop in the background, November 1964..

The 'V2s' were interesting, some dozen of them had recently come down from the Heaton area for scrapping, their tenders being adapted for further use. They were quickly despatched having all gone by the end of the month, but in doing so gave some Great Western types an extra few months of life.

As said, overhauls of steam locomotives came to an end at the close of 1964. A handful of steam locomotives continued to linger around the Works, a few reserved for preservation lingered on the dump whilst some pannier tanks were retained for shunting duties. By the end of 1965 they had all gone.

From my own recollections and reading through copies of the RCTS 'Railway Observer' I fancy five Stanier 5MT Moguls and some twenty three 4MT Ivatt Moguls passed through Works, not including a few 'Crabs', '4Fs' and 'Jinty' tanks that arrived for scrapping.

Although I photographed these foreign interlopers I only did so because they were there. Now some fifty years on I'm glad that I did, as it is my own small photographic record of an interesting oddity in Swindon Works long history.

The Dam Busters remembered 16th/17th May 1964

Peter Askey, John Durrant and the author as pfotographed by Paul Wells, Weymouth loco shed 17th May 1964.

Train spotting still had some time to run before its inevitable demise and one particular jaunt was a weekend ride down to Bournemouth and Weymouth loco sheds. The planned weekend was the 16th/17th May 1964 which turned out to be the twenty first anniversary of the Dam Busters raid. For this reason we decided to kick off at midnight on the Saturday thinking ourselves to be on 'ops'. It certainly felt like it. This jaunt for us would be an epic of major proportions bearing in mind that up till then we generally rode no further than work, pictures, pubs and local shed bashing trips.

Overnight shed bashing excursions by train was one thing, but on our bikes? I for one was seriously worried.

The Dam Busters might have had to fly over war-torn Germany at night, we now had to ride all the way down the old A30 and A31 roads to Bournemouth. On our bikes. At night.

Four of us, Peter Askey, John Durrant, Paul Wells and myself were up for it but we were already handicapped with two bikes down already. This left only Peter's Japanese Honda Benly and my own German Zundapp, in the circumstances not the most patriotic of machines. But at least the tyres were British. Important that.

For practicalities sake the 'Black Prince' outfit was resurrected and I was back to my NH specs again having smashed my newly purchased, and what I thought quite stylish, heavy black-framed glasses.

The traffic that Saturday night was extremely heavy and the roads very narrow making for a miserable ride down, having to continually overtake slow moving traffic whilst suffering endless headlights coming the other way.

Following a stop at a rather dingy overnight café near Basingstoke we were eventually onto the

Bournemouth loco shed.

empty roads crossing the New Forest which made for exhilarating running, the bike's air cooled engines responding well to the cold night air.

So we made it to Bournemouth safe and sound and with the sun coming up we rewarded ourselves by stopping off at the first open café for a decent early morning fry up and strong hot tea.

With a new day dawning we rode on paying our respects to Bournemouth and Weymouth loco sheds. By this date Southern types were limited to Pacific classes save a couple of Moguls on Weymouth and a few dumped 'M7' tanks on Bournemouth. We wandered around Bournemouth West station at our leisure, the place being totally empty, as was Branksome loco shed other than another five withdrawn 'M7' tanks out in the yard.

Twenty one years previously the Dam Busters had made history, but at a cost of half the squadron.

My only problem was struggling home with a broken clutch cable.

But for us it was an epic.

Branksome loco shed.

Weymouth loco shed.

The Mysterious Case of Engine No.1151

By the summer of 1964 Llanelly loco shed was one the last outposts of steam in West Wales. Being some way west of Swansea as a trip it had its limitations. A train fare of around a fiver and a five hour journey each way was some deterrent.

A long way to go and a lot of money to fork out for one shed, but it was a fair chance that Newport Ebbw loco shed could be done on the way back.

So after a degree of thought Paul and I decided to go and see what West Wales had to offer. Amazingly we never even bothered to apply for a permit.

Llanelly was a typical GWRly twin turntable brick built loco shed and on the day of our visit 12th July 1964, my 19th birthday, held some forty two steam locos and thirteen diesels. I suppose the three 'Manor' Class locos and five 16XX pannier tanks on shed just about made it worth the train fare even if the eleven former LMS Class 8F's didn't.

Llanelly loco shed, July 1964.

R S Hayes' scrap yard. Paul, on left, being careful as to what he might tread in. July 1964.

But two things were to change that, the first coming across a scrap yard set down from the main running lines as our train approached Bridgend on the outward run. Something we hadn't bargained for, and could easily have missed. What's more it was full of steam locomotives.

So with Llanelli decidedly 'bunked' we were soon heading back to Bridgend station to find our scrap yard. With the lure of all those unknown locomotives just sitting there waiting for us it wasn't long before our 'nose' for train numbers had us scaling the scrap yard fence whilst wondering if any large dogs were running about.

The scrap yard turned out to owned by R S Hayes Ltd a largish site being set down and running parallel to the main running lines. Twenty seven assorted Great Western types were scattered about with three oddball industrials and to shunt this lot around a Fowler industrial diesel resided up one end of the yard. Scrapping was underway with several unidentifiable hulks having been reduced to boiler parts and wheelsets whilst an upside down Class 'M7' bunker resided on top of some Gresley carriage bogies. And other assorted chunks of metal ...were just that.

With loco numbers noted and photographs duly taken we would have been on our way save for a sudden 'poop pooping' going on up on the main line. Obviously a steam locomotive.

With our curiosity aroused we clambered up the embankment to find a closed railway station, well a single platform actually, lacking in any buildings whatsoever and the strangest of trains. What

Above and below: Ex P&M railway No1151 (w/d 8/63) at the long since closed Tremains Halt, July 1964..

met our eyes was a short train of flat wagons and a brake van headed by a small 0-4-0 saddle tank, obviously recently bereft of its Great Western cast cab side number plates

With formalities observed, click click, we were soon on our way but this little loco was a mystery. Obviously of Great Western Railway parentage but originally from one of the smaller Welsh Railway companies taken over at the 1923 grouping.

Confirmation came later. She was a former Powlesland & Mason Railway Peckett saddle tank becoming Great Western No.1151 withdrawn in August 1963 from Swansea (East Dock) and sold to R S Hayes in January 1964.

They in turn used it as their yard shunter, it being noted shunting the yard in August 1964. R S Hayes Ltd sold out to Birds Ltd in August 1965, the little Fowler diesel shunter being scrapped in late 1966 whilst No.1151 lingered on till January 1967. The yard closed down c.1968

The station, or platform, was known as Tremains Halt and was opened early in the Second World War to serve the newly opened Royal Ordinance shell filling concern which occupied the scrap yard site during the war years. At cessation of hostilities both the shell filling factory and the halt closed.

Today, nothing remains of the little halt or the scrap yard.

But why and what was No.1151 doing up on the main line in July 1964 and what, I wonder, happened to loco's number plates?.

In the end not a bad day for my 19th birthday.

Last Orders - 1965

When my first book was published in 2010 I included a postscript titled 'Last Orders' which described our final days of trainspotting during the opening months of 1965. I thought it might be worth having another bash at this article although now enhancing it a trifle to show how our enthusiasm for the railways had slowly drained away.

White van man had allowed me the pleasure of riding my BSA Gold Star motorbike splat into him shortly before Christmas 1964 so when we took ourselves off on a little excursion to Old Oak Common, Willesden and Southall loco sheds on the 24th January 1965 I was without transport. So being relegated to being a pillion passenger to either Paul or Peter's motorbikes, the latter was the better bet he being less inclined to get embroiled in any spontaneous two wheel 'challenges' with other young tearaways.

At Old Oak Common an old brick shed was provided for motorbikes so we casually looked round to see what else was about before wandering down to the loco shed. On this occasion there was a bright red and very stylish lightweight Italian job in amongst the more mundane British offerings. Someone at Old Oak Common had style.

The author, Paul Wells and Peter Askey (lower picture) at Old Oak Common January 1965.

Walking around and looking down on the loco shed itself it became immediately apparent that demolition was well advanced with one of the four covered turntables cleared with a three-road diesel servicing depot being erected on the site. Out in the shed yards much was in disarray with track work either out of use or already lifted. The coaling stage was partly operational and many of the ancillary buildings around the depot had already been cleared.

Forty diesels locomotives were scattered around the site. The former workshops, known as 'The Factory', had already been turned over to diesel traction as had the extensive 1930s-build carriage sheds located alongside the steam shed itself.

A nameless 'Castle', No.7022 and one of the last to be withdrawn. Old Oak Common, January 1965.

Old Oak Common's coaling plant, January 1965.

Many diesels were stabled around the remaining turntables, the majority being diesel-hydraulic 'Warships', 'Westerns', 'Hymeks' and North British Class 21s, as well as a handful of diesel-electric Sulzer Class 47s and Class 08 shunters. Sorry about talking TOPS in 1965, but it comes easier to my lap top finger.

Steam was mainly in poor condition and totalled 30 locomotives comprising mainly of former GWRly classes. 57xx and 94xx pannier tanks formed the majority on shed with a single 61xx Prairie tank. Tender locos were limited to two 'Castles' Nos.7022 and 7034 and six 'Halls'/'Modified Halls', all mostly stripped of their name and number plates. We had the distinct impression that the old order had simply given up the ghost and there would be no accolades for steam's departure which occurred just two months later.

From Old Oak Common a short ride would take you over the Grand Union canal to a left-hand turn by an old tin church which led to a short tarmac drive leading up to the rear of Willesden loco

shed. Whilst the canal threaded its way between the left-hand side of the loco shed and the huge cooling towers of Harlesden power station, a small wagon works and square built roundhouse was located to the right of the tarmac drive and on this visit it contained only a few diesel locomotives including early LMSRly/English Electric Co-Co No.10001.

The now depressingly run-down 12-road long shed held some 39 exceedingly unkempt steam locomotives including former LMS Black 5s and 8Fs, with several BR Standard tender types including eight Class 2 Moguls. Large LMS Stanier/Fairburn tanks were still in evidence as were two 'Jinties'. Of the 42 diesels on shed Classes 08, 11, 20, 24 and 40 - more TOPS talk - were well represented. Other than those diesels in the yards and resident in the roundhouse, the remainder were to be found stabled along two roads of the smoky, greasy, dusty environs of the long shed.

Willesden's steam days were obviously numbered, the shed finally closing in the September by which time the nearby diesel and electric depot had opened, interestingly No.10001 was stored over there for many years prior to scrapping.

Before riding over to Southall we stopped off at a strangely cold and empty Ace café. The Ace lacked its usual atmosphere, the hours of darkness seemed to suit the place better. Perhaps turning up on a couple of Japanese Honda Super Hawks, a red-un and a blue-un, didn't help. In those days riding Japanese bikes still went across the grain. We didn't linger.

Bunking into Southall shed even in the middle 1960s demanded some discretion so we wandered in through the rear yards, having to park the bikes in a side street and walk along a long footpath which worked its way under the main running lines and then between the high walls of the giant AEC concern and the loco sheds rear yards and turntable. Never, ever, did I see a loco on that turntable.

Adjacent to the rear yards were open fields which were always home to several donkeys,

Diesel locomotives scattered around the old Willeden steam shed on our visit, January 1965. These include, from top to bottom Nos.10001, D307, D2518 and 12090.

these being friendly souls and always appreciated a bit of extra company, unlike the Southall shed foreman. He certainly didn't want ours. It was always best to get some photographs in and around the rear yards before attempting to dodge the Foreman in the loco shed itself. However on this day there was no sign of him so we wandered where we pleased, the shed being surprisingly active. Forty nine grimy steam locomotives were 'on shed' including former GW classes 28xx, 45xx, 57xx, 61xx - all 12 of them - 'Granges', 'Halls' and 'Modified Halls' and even a single woebegone 'Castle' No.5042. Standard Classes included a single Class 5 and ten 9Fs.

A solitary Class 47, sorry Sulzer Type 4, diesel locomotive idled away in the top yards whilst nine dumped hulks including three 'Castles' and a old 57xx condensing tank eked out a existence at the rear. Southall shed closed 12 months later.

Southall loco shed, January 1965.

Top left: 61xx class No.6125.
Middle left: 'Modified Halls' Nos.6986 *Rydale Hall* & 6974 *Bryngwyn Hall.*

Lower picture: A deserted Reading loco shed, January 1965.

Above: A quick glimpse to the rear of Swindon loco shed, the old stock shed and a few of the gas works buildings (extreme left) with new industrial construction in middle background. Of the many steam locomotives that had been dumped around here only two, a 'County' and a 'Hall' remain. They would not linger.

Left: Gloucester (Horton Road) coaling plant and shed yards. January 1965.

With Peter's interest draining away as the day progressed and John not even bothered to put in an appearance it was left to Paul and myself to undertake two further planned trips, one to Barry dump, the other to Eastleigh loco shed. And at the time we thought that would be it.

The pair of us pushed off to South Wales and Barry dump on the following Sunday, the 31st January. The only trouble was that the weather had taken a turn for the worse, it being bitterly cold. So we both wore our motorcycle clobber, but went by train.

By this time both Slough and Reading loco sheds were devoid of steam, being reduced to stabling points for a few diesel shunters. On passing Swindon and taking the Gloucester line a few dumped locos were noted around the loco sheds coaling plant whilst the stock shed appeared to be empty other than a 'County' and a 'Hall' dumped outside. Gloucester Horton Road shed proved busy, the yard seemed active enough with mainly Midland types including Class 4F No.44222, a regular Somerset & Dorset locomotive. At Severn Tunnel Junction a huge dump of withdrawn locos had collected at the western end of the loco shed yard, no doubt destined for the scrap yards of South Wales.

On arrival at Barry a quick walk to the former steam shed found several diesels including six Class 37s - Tops Talk again - and, interestingly, former GW type shunters Nos.15101/2/3.

Barry Dump, West Pond area.
January 1965.

Above: The cut up remains of a tender locomotive at Barry, January 1965.

Left: In the far background can be seen the road/rail viaduct built to connect Barry town to Barry Island when this area was a large water pond.

Barry dump itself held 108 locomotives mainly assorted ex GW types including one small pannier tank No.1368 which sadly did not survive. Southern types had now appeared as had a Midland 'Jubilee' and two SDJRly Class 7Fs. Unusually the dump held seven Longmoor Military Railway Austerity 0-6-0STs of which two were already being broken up.

Whilst we were glad of our fur lined gloves and boots we were damn happy to get back to our train's heated buffet car and steaming hot cups of tea, even a British Railways curled up sandwich looked appealing. Or possibly a pork pie.

Some days later processing the films turned out to be a disaster. My film came out somewhat thin so at least Paul's had the advantage of an extra minute …

Whilst we froze at Barry with what little enthusiasm that was left, Paul and I were off again the following Sunday, the 7th February, to Guildford, Salisbury and Eastleigh. A Southern bash.

As I was still bikeless I rode pillion on Paul's 305cc Honda, but once again the weather put the kiss of death on the day, dull and miserable it was and by the time we were half way down the old A3 to Guildford the rains came.

Guildford shed contained 27 steam locomotives and a few diesels. The shed pilot was the usual 'USA' tank No.30071, the bulk of the remainder being 'U' or 'N' Class Moguls. Photographic opportunities, if you be so inclined, were few with mostly tenders poking out of the unusual open

Eastleigh loco shed. February 1965
An LMS Class 8F with 'West Country' Class No.34017 *Ilfracombe*.

semi-roundhouse.

On to Salisbury shed which managed a meagre 21 steam, the only Southern types being light Pacifics, the rest being BR Standard Class 4s. Eight diesels including three 'Warships' contributed to the misery. No photos here either, you have to be determined to photograph in sheeting rain.

With the pair of us now standing in the somewhat dark dank and desolate loco shed and enthusiasm fast ebbing away it was fifty-fifty whether to call it a day. But deciding to carry on to Eastleigh was to have its highlights. Paul had the ignominy of being overtaken by a car, a Austin Healy 3000, the proper job. I must have had total faith in Paul's riding abilities to go chasing cars in the pouring rain. It was, in the slang of the time, 'a right little burn up'! Anyway we had the better of him and arrived at Eastleigh somewhat the sooner, but at least the rain had eased off. Well at least it did till time for us to depart.

Eastleigh was dull, misty, miserable and wet. Surprise there then. The two of us were just about done for and we hadn't even been around the shed yet. No steaming hot cups of tea for us here, all the cafés were closed. We'd even forgotten the thermos. Wet and miserable we trudged off leaving the Honda in the bike shed to find some 109 steam locomotives scattered about but perhaps due to the dreadful weather and the fact that we were totally fed up the shed radiated a strange melancholy

A stone-cold 'Jubilee' Class No.45699 *Galatea* alongside Eastleigh shed.

Eastleigh loco shed, February 1965.

Above; Wearing motorcycle boots can have some advantages as Paul has no problems negotiating the neglected shed yards.

Left: No.34015 *Exmouth*.

feel to it. Not that it was much of a shed anyway, large yes, but to me the place resembled nothing more than a large barn. And cosmopolitan too, BR Standard classes now proliferated over all others. Surprisingly some 20-odd Midland locomotives were littered about from Ivatt 2MT 2-6-2Ts and 4MT Moguls, to over a dozen 8Fs and even a stone-cold 'Jubilee'. The place wasn't even Eastleigh any more. Southern types just about numbered 40, the majority of these being light Pacifics, many of which were in the lines of dead locomotives dumped around Eastleigh's rear yards. Several had their rods off with a few of the 'flat tops' sporting gaping holes where their nameplates had been crudely cut out.

One oddity dumped in a quiet corner was, interestingly, diesel shunter No.15201 which had been withdrawn a few months earlier. Built in 1936 she was the Southern Railway's first diesel locomotive to enter service and carried their 'No 1'. Following withdrawal she apparently lingered on for several years being put to use as a generator.

We watched 'flat top' No.34079 steam off shed into the mist and the rain and that was that. All that was left was a wet miserable ride home. Other than that Paul's bike excelled itself, its engine never missing a beat all day.

Unsurprisingly the films came out as uninspired as the day itself, not, as it turned out, a good end to one's photographic endeavours.

For me interest had now totally evaporated but, surprisingly, another two shed bashing trips were to be made during the summer of 1965, and on the motorbikes. Not that anyone bothered to take cameras and on reflection I'm surprised I even took a notebook. Following retrieving my crash damaged BSA Gold Star from a local back street garage and repairing it ourselves I took an impromptu solo flight down to Eastleigh one bright and sunny June day.

Sixty four locomotives were present the majority being, again, BR Standard classes plus a handful of Southern locos, some 'USA' tanks, 'N' and 'U' Moguls, even a single 'S15' mixed in with a gaggle of light Pacifics. On this visit only a few Midland locomotives were about, including five Ivatt 4MT Moguls residing on the scrap line, but no doubt waiting Works for repair.

Remembering the loco shed of only a few years previous, an Eastleigh of 'Lord Nelsons', 'Schools', and 'King Arthurs' etc., endless BR Standard types seemed bland by comparison. Boring even. My disinterest returned, even on such a warm and sunny day. Compared to the previous January visit the rear yards had now been mostly cleared of the endless lines of dead locos.

My enthusiasm for the diesel depot didn't amount to much as I never bothered to pay the place a visit.

The ride home was enjoyable as I had the old Goldie flat out under the famous Spitfire bridge on the Winchester bypass only to be nicked for speeding nearer to home.

My Eastleigh excursion must have revived some lost enthusiasm in the others as the following weekend the old gang of Peter, John, Paul and myself took ourselves off on our bikes for a ride

While 'Battle of Britain' No. 34079 *141 Squadron* works off Eastleigh loco shed into the murk. Paul and I get ready for a long wet bike ride home, January 1965.

out to Oxford and Banbury. Other than my notes I remember little of the day. Oxford's old wooden loco shed, rumoured to date to the age of the broad gauge, was considerably run down, possibly even near to falling down. Thirty six locos were in steam with another 20 rotting away in sidings near to the coaling plant. Despite the appalling condition of many of the locomotives there was a good variety of former GW classes including a 'Castle' four 'Granges' and two 'Manors'.

Riding up to Banbury we found the locomotives, 38 of them, in much the same state as Oxford loco shed. Both sheds were beginning to look pretty run down with heaps of ash and debris scattered around, but both sheds had still just over a year to run before closure. British Railways Standard classes and Midland jobbies ruled the roost at Banbury with only 13 ex-GW types, including five 56xx tank locos. Odd that. With a handful of withdrawn locos stored in sidings at the rear of the shed one, a 'Hall' No.6906, was being cut up on site.

On the spur of the moment we decided to run over to Woodford Halse. On parking the bikes up we walked over to the loco shed to be stopped in our tracks by the authority who appeared out of a shed office. Not having a permit he threw us out. This was the first time we had come across anyone in authority on the day and were somewhat surprised. There was no talking him around, he being totally adamant so we went on our way without argument ... what would be the point, as the shed was totally empty.

Woodford Halse had closed that month.

Thrown out of an empty shed! What a way to end things. Perhaps the man thought us to be leather jacketed vandals but one thing was for sure ... we weren't trainspotters any more. An era had passed.

The 4.15 to Bicester - Last Steam out of Paddington, June 1965

June 1965 would see the last scheduled steam train out of Paddington, the 4.15 Bicester service which gave way to diesel traction that month. Knowing dieselisation was on the horizon Paul Wells and I took the train in late 1964/early 1965 and it would be the last time that we would be steam hauled by British Railways. 'Grange' Class locomotive No.6853 formerly *Morehampton Grange* was photographed by Paul at Princess Risborough station before we carried on up to Bicester. Our locomotive had lost all its number and nameplates. Of my photographs taken on that day there is no trace. Having just taken the train to say we had done it Bicester had nothing to offer other than Eddie Dows motorcycle shop which specialised in the BSA Gold Star motorcycle. We just had time to gaze upon several polished examples of the beast and the many accessories on offer before we caught our DMU home. For me the beginning of the end of one era ..... and the beginning of another.

The Spring of 1966. Willesden Loco Shed … empty.

My little 98cc Excelsior motorcycle at Willesden loco shed.

By early 1966 my motorbike was in the garage at home being 'prepared' for my road racing debut. Well put it this way - it was off the road. For transport I had purchased an elderly rigid framed 98cc two stoke Excelsior motorbike. So taking it for a spin one day I found myself at Willesden loco shed which had closed some months previous. I just wondered what had happened to the place. No particular reason why I took my camera a 35mm single lens reflex, for within months it went to finance the bike racing. Parking the bike up against a yard lamp ladder I wandered around a completely deserted site still overshadowed by the cooling towers of nearby Harlesden Power Station.

It seemed incredulous to me that just over a year previous the shed was still very much alive with some forty grimy steam locomotives and countless diesels scattered about. A mere eight years previous Buster and I had first screwed up our courage overcoming a bad dose of the butterflies to bunk into the place. The square built roundhouse I remembered as if yesterday, we slunk around skirting the walls hoping they might just swallow us up. It was with great trepidation that we finally approached the steam locomotives positioned around the turntable. At ground level a live steam locomotive makes an incredible impression on a thirteen year old boy and one not likely to be forgotten.

Buttercups and daisies, or just weeds?

Willesden shed, located in NW London was of the 12-road dead-end variety and opened in 1873 by the London & North Western Railway to relieve an overstretched Camden Loco Shed situated near to Euston station. Following Willesden opening Camden then became the provenance of main line express workings which it remained till closure.

A large three-road repair shop was located at the rear of Willesden's loco shed and a mechanical coaler and the square shaped covered roundhouse were added in the 1920s. Extensive carriage sheds were situated alongside the loco shed but these buildings were removed in the early 1960s.

During the summer of 1962 Neasden loco shed had closed and Willesden inherited all the BR Standard Class 'Britannia' Pacifics which worked the Nottingham services out of Marylebone station. By early 1963 further 'Britannias' were then allocated to Willesden shed having been displaced by diesels on the Eastern Region

Dieselisation of the West Coast main line out of Euston commenced in the early 1960s and Camden closed to steam in September 1963, its

Willesden 12-road long shed and roundhouse on closure.

remaining allocation of three 'Coronations', Nos. 46239, 46240 & 46245, being transferred to Willesden. These were to be the only examples of the class to be allocated at Willesden and No.46245, being the last of the class to receive a general overhaul, was always kept in excellent condition.

Through 1963/64 up to half a dozen 'Coronations' and a dozen 'Britannias' could be found on shed, with equal numbers of 'Royal Scots' and 'Jubilees'. Taking in Willesden's staple diet of freight

The turntable, now cut up and loaded up ready for the scrap man.

Willesden coaling plant as photographed from the relative safety of a yard lamp post

work, ECS duties and shunting turns over 100 locomotives could now be found on shed.

But Willesden's Indian Summer of main line steam wasn't to last. By late August 1964 the 'Coronations' had gone with the 'Britannias' departing by early 1965.

With all watering facilities removed from Euston station in the summer of 1965, Willesden's ECS duties came to a end, its allocation of Stanier amd Fairburn tank being put into store or transferred away. The last local coal workings, 'Jinty' hauled, ceased in July 1965, the last turn believed to be worked by No.47432.

The end of steam then came rapidly with closure in September 1965. The nearby Diesel Traction Maintenance depot had opened early the same year but diesel locomotives continued using the now closed steam shed yards till year's end.

Several condemned locomotives also remained on shed but by November 1965 only 'Jinty' No.47432 remained, and this had gone by January 1966.

On this, my last visit, the long shed was totally empty other than the pigeons nestling in the roof, whilst the contractors were already on site in the roundhouse taking out the turntable. The stationary boilers had already gone.

The whole place was deathly quiet. Not a soul stirred. Except for those pigeons. Oddly enough even the vandals hadn't paid a visit. On this occasion, and with Neasden in mind, I felt no desire whatsoever to scale the coaling plant, limiting my picture taking to climbing up the odd yard lamp post.

Hunting around for souvenirs never entered my head, well why would it? After half an hour or so I kick started the little Excelsior into life and was on my way home.

It wasn't long following my last visit that the site was completely cleared to be eventually redeveloped into a Freightliner depot. Some 20 years later even Harlesden's power station had had its day, its cooling towers coming down severing another link to an age now gone.

Our part in the downfall of the British motorcycle industry

Motorcycling's salad days of '63

Peter Askey, top picture, runs his little 125cc Honda Benly through Greenford suburbia whilst John Durrant takes the author's 250cc Zundapp Trophy for a spin through Denham Village.

Being teenagers. motorbikes had a greater attraction to us than just our day to day transport. The antics of the original leather jacketed 'coffee bar cowboys' and 'ton up' lads to the Rockers of the 1960s gave all things motorcycling a bad press. So another reason to own a high powered motorcycle. Coffee bars as well as transport cafés had a bad reputation for being home to all manner of young people from beatniks, bearded angry young men 'square man, square' to those anti-social tearaways on bikes. Day release at Acton college, West London, would find myself and fellow students frequenting the local coffee bar. This establishment was considered to be 'in'. Frothy Expresso coffee. God we lived life on the edge.

Catering for the working man in the early 1960s could be pretty basic with transport cafés viewed as greasy spoons fit only for commercial drivers ... and 'ton up' lads alike. Most folk whilst out for a spin in the car wouldn't go near a transport café with a barge pole, let alone step foot inside. So for us an even greater attraction. With our collection of motley bikes even we shied away from such establishments for fear of being ridiculed. Well either that or hide them round the corner.

Whilst my Dad's old sheepskin jacket or my PVC 'Black Prince' outfit might at a push just qualify for café culture, John and Paul wore something called 'Combo' jackets a sort of olive green imitation American GI Combat jacket. Meanwhile dear old Peter Askey was still riding around looking like something out of an old British 'B' movie in grey trousers, V necked jumper and a cravat.

Then literally overnight, well 1964 actually, we all became anti-social tearaways ourselves. Possibly the newly aquired leather jackets had something to do with it, the bigger noisier bikes didn't seem to help either. We had become ton-up boys ourselves, or worse … Rockers. And by 1964 what most Rockers wanted was a 'café racer', a road going version of a racing bike. Customising standard road bikes to resemble racing machines became big business, not that we saw it that way at the time.

As for our bikes, 'Ginger' Baker and myself went the way of the BSA Gold Star whilst John

Ton Up Lads, Rockers & Cafe Racers
The top picture taken sometime in the late 1950s features our 'ton up' lad at the Busy Bee transport cafe astride his stock standard Triumph motorbike. By the early to mid 1960s the 'Rocker' had evolved his machine being the customised cafe racer and never more so than the Norton Dominator, lower picture, as marketed by Paul Dunstall. For many this was the ultimate cafe racer.
(Acknowledge Busy Bee MC Club and 'Rockers' by Mike Clay)

Durrant and Clifford Dart, aka 'Deem', went Velocette. Single cylinder machines and British through-and-through. Meanwhile Peter Askey and Paul Wells were lured away by the orient with promises of new technology. It went by the name of Honda. Modern overhead camshaft engines. Electric starters, indicators and that sort of thing. Fast, reliable … good brakes … no oil leaks. The motorcycling equivalent of those up-start diesels.

As for customising, the Gold Stars were already the business but John and Paul gave their bikes the treatment, although John kept the Velocette's traditional fishtail silencer. Less its baffles of course.

So for us no more hiding our bikes around the corner, we could now park up at transport cafés with confidence, that is if you could get into the forecourt. We rode out to West London's cafés such as the Ace, the Busy Bee and The Celler just to be there. We embraced such places, they exuded noise, youth and atmosphere. Hours would be spent drinking tea or coffee whilst putting the world to rights or arguing over bikes and road tests. Transient friendships would be made and lost, stories of 'daring do' swapped and indulged in and fanciful top speeds believed … or not.

Riders on all manner of machinery came and went, their bikes to be mulled over, discussed, critised and debated. Some lads, more affluent than most, rolled in on beautiful customised 'café racers' whilst others rode up on total heaps of shit.

All human life washed up at a transport café. Who cared. But vandals and troublemakers, never … decent chaps … mostly.

Departing demanded some ritual. Style was required. With much revving of engines, fancy footwork and slick throttle work we would take off. And perhaps a hint of castor based racing oil in the petrol to give your bike that certain racing ambienence.

But we were very keen. Engines would be stripped down and anything in sight would be polished and lightened. Attempts at engine tuning would be indulged in with plenty of experts on hand to help improve your bike's performance, whilst emptying your pocket at the same time.

There were distractions. I distinctly remember a few girls being around. Some leather clad as well. I don't know if they were as notorious as the press made them out to be as we were never lucky enough to talk to them.

Whilst out on the road we would occasionally have a bit of a thrash amongst ourselves in certain knowledge of our limitations, but you were on your own mixing it with other lads. Anyone getting past you was obviously mad and having second thoughts could save you from disastrous consequences. Discretion, something rarely admitted to, played a big part as you soon found that

A rather cheeky 1960's Honda advert.
(*Courtesy John Durrant*)

some lads seemed to possess total confidence in their doings, body language said it all … move out my way … I'm a coming through …

Other road users certainly knew we were coming … and then going. A bloody menace. Many a bike's silencer would be 'de-baffled' and if the bike didn't go any faster it would certainly sounded as if it did. For some unaccountable reason the coppers always had a down on you even if some of the traffic cops could be quite friendly whilst they nicked you for speeding or in my case on one occasion, low flying.

The occasional prang would enlighten our lives but Lady Luck would always cast a benevolent eye on us. This was possibly a short term contract.

On one occasion Peter was passing Northolt aerodrome on a wet and greasy A40 Western Avenue with Paul on the pillion clutching Peter's mothers brand new and highly prized Bush radio. Next thing they found themselves spinning around and around on their backsides Peter casually noting his mother's Bush radio spinning past between the pair of them. The radio survived, the Honda Benly's engine didn't …

One of 'Ginger' Baker's chums, Alan I fancy, certainly didn't go down the road of customising bikes, his BSA 650cc Rocket remaining in full touring trim. It really was the immaculate conception and forever fearing the worst he eventually fitted large sturdy chrome plated crash bars to the bike both front and rear. After fitting the wretched things we took off for a spin from The Polish War Memorial on the Western Avenue (A40) up to the Busy Bee. Come the first bit of fast cornering he lost control and fell off obviously being unaware of the effect that such heavy things would have on the bike. It was an amazing sight to see the 'immaculate conception' sliding down the road sparks flying off those great crashbars. However much to our amazement the bike itself suffered no great damage and fully justified their fitting. Or so he would have us believe. We were not surprised when shortly after he sold the bike and bought a car.

'Deem' one dark night attempted the racing line on his Velocette Venom Clubman through the arches of Brunel's famous West London Wharncliffe Viaduct. Sadly for Deem he failed to find the racing line depositing both himself and the bike in a heap on the kerb by one of the viaduct's brick arches. No doubt Brunel would have been amused.

I certainly wasn't amused at the bottom of Hillingdon Hill, Uxbridge one evening when white van man allowed me the privilege of riding my Goldie splat into him as he pulled out from a side street. For a bonus John, my pillion passenger, received free flying lessons as he cleanly skimmed over the van's roof. Whilst enjoying this new found but brief sensation my bits and bobs had to contend with my bike's large circular steering damper knob. Ouch …

Sometimes there was more a hint of comedy.

You may remember 'Ban the Bomb Bob' from a previous chapter, well despite his political leanings he eventually got himself a job as a dustman from then on becoming known as 'Bob the Dust'. With money in his pocket he gave up thumbing lifts and bought a cheap but somewhat smoky two stroke Francis Barnet motorbike.

Picking up Peter from college one evening they pushed off to the Busy Bee café to meet us lot. Perhaps due to his lowly transport he decided to impress the assembled lads at the 'Bee' with a 'grand entrance'. The pair of them charged in with some style but sadly Bob took the lorry entrance only to drop into one of the deepest pot holes imaginable causing him to lose control in spectacular style. As both he and Peter were thrown off the bike the throttle decided this was the best moment to stick open, thus covering the 'Bee' with clouds of blue exhaust as well as quantities of dust and dirt. This rapidly descended over the assembled ensemble to be shortly followed by Peter's college work which gradually floated down over the forecourt.

Us lot, 'The Rabble'

Paul Wells 250 Honda

Ted Reading 499 BSA Gold Star

John Durrant. 350 Velocette Viper

Clifford Dart 499 Velocette Venom

'Ginger' Baker 499 BSA Gold Star

Peter Askey whilst out on a spin.

On that same night Peter spilt all our mugs of tea over a group of hard looking lads one of whom proudly proclaimed himself to be the 'Highwayman from Muswell Hill' as studded into the back of his leather jacket. Not knowing from which direction the hot tea came from this then started something of a fracas. Bob and Peter fled the scene and were last seen with Bob frantically kicking over the Francis Barnet for all his life's worth then disappearing up the Watford By Pass looking desperately behind them.

One last anecdote concerned 'Ginger' Baker and his Goldie. Being a 'ton up' lad in search for extra speed and defying the best efforts of the BSA technical department he once spent all one day ramming the baffles out of his bikes silencer with his mothers broomhandle. On our arrival 'Ginger' was distraught, on cranking up his Gold Star it no longer had its characteristic 'twitter' to its exhaust. To him a 'twitterless' Gold Star was beyond belief, Mothers broom handle hadn't faired that well either now being ingrained with black soot and utterly ruined. Mother was not best pleased. Nor was 'Ginger'

For us lot life in the fast lane was to be somewhat short lived, time, and life, had moved on and probably for us just as well as we all went the way of rusty cars, pubs, and dance halls. Our parents thought car ownership and drink driving considerably safer and tended to ignore the litany of dented wings, bumpers and door panels. 'Ban the Bomb Bob' reverted to form going hitch hiking through Europe never to be seen by us again.

As the 1960s came to an end changing traffic patterns, motorways etc resulted in the old roadside transport cafes fading away while increasing affluence saw two wheels giving way to four. Hippies and 'Flower Power' became the thing, drugs and all that. In later days on passing the 'Ace' a handful of bikes would still be seen, American chopper things with high handlebars. Easy Riders. We never went there.

The 'Busy Bee' closed in 1968 to become a glitzy neon lit restaurant its forecourt resounding to the exhausts of Jaguars, BMW's and the like until closure and demolition in 1988. The Hilton hotel then took over the site but that old forecourt still remains as the car park the actual 'Bee' site having been grassed over. The 'Ace' closed in 1969 to become for many years a tyre depot until its fortunes were revived the old cafe having now been lovingly restored to its former glory. And as for the demise of British motorcycle industry, well they didn't really need our help for they managed to do it all by themselves.

The end of an era.
The Busy Bee and Ace Café in the 1980s.
(Courtesey Busy Bee M/C Club and Barry Cheese)

The BSA Gold Star -
A very British Motorcycle

Bernard Codd sits on his Gold Star having just won the June 1956 Isle of Man 500cc Clubmans TT, the picture originating from a care worn copy of the then weekly magazine 'Motor Cycling'. Bernard also won the 350cc Clubmans TT race also on a Gold Star. Left is a Silverstone race programme cover of 1959 featuring Gold Stars, a bike that like no other dominated Club racing through the 1950s.

Courtesy Charlie Williams

Courtesy Derek Harmsworth

BSA Gold Star Clubmans

Two pictures of BSA Gold Star Clubmans bikes, the top is a young Charlie Williams on his 349cc Gold Star outside the Ace Cafe in 1962. At that time I was still riding a moped and too scared to go there. Charlie appeared in the 1963 film 'The Leather Boys', a film that us lot thought unforgivable when a race to Edinburgh and back was won by a sheepskin clad chap riding a two stroke 250cc Aerial Arrow. Unbelievable. The lower picture is Derek Harmsworth on his 499cc Goldie whilst taking part in the 1967 National Rally, the same year in which he rode the bike down to Monte Carlo. The bike has a 'C' plate but thats another story. I have to admit an interest in this bike as I'm now its present owner.

Clive Wall approaches Bottom Bend at Brands Hatch on his 500 Goldie during a production bike race in 1965.

The BSA Gold Star was a typical British four stroke single cylinder machine of the early post war years the engine being of overhead valve design operated by pushrods.
The Gold Stars' history went back to the late 1930s when a 499cc BSA Silver Star won the coveted Gold Star trophy at the Brooklands race circuit in 1937, so for the following season the Gold Star was born. However, the Second World War bought any further developments to a halt but when production was resumed following the end of hostilities the girder forks were replaced by the modern telescopic variety and by 1953 the plunger frame had given way to the swinging arm version.
The bike was available in either 349cc or 499cc capacity and production ceased in 1962, or 1963 depending on which account you read. But what put the Gold Star above all other bikes of the period was that not only was it sold as a standard touring road bike but was also available for the competitive motorcyclist in trials, scrambles and road racing trim. However what was to make the Gold Star a legend in motorcycle circles was its availability in Clubmans' trim which meant a racing bike in all but name and fully road legal. And all supplied direct from the factory.
The Gold Star in its Clubmans' guise took its name from the Isle of Man TT races which introduced the Clubmans series in the late 1940s for production road bikes. By 1957 this was abandoned due to the events total dominance by BSA and its Gold Star. Another notable event was the Southampton & District Nine Hour Endurance race introduced at the Thruxton circuit in 1955 which was once again dominated by the Gold Star Clubman till 1957 when the event was reconfigured as the 500 Mile race.
Throughout the 1950s the Gold Star made a name for itself in all forms of competitive events, in scrambling both at Club and National level whilst in road racing it was a serious contender at Club meetings although at National level it was more than outpaced by the 'over-the-counter' overhead camshaft 350cc & 500cc Manx Nortons and the 350cc AJS 7R and 500cc Matchless G50. Despite this many famous racing stars started their careers on BSA Gold Stars.
Over the years the engine would undergo considerable detail design changes and by 1955 the final version of the distinctive Gold Star clubman machine had arrived. Large fin alloy engine, large bore Amal GP carburettor with remote float chamber, racing clip on handlebars with rear set footrests, a swept back exhaust pipe with semi-megaphone silencer which when combined with sports camshafts gave the bike a characteristic twitter to its exhaust note. Remember poor old Ginger,

previous chapter.
As the 1960s progressed the Gold Star became rapidly dated in sporting events and competition versions of the bike, many now in poor order, could be had at reasonable cost. Meanwhile out on the road the Gold Star Clubman still commanded high prices due to its racing heritage which would lead it to be forever associated with the original 'ton up' lads or their 1960s equivalent 'Rockers'
But even here she would come up against large capacity twin cylinder bikes like the Triumph Bonneville or the Norton Dominator SS. These machines had speed and greater flexibility for riding on the road. However the old 'Goldie' was still a much respected machine despite some of its 1950s big single idiosyncrasies such as valve lifters, manual ignition advance and air slides. Not forgetting the close ratio gearbox. Starting the beast could prove interesting requiring something laughingly called a 'long swinging kick' with resulting fear of 'kick back' from an over advanced ignition.
The Gold Star was a beast that could bite back.

The Gold Star Clubman's racing swansong. Goldie's in action during the mid 1960s.

Three trainspotters go road racing

Following a few years of going our own separate ways, meeting up with my old school mate Buster again now found him wildly enthusiastic about motorbike racing. His own motorcycling days were now behind him, he now being the owner of an elderly blue half-ton Austin A55 van. A vehicle with little in the way of suspension.

So it was sort of natural that come the Easter of 1965 Buster and I would be seen bouncing our way in his old van down to Brands Hatch to watch the season opener. The day became one of those life changing affairs, it wasn't so much watching all the racing stars scratching round, but a race for road or production bikes then taking in all the frantic activity in the race paddock. I knew there and then that I wanted to be on the that side of the fence, so for the rest of the year I went to as many race meetings as possible.

1965 'King of Brands' road race programme.
(Courtesy John Durrant)

This racing thing had so far passed us all by as we all though we were doing it anyway. Roads now took on a different meaning and everything including roundabouts had to be taken on the racing line. Sometimes with startling results. It turned out that Paul proved to be the most proficient at being the last into a bend and first out. This became the order of the day. The down side of all this was being nicked three times in quick succession by the coppers. This persecution by the officers of the law could not continue for I was rapidly running out of points on my driving licence.

Straight line sprinting was another motor sport popular at the time. I having already been to a National Sprint Association meeting at Debden, Cambridgeshire, with Alan Jones my enthusiastic motor biking guv'nor. Debden was a former war time RAF fighter command base and during the Battle of Britain was in the thick of the action against the might of the Luftwaffe. That was now 20-odd years past and being no longer required was either abandoned or was put to some minor uses. Officially I think this meant being under a 'Care and Maintenance' basis. Anyway we simply drove in past the empty guardhouse, empty admin blocks and hangers to come across a huddle of vans, motorbikes and enthusiastic sprinters out on the runway. The bikes themselves looked more like mechanical monsters having little in common with bikes as I knew them. Sprinters went for pure function with little concern for aesthetic beauty, although unlike road racers they seemed to have a flair for giving their machines names. But no pictures or description could do justice to the ear shattering noise these two wheeled beasts made blasting off from a makeshift start line, tearing up the old runway at full throttle heading towards a pair of chequered boards some way distant. But unlike organised motor cycle race meetings this event was a cheerfully casual affair and for us it was all free.

Much impressed by all this 'Deem', Paul and myself eventually decided to give it a go by entering a National Sprint Association standing quarter mile sprint at Duxford. Another seemingly abandoned RAF airfield. This would be 1966. I think they filmed the 'Battle of Britain' there the following year, and blew up a hanger. With safety at an understandingly low priority, a second-hand race approved 'pudding basin' crash helmet was purchased to go with my leather jacket and jeans, de rigour of my Rocker days. The day turned out to be wet and miserable. Well it would rain wouldn't it? We rode up in the rain, spent the day hanging around in the rain, put in a few miserably unimpressive runs in the rain then rode home in the rain. Believe me old airfields offer nothing in the way of shelter from the elements. Getting wet, we thought, was not conducive to competitive sport.

A few months later I again rode the bike down to Brighton having entered the High Speed trials along the sea front. This time around the weather behaved itself, only for me to cook the bike's

John Durrant 125cc BSA, Snetterton 1967.

Paul Wells 350cc Honda, Brands Hatch 1967.

Ted Reading 499cc BSA Gold Star, Silverstone 1966.

Duxford & Brighton sprints 1966

'Deem' (top) and the author dabble at sprinting, which taught us one thing ... buy a van.

clutch in heavy traffic on the ride down. And then I had to get home let alone sprint the bike along the sea front.

My road racing debut had occurred some months earlier with the British Motorcycle Racing Club meeting at Snetterton, Norfolk. I had entered my bike in the production bike race, coercing Buster to take us up in his van. This was luxury I could get used to. Rudimentary cooking could be undertaken and no worries about the bike especially as I vanished into a cornfield.

But even with help from my Dad, competition work taxed what mechanical skills I had to the absolute limit. With much burning of the midnight oil I achieved very little in the way of results, it being an achievement to actually finish. Sprinting was no better, seemingly to be a matter of something called 'gearing'. Whatever that was.

Initially Buster had sort of volunteered himself and his van to further my racing career, but thinking that bike racing, or my version of it, should have been more exciting sold me the van for £15.

This racing thing was becoming infectious, so by the following year, 1967, John had purchased a much modified 125cc BSA Bantam racer and capable of near 80mph. She really was a lovely little bike. 'Deem' on the other hand 'constructed' his own version of a Bantam racer while Paul put his road going Honda on the track, stripping it down to the bare essentials and shodding the machine with second hand racing tyres. Peter thought the better of it starting a love affair with sports cars.

John and 'Deem' entered the Bantam Racing Club's 1967 seasonal opener at Snetterton in Norfolk which unsurprisingly turned out to be bitterly cold affair. I went along as the 'spanner man'. This little excursion was to be overnight but no great attention was made of this fact. Travelling overnight was no great problem as in our old trainspotting days you simply bedded down for the night in a station waiting room or even on a train. Heating generally came free. However sleeping in a heater-less van on a bitterly cold night with nothing in the way of extra clothing or bedding is not to be recommended. Such things never entered our heads. 'Deem' drove us up in the old Austin A55 van. Well that

Bantam Racing Club Snetterton 1967
John and 'Deem' poking about with John's BSA Bantam.

Brands Hatch, 1967.

The author sits on his Goldie, John is the 'spanner man' and Paul stands by his Honda. Don't you just love his tool box cum bike stand.

proved to be interesting. On the way up on the old A11 'Deem' did his best to kill us all with some remarkable, even imaginative, overtaking. You can only keep looking at oncoming headlights for so long before you close your eyes and start praying. 'Deem', it had to be said, seemed unperturbed by such excitements.

Having missed our fate the first time round it now seemed we were to freeze to death, so with teeth chattering away we had no option but to go for a quick trot round Snetterton's two and a half mile track whilst the sun came up. Unsurprisingly we were to be totally alone on the airfield's old runways. Being a former wartime American bomber base we wondered if we might catch the ghostly echos of Snetterton's war time past. Well we didn't.

As it turned out Snetterton was to see 'Deem's' racing career over before it started, he managing only a lap and a half in practise before he had the ambulance pulling out. We were soon to find out why. 'Deem' had thrown his bike away on a long fast right hander. Finding him now laying prostrate in the First Aid hut John reduced us to tears by asking how the bike had handled.

Even more humiliation was to come 'Deem's' way, suffering gravel rash on his lower face the Doctor gave him injections causing his lips to swell to enormous proportions. Mick Jagger or even Botox had nothing on 'Deem', this man was forty years before his time. A few days later whilst down the pub 'Deem' announced his retirement whilst sipping his beer through a straw. This was a pity as we all believed he had potential, the consensus was that 'Deem' and Paul were totally fearless on the road. Not the best qualification in the world maybe but we thought it helped and it has to be said that Paul would be the one to go on to have the greatest racing successes.

The author sitting in our £25 Bedford, a van with a mighty thirst for oil. 1968

By the end of that year we had all learnt something of the art of road racing and your author for one thought he had arrived on the production racing scene even if I was riding my beloved but outdated BSA Gold Star. So I should have sold it. But I didn't, and worse still, through the winter we all deserted the bikes for our local dance halls, suits, and an alternative lifestyle in pursuit of the ladies. In that I was lucky in meeting up at a local dance with one Iris Rossiter who became the love of my life and my financial sponsor. Not only that but my sponsor provided a home for my bike in her parents garage as my

Dad wanted his own one back. More importantly, my sponsor provided replacement transport ... a pale blue Bedford van for £25 with working suspension but unbeknown to us a dreadful thirst for oil.

It might be mentioned here that on several occasions whilst racing the motorbikes we were to be reacquainted with the police who would take a great interest in stopping us late at night and poking their torches inside our overloaded vans to reveal our bikes. All would be explained ... eventually.

Anyway, sadly I failed to impress my Iris, firstly by not having the bike ready till half way through the season and secondly by then managing to throw the thing down the road at Cadwell Park. Picking myself up and being somewhat dazed a very young and overly enthusiastic St Johns Ambulance volunteer rushed up to my aid. Sadly his medical assistance didn't match his enthusiasm for the contents of his First Aid bag contained nothing more than his mother's sandwiches. Bless him though, he stood there as proud as punch in his St Johns' uniform.

On the bike's eventual return to the track it obviously felt somewhat aggrieved at my treatment of it so paid me back with ignition problems which eventually turned out to be a duff magneto. Sadistic things magnetos, they can take a long time dying.

John Durrant and Paul Wells faired much the same through this period although they at least managed to stay on their machines. John had put in some decent rides but retired at the end of the year selling the little BSA to Paul for fifty pounds in the pub one night. Paul in turn certainly put the little bike to good use scoring some highly creditable performances in the Bantam Club, but whether John got the full fifty quid for the Bantam is still up for debate.

The Author, his Gold Star and Iris.

The Author on his 499cc BSA Gold Star Snetterton September 1967.
Finished 7th overall and 1st 500 home in Production Class Race.
Iris astride the Goldie during the winter 'preparations' of 1967/68
Sadly all to no avail.

Of the three of us, Paul was without doubt the most proficient and determined rider, but by the end of the 1960s the racing thing had had its day. Competitive sport like anything else you put your heart and soul into is totally demanding and never cheap.

John had gone and despite Paul having some outstanding rides on his now overbored 350cc Honda, continual mechanical problems culminated in him investing everything into a competitive 250cc Bultaco racer which financially broke him - and that was that.

With my own finances at a all time low and no ready cash to sort the Goldie out, any common sense that I was ever born with totally deserted me by buying an old 600cc Norton Dominator 99SS on the credit. Sadly it did nothing but vibrate itself to pieces so that and the terminally dead Gold Star went the way for an even older and totally uncompetitive 350cc racing Gold Star special. God knows why. She was a lovely old dear but really didn't have much in the way of speed. Anyway for 1970 the two of us plodded round a few times with me once again more at the back of the field than anywhere else. However, to be honest, I had lost interest and was simply going through the motions. It is said that every dog has it's day and I was fast coming to the conclusion that I had long had mine.

Selling the old thing turned out to be an event. Having eventually found a prospective buyer, he wanted to test ride it so we took him and his chum who had just built up a Velocette down to Brands Hatch. The old Bedford van's thirst for oil forced an unscheduled stop at a garage which being closed precipitated a frantic search through the waste bins looking for used oil cans. With sufficient dregs of oil squeezed out of every used oil can we could find, we managed to get back on our way. Desperate stuff though.

All then went well with the two chums till they both went out together. Can't remember which one went down first but it was a very subdued drive home. Whatever, he bought the bike and I retired … for the moment.

The old Bedford van was despatched shortly after when its owner demolished some twenty feet of her neighbour's front garden fencing.

Well, in all fairness, it was her van.

Left: The 600cc Norton 99SS

A machine best forgotten!

It's 1970 and the pair of us just plodded round….

My 350cc Roland Pike BSA Gold Star special. Cheap and uncompetitive at the time it would now be deemed a 'Classic', with a price tag to suit.

A short photographic excursion into the 1960s world of aircraft, ships and boats

A Princess at Cowes, Isle of Wight

The Askey family generally went to the Bournemouth and Lymington areas for their holidays and a boat trip over to the Isle of Wight produced this interesting picture taken by Frank, Peter's Dad. in July 1964. Some fifty years later whilst looking through Frank's colour slides there was, at first glance, nothing much of note. Then on examining one particular slide, holding the middle distance there looked to be a rather large aeroplane … something which turned out to be a Saunders Roe 'Princess' flying boat.

By the time of Franks photograph, taken in the summer of 1964, this particular flying boat had been cocooned against corrosion for ten years at the Saunders Roe factory site along the River Medina at Cowes on the Isle of Wight.

Three examples were built in the late 1940s for the transcontinental route, but time had overtaken the concept of the flying boat in favour of land based aeroplanes.

Our Princess, registered G-ALUN, first flew in 1952 but with the scheme abandoned she was cocooned at Saunders Row factory site whilst the other two unfinished airframes were likewise cocooned, but at Calshot Spit on the mainland.

All three Princesses were finally to be purchased in 1966 but on stripping off the protective cocooning they were all found to have suffered from serious corrosion.

Not surprisingly the deal fell through.

The two unfinished airframes were scrapped on site at Calshot Spit whilst G-ALUN was towed across the Solent in 1967 for scrapping at Southampton. It is understood that the cockpit section remained intact for many years in use as the scrap yards office. That must have been the most spacious and expensive office of all time.

Matters aeronautical - Over our heads

Dull, miserable rainy days would find our Greenford, West London home under the flight path of London Airport resulting in a constant stream of low flying aeroplanes passing directly overhead. With the dawning of the 1960s we had a succession of propeller jobs Avro Britannias, Lockheed Constellations, Boeing Stratocruisers and endless whining Vickers Viscounts to name but a few. I think I once saw an Avro York. The only jet in those early days was the De Havilland Comet a futuristic aeroplane something akin to Concorde of later days. By the end of the 1960s the propeller jobs had had their day. The top picture features a BOAC Argonaut, a Canadian version of the American Douglas DC4. BOAC operated them from 1949 to 1960.The lower picture is of the more common Bristol Britannia, the whispering giant, which BOAC ran from 1957 to 1965. The picture above however features the military version of the Britannia which the RAF operated till 1976.

Matters aeronautical - Jets

The De Havilland Comet, top picture, would be the first jet airliner to take to the skies BOAC taking delivery in 1952. Sadly the initial Comets were to become an aeronautical disaster with five examples crashing due to structural failure. As a young boy I remember the intense press coverage and newspaper headlines. BOAC continued to fly later variants of the Comet till the mid 1960s the aircraft remaining in service with other UK airlines till 1981. The Avro Vulcan, lower picture, was introduced into RAF service in 1957 as a high level strategic bomber designed to deliver our nuclear deterrent. In this role the Vulcan was turned out in all over anti flash white. In those Cold War days we had a four minute warning of nuclear attack something that gave much comfort to us all. Oh, and take cover under the kitchen table. With improvements in Russian radar and missile technology the Vulcan became obsolete and by the early 1970s took on a low level nuclear tactical strike role taking on a green gray camouflage colour scheme. The Vulcan was finally withdrawn from RAF service in 1984.

All four pictures from 'The Collection'.

I must go down to the sea again, to the lonely sea and the sky,
And all I ask is a tall ship and a star to steer her by.
Sea Fever, John Masefield

Well I have never had a tall ship nor a star to steer her by. However my Dad did have something, a converted lifeboat, moored up at Strand on the Green on the River Thames. I remember little of her other than the disagreeable toilet arrangements up at one end. Later in life I did pass by Southampton Docks on trainspotting excursions and remember seeing on several occasions those great ocean liners from our train. My first actual incursion into Southampton Docks was with Peter Askey in October 1961. This was on another trainspotting trip to Eastleigh and we had Merchant Navy class No.35030, my last MN cop, to take us on our way. Following Eastleigh we journeyed on down to Southampton and somehow managed to gain entrance into the docks. I seem to recall policemen on the docks entrance but I suppose we just walked on through. The small loco shed took some finding and we were rewarded with several 'USA' and Class 'E2' tanks. It could be said that there was no way you could miss the then famous Ocean Terminal, but I did. It didn't even register but then I was only sixteen and my interest in those days only extended to loco numbers. Everything else was taken for granted. Some sixteen years later, 1977, the four of us, Peter Askey, Paul Wells, John Durrant and myself were again at Southampton Docks this time to photograph the loco shed site, now long since demolished. From near this vantage point you could view the Ocean Terminal in its entirety and despite its art deco styled southern end from a distance it looked little more like an extremely long warehouse. The days of regularly scheduled transatlantic crossings were now long past and I seemed to remember the terminal was showing her age. But, for my sins, I failed to record it something which is something I have always regretted. The Ocean Terminal finally closed in 1980 and was demolished three years later. The following year I came back to photograph a vacant site.

The following pictures of ships, boats and other things afloat come from 'The Collection' which is described in the front of the book. Thus we know nothing of the photographers. But I tip my hat to them. The majority of the pictures originate from colour transparencies a few of which are process dated to the 1960s. Some photographs were dated by inspection and a fair bit of deduction. Or my imagination. One thing that I was not aware of was that shipping companies used their ships funnel, or stack, colours to identify their ownership. Cunards were, for example, always bright red with two thin black strips. The tops of funnels were always black for obvious reasons. Another factor concerning ships was their identification, or prefix to the ships name, such as RMS, SS, MV etc. These are included where known. Of the photographs, the ocean liners are at Southampton Docks, both of Cunards Queens being berthed in the Ocean Dock. Of the cargo boats unless where stated I have little knowledge of location or date.

The Ocean Terminal, Ocean Dock, Southampton as reproduced from an old postcard, origin unknown.

The Cunard Queens and Ocean Liners

To me there would be nothing more romantic than to travel down on a steam hauled boat train to Southampton Docks Ocean Liner terminal to board one of the great ocean liners for a transatlantic voyage across to America.

As the 1960s dawned this was still the way of it but by the end of the decade safe air travel became 'the way to go' with jet airliners replacing their piston engine equivalents. Everyone could now start to cross the pond in hours and not days and with the beginning of non-stop flights travelling times became even quicker. Depending on circumstances and financial wealth it could be said that speed had overtaken style.

To some extent the old ways still exist today. Scheduled year round transatlantic crossings may be something of the past but Cunards *Queen Mary 2* still sails from Southampton Docks to New York a dozen times or so each year. There is even the occasional boat train, sometimes steam hauled, that can still take you out of London to Southampton Docks but the liner will be more for cruising....and that's something totally different.

The great ocean liners came into being in the mid 19th century and not only carried passengers, both rich and poor, but also mail and cargo. The North American route to the USA from the UK and Europe was the most famous of all the great shipping lanes around the world. However with the arrival of air travel the days of the great transatlantic liners was over and those that could not be readily converted for cruising would, with few exceptions, be sold off for scrap.

It has been said that the 'golden age' of the ocean liners was the inter war years with a brief but busy period following the Second World War. With each shipping line doing their utmost to cross the Atlantic in the quickest time possible, the unofficial 'Blue Riband' was the most highly prized accolade that a transatlantic liner could hold. This represented the fastest west bound crossing from Europe to the United States and the *Queen Mary* held the Blue Riband more often than not from 1936 through to 1952. However in that year the *United States* took the award on its maiden voyage crossing the Atlantic in 3 days 10 hours and 40 minutes at an average speed of 34.51 knots. A record that it held to the very end of the transatlantic liner itself.

The *Queen Mary*, at 81,000 tons, was built by J. Brown & Sons, Clydebank, Scotland for Cunard's transatlantic route and was launched in September 1934 undertaking her maiden voyage in May 1936. During the Second World War she 'did her bit' serving as a troopship both in the Far East and the North Atlantic. She acquired the nickname the 'Grey Ghost' due to her all gray camouflage scheme and on one particular voyage transported some 16,687American troops, something of a record. At the end of hostilities and following the repatriation of American troops she was eventually 'demobbed' in September 1946 and following a complete refit returned to Cunard Line in July 1947. There she remained on the Southampton, Cherbourg to New York run till her retirement in 1967 being sold on to become a tourist attraction at Long Beach, California where she still resides today.

The *Queen Elizabeth*, at some 83,600 tons, was also built by J. Brown & Sons on Clydebank for the Cunard line. She was launched in September 1938 and started her life in somewhat different circumstances to the *Queen Mary*. Her maiden voyage was also to the USA but undertaken in a cloud of secrecy during February 1940 and like the *Queen Mary* spent her war as a troopship initially in the Far east then on the North Atlantic route. Following the Second World War she was refitted and rejoined Cunards in October 1946 on the Southampton, Cherbourg to New York route. During 1965 she was adapted for both cruising and the transatlantic route in which roles she performed till 1968 when Cunard retired her being replaced by the *Queen Elizabeth II*. Unlike the *Queen Mary* retirement was not a happy experience, initially sold to an American concern and was berthed as a tourist attraction at Port Everglades, Florida. Sadly this venture failed and she was bought up by a Far Eastern business man sailing from Florida to Hong Kong in 1970. During a subsequent refit she caught fire and capsized in Hong Kong harbour in 1972 the burnt out hulk being partially scrapped above the water line during 1974/5.

Cunard's replacement for the old Queens was the *Queen Elizabeth II* which entered service in 1969 at a time when most shipping companies were bowing to the inevitable and pulling out of the transatlantic route. For the Americans the United States Line's *United States* ceased sailing in 1969 whilst on the European side of the pond 1971 witnessed the end of an era for the Holland America

QUEEN MARY

line's pre war *Niew Amsterdam* and the equally elderly North German Lloyd lines *Bremen*. As well as these well loved old dears a new generation of ocean liners faired no better with French Line's 1962 build *France* being controversially retired in 1974 and Italian Lines 1965 build *Leonardo da Vinci* finally pulling out in 1977. From then on Cunard alone would continue regular scheduled transatlantic sailings with the *Queen Elizabeth II* as well as taking in an excursion down the Falklands way on the early 1980s. She was replaced by the *Queen Mary 2* in 2004 and from then on concentrated on full time cruising till sold in 2008.

RMS Queen Mary & *Queen Elizabeth,* Ocean Dock, Southampton

SS United States & *SS Niew Amsterdam*

At 47,000tons the *SS United States*, opposite. was built for the United States Lines and made her maiden transatlantic voyage in May 1952 taking the prestigious Blue Riband from Cunard's *Queen Mary*. Retired in 1969 she was laid up till 1978 when her owners finally sold her but she still remains to this day rusting away on the Delaware River, South Philadelphia.

The *SS Niew Amsterdam,* above, at some 38,000 tons was built for the Holland America Line undertaking her maiden voyage in 1938. She was 'enlisted' by the British during the Second World War as a troopship and following the conflict underwent a complete refit returning to the transatlantic route in 1947. The *Niew Amsterdam* continued in this role till 1971 by which time she had also been adapted for cruise work in which guise she worked till 1973 when finally retired and broken up the following year.

MV Royal Daffodil

This ship deserves a page all to itself. The MV *Royal Daffodil* weighed in at 2000tons and was built in 1939 by William Denny and Sons, Dumbarton for the General Steam Navigation Company. She managed a few trips from Tower Bridge to Ostend prior to the outbreak of the Second World War. Quickly requisitioned by the Royal Navy she took part in Operation Dynamo, the evacuation of Dunkirk in 1940, making seven trips across the English Channel bringing home some 9,500 soldiers. And not without incident, suffering bomb damage as well as machine gun attacks. The *Royal Daffodil* continued to have a interesting war. Following the end of hostilities she had a complete refit and returned to cruising from Gravesend or Tilbury even taking part in 'No passport' trips to France during the late 1950s. Musical entertainment was provided including live performances from the top stars of the time including Gene Vincent and Jerry Lee Lewis. Sadly these jolly japes were to prove unprofitable and in 1967 she travelled the English Channel for the last time to Belgium for breaking up. The *Royal Daffodil* lived through interesting and dangerous times. Rock & Roll music might just do some peoples head in but it's a long way from being bombed and machine gunned. The *Royal Daffodil* saw it all.

Paddle Streamers

PS Queen of the South

Built in 1931 by Fairfield Shipbuilders & Engineers, Govan for the London & North Eastern Railway she was originally named *Jeanie Deans* and weighed in at 635 tons. She worked summer cruises around the Firth of Clyde until the outbreak of the Second World War when she was adapted for minesweeping. Following the war and a complete refit she returned to summer cruising till being retired at the end of 1964. Then sold to the Coastal Steam Packet Co and renamed *Queen of the South* she commenced cruising on the River Thames in 1965. Sadly continual technical problems brought this to an end in 1967 whereupon *Queen of the South* was towed to Antwerp, Belgium for scrapping. This was something which apparently caused a stir in the world of paddle boat enthusiasts to the extent that not another of these grand old paddlers would ever again go for scrap.

Ferry Boats

SS Caesaria and SS Sarnia Weymouth Harbour

SS Caesaria and SS Sarnia

The *Caesaria* and *Sarnia* were sister ships built by J. Samuel & Sons, East Cowes, Isle of Wight for the British Transport Commission, Southern Region's Weymouth to Channel Islands ferry service. Boat trains, two per day in each direction, would traverse the quay branch from Weymouth harbour station to the main line adjacent to the town station and from there onto Waterloo station, London.

The *Caesaria's* maiden trip was in November 1960 and the *Sarnia's* in June 1961. On both these occasions special cruises to or from Southampton were put on for the press and invited guests. For the *Caesaria's* maiden cruise a Pullman train was put on running from Waterloo to Weymouth harbour the passengers then travelling back to Waterloo from Southampton. For the *Sarnia's* maiden cruise the reverse occurred the passengers embarking at Southampton with the Pullman train then running from Weymouth harbour station back up to Waterloo.

Both ships received a reversed version of the British Rail 'arrows of indecision' logo on their funnels in the mid 1960s with 'Sealink' being painted on their hulls in the early 1970s

But with the introduction of older ferry boats converted to roll-on roll-off car use in 1974 the *Caesaria* and *Sarnia's* days were numbered. The *Caesaria* was retired in 1975 with the *Sarnia* going two years later. However time was not yet up for *Caesaria* as she continued on the Dover/Folkestone to Calais ferry service till being finally retired and sold off to a Hong Kong concern in 1980. Renamed the *Aesavea* she possibly worked for some time as a hotel ship before being broken up in the Korea in 1986.

The *Sarnia* on retirement in 1977 was sold off to a superstore being renamed *Aqumarket*. She worked for a very short time as a floating duty free supermarket off the Belgium coast before being bought up by a Greek concern and renamed the *Golden Star*. She was sold on again in 1981 to a Saudi Arabian company working between Port Said and Jeddha but was broken up in Pakistan by 1987.

The Weymouth quay branch closed to goods in 1974 and to regular passenger services in 1987, fuel tanker deliveries ceased in 1983 with the last enthusiasts special running in 1999. Since then there have been several attempts to reopen the line but all, so far, to no avail.

MV Earl William

OK, I own up this picture is from the family album. Taken at Weymouth during May 1982 the photograph shows Iris and the children standing in front of the *MV Earl William*. At 3980 tons she was the new order in ferries, a purpose built car ferry. Named *Viking II* she entered service in July 1964 with Thoresen Shipping having been built in Tonsberg, Norway. By 1976 she had been sold to British Rail (Sealink) being renamed *Earl William* and by the early 1980s was working the Weymouth to Channel Islands route. This she did till displaced in 1987 then serving as an immigration detention centre at Harwich for a year before returning to ferry duties on the Liverpool to Ireland route. By 1992 she was working foreign waters having been sold to Ardonis Shipping and then sold on several times after that eventually becoming a hotel ship in 2006 on Trinidad and Tobago. During 2011 whilst being towed she was involved in a collision and eventually sank.

SS St Andrew

The *SS St Andrew* was built in 1932 by Cammell Laid for the Great Western Railway's Fishguard to Rosslane, Southern Ireland ferry service. She weighed some 2700 tons. During the Second World War she served as a hospital ship. *St. Andrew* covered many WW2 campaigns beginning with Boulogne, Calais, Dunkirk, Malta, Salerno, Algiers, Bizerta, Anzio, Taranto, Catania, Bari, Ancona, and Syracuse. Her Mediterranean record was phenomenal, sailing over 46,000 miles and rescuing 15,145 wounded men. *St. Andrew* had the dramatic experience of going to the rescue of and watching the sinking of *St. David,* her GWR sister ship, with the ship's fellow colleagues and friends on board. It was during this desperate action that *St. Andrew* had a narrow escape from a bombing attack that left her slightly damaged but badly shaken. Whilst continuing on her humanitarian mission in the Mediterranean she struck a mine in 1944, and had to be towed to Taranto, the damage was so great that it effectively put an end to her Mediterranean service, she was compelled to limp home in stages where it took months for repairs to be carried out. She was returned to the Great Western Railway in 1946 resuming her ferry duties on the Fishguard route. Not the most practical of ferry boats for shipping cars they having to be craned aboard in rope slings, note the inset picture of the Austin A40. No doubt this caused a few worrying moments to their owners. The *St Andrew* was retired and scrapped in 1967.

MV Brading

Following the Second World War the Southern Railway ordered two ferry boats to replace its war time losses and aging paddle steamers on the Portsmouth to Ryde, Isle of Wight service. Built by William Denny of Dumbarton the two ferries *MV Brading* and *MV Southsea* came in at around 980 tons and were launched in 1948 and so went into service with British Railways (Southern Region) They both continued in service till made redundant by car ferries , the *Brading* being retired in 1986 initially being stripped of parts for her sister ship. After being laid up for many years she was finally scrapped by Pounds Shipbreakers, Portsmouth in 1994

HMS Vanguard

HMS Vanguard

HMS Vanguard was at 44,500 tons the Royal Navy's biggest fastest and also its last battleship. Built by John Brown & Co, Clydebank she was laid down in October 1941 and following several design alterations was launched three years later. Her main armament was 8 x 15in. guns which interestingly enough originated from two WWI battle cruisers which were converted to aircraft carriers in the 1920s

She was commissioned in May 1946 thus seeing no action in the Second World War her first major duty was to become one of the largest Royal Yachts ever, taking the Royal family on tour to South Africa in the late 1940s. Talk about flying the flag.

With the days of the battleship deemed to be over, following its 1955 refit she was put into reserve being finally decommissioned in June 1960. On her final departure from Portsmouth, the location of our photograph, to Faslane Scotland for scrapping, large crowds thronged the waterfront to wave the grand old lady farewell. She was broken up over 1961/62.

HMS Ark Royal, Portsmouth Navy Day August 1966

HMS Ark Royal was laid down in May 1943 at Cammell Laird and was to be one of a class of four aircraft carriers. Two were cancelled at the end of the Second World War whilst construction of *Ark Royal* and her remaining sister ship *Eagle* was suspended. *Ark Royal* was finally launched in May 1950 being commissioned in February 1955 by which time she had been considerably redesigned and incorporated the first angled flight decks on a British carrier. Her initial compliment of aircraft included Sea Hawks, Sea Venoms, Gannets and various helicopters Our pictures show *Ark Royal* at the Portsmouth Navy Day in August 1966, the Sea Vixen on display being from 890 Squadron. By 1970 Phantoms, Buccaneers and Gannets were the order of the day. With the decision to end fixed wing aircraft on carriers the days of *Ark Royal* were numbered, she being decommissioned in February 1979. The following year she made the journey north of the border to Stranaer for scrapping and on arrival the partial hulk of her sister ship *Eagle*, which had been decommissioned back in 1972, still remained. *Ark Royal* was broken up between 1980 to 1983.

HMS Bulwark & *HMS Leviathan*, Portsmouth Navy Day August 1966

An interesting picture of two aircraft carriers taken at Portsmouth during the August 1966 Navy Day, but not forming part of the event itself. Looking across *HMS London* and berthed alongside the dock wall is *HMS Bulwark* whilst *HMS Leviathan* is in dry dock.

HMS Bulwark was one of four light aircraft carriers known as the 'Centaur' Class laid down during the closing stages of World War Two. *HMS Bulwark* was launched in 1948 and like its sister ships work was then suspended. She was finally commissioned in 1954 and by 1960 was converted to the role of a Commando carrier till being placed in reserve in 1976. Recommissioned as an anti-submarine carrier in 1979 she maintained this role till being finally decommissioned in 1981, remaining at Portsmouth till 1983 when she was towed to Scotland for scrapping. Two of her sister ships were decommissioned in the 1960/70s and scrapped whilst the remaining carrier *HMS Hermes* served in the Falklands and was later sold to the Indian Navy were she still remains.

HMS Leviathan was one of six light fleet carriers of the 'Majestic' Class which were all laid down in 1943 and launched by 1945 whereupon construction was suspended. Five of the class were eventually completed, two being sold to the Australian Navy, two to the Canadian Navy and one to the Indian Navy. However *Leviathan* was never completed being towed to Portsmouth during the late 1940s remaining there as an accommodation ship till the decision was made to scrap her. To that end following removal of her boilers she was towed to Faslane, Scotland in 1968 for scrapping.

HMS London, Portsmouth Navy Day August 1966

One of a class of eight 'County' Class guided missile destroyers built in two batches of four from 1959 to 1970. These were the first such ships to be supplied to the Royal Navy. *HMS London* was built by Swan Hunter, Wallsend and was laid down in December 1960 launched one year later and commissioned in October 1963. Our photograph was taken in August 1966 at a Portsmouth Navy Day. Of the first four destroyers of the Class all were decommissioned by the early 1980s. Three were eventually disposed of although one lingered on in the role of a static training ship at Portsmouth till 1996. *HMS London* itself was to have a further lease of life being sold to the Pakistani Navy in February 1982 becoming their *Babur.* She was finally decommissioned in 1993 and sold for scrap in 1995. Of the second batch all four were sold to the Chilean Navy during the 1980s the last being decommissioned in 2006.

Freighters or Cargo Boats

Whilst the great ocean going passenger liners succumbed to the jet aeroplane in the '60s, so the traditional freighter, or cargo boat, went the same way when containerisation came in during the following decade. Whilst various forms of containerisation had been around for many years it was not till the mid 1950s that this form of cargo handling started to take off. Early containers around the world were not compatible but once this problem had been overcome with standardised container dimensions, containerisation became a simpler and quicker method of transportation of cargo. Containerisation had a huge effect on the nation's docks with traditional docks such as London and Liverpool suffering badly whilst smaller docks such as Felixstowe expanded.

Glenartney

Built by the Caledon Shipbuilding & Dry-dock Company, Dundee in 1940 for Glen Line. She came in at 9795 tons and initially worked as a commercial freighter till requisitioned by the military becoming a fast supply ship serving on the Malta run in 1942, progressing to the Pacific by 1944. Returned to Glen Line in 1946 she worked the Far East run till sold for scrap in 1967.

MV Otaki

Built by John Brown & Sons, Clydebank in 1952 at 10934 tons as a refrigerated cargo ship for the New Zealand Shipping Cargo Co. Sold on in 1973 to the Federal Steam & Navigation Company she would be resold on several times again before being broken up in 1984.

SS Autolycus

Built by Vickers Armstrong at 7700 tons in 1948 as a refrigerated cargo ship for the Blue Funnel Line. Sold on initially to the China Mutual Company in 1974 and several owners after this carrying the name *Gulf Trader* at some time. She was broken up in 1978.

Glenalmond

One of four express cargo ships known as the 'Priam' Class built for the Glen Line in the mid-1960s. At 12294 tons she was one of two of the class built by Mitsubishi Heavy Industries, Japan being the first ship to be built in a Japanese yard for a British company. The other two were built in British yards and the Class was technically very advanced for the time. The *Glenalmond* worked the Europe to Far East routes. Made redundant by containerisation in the 1970s she was sold on in 1973 to several foreign shipping companies being renamed *Patroclus* and then *Rejab*. She was broken up in 1984/85.

MV Ipswich Purpose & Ipswich Progress

Two sister ships photographed together at an unknown UK location. Both general cargo ships they were built in Bremen, Germany. The *MV Ipswich Purpose*, left in picture, was built in 1955 whilst the *MV Ipswich Progress* followed in 1961. When photographed in the early 1970s they were registered to a Rotterdam company before being sold on but within a few years they had both sunk within a short time of each other. The *Progress* went down in 1976 following a collision on route to Amsterdam whilst *Purpose* followed suit in 1977 foundering near Alexandria.

The *Vega, Queensland, and Atlas*

Three ships of which I can find little about. The top and middle pictures show the *Vega* and the *Queensland* both of which appear to be coastal bulk traders. The *Vega* looks to be a modern ship, has two derricks on board which suggests she might be used to moving cargos at small harbours with little in the way of handling.

Whilst the *Vega* might prove elusive the buildings behind give the clue to the location, these being the East Anglian flour mills of E .Marriage & Sons at Felixstowe Docks. Opened in 1907 the mill went on to be successful in the importation of wheat and the export of flour. Disaster struck in June 1940 when an RAF bomber crashed into the mill putting it out of action for several years. Always known locally as Marriages Mill it closed in 2005 and was demolished two years to make way for dock improvements.

MV Vega Felixstowe Docks

Queensland

SS Atlas

Meanwhile the *Queensland*, sitting high in the water, seems to be the sort of boat that gets its hands dirty on coal or coke. Or even limestone, who knows. And as for the *Atlas* what a dear old tub she is, a traditional cargo boat nearing the end of its days. Who knows how many of these old tramp steamers once plied our seas and oceans transporting all manner of cargoes. But no more. Possibly.

MV Esso Dover

The Esso Company, or Exxonmobil, to give the company its correct name has since its early days as the Standard Oil Company and its English branch the Anglo American Oil Company have run a considerable shipping fleet from ocean going to small coastal tankers.

The *Esso Dover* was one of the latter built in 1961 at 490 tons by J.Bolson & Sons of Poole, Dorset and worked, amongst other duties, from the large storage wharves at Purfleet on the River Thames to various coastal ports around the UK.

She was sold off in 1980 firstly to Cherry Marine being renamed *Cherryhobs* who shortly afterwards resold her onto a St Helena concern who renamed her the *Bosum Bird*. She finished up being a floating fuel store on the Ascension Islands and was scrapped in 2001 at Mombasa.

MV Steyning

Built by Clelands Shipbuilders, Wallsend in 1965 as the *Glanton* for the Sharp Steamship Company. Sold on in 1971 to the Stephenson Shipping Company they renamed her *Steyning* and she stayed with them for ten years before being sold on to a Panamanian concern who renamed her *Julia*. She was broken up at Aliaga in 1988/89.

A Thames Sailing Barge

The Thames sailing barge was a commercial sailing boat that reached its zenith at around the turn of the 19th/20th century. At that time some 2000 barges were registered but there popularity declined especially after the Second World War leaving only a handful at work by the 1960s. Generally they had a crew of two and their cargoes could vary from bricks, rubbish, sand, coal and grain. They worked not only on the River Thames and it's estuaries but from the North of England to the South Coast.

Characteristically they were flat bottomed boats fitted with leeboards and were ideal for shallow waters and rivers. As such they could dry out in tidal waters without heeling over as can be seen in our picture the location of which remains unknown

Our particular barge, a 150 footer, carries the name *Will* and was built in 1925 at Great Yarmouth being originally named *Will Everard* and owned by F.T. Everard & Sons of Greenhithe. She was sold on in 1966 being renamed *Will* so this dates the photograph to some time after 1966.

This picture was taken by our two touring motorcyclists who we came across earlier in this book. However they have now progressed to a car. The motorbikes have seemingly gone the way of a F Series Vauxhall Victor which appears in several of the negative strips which includes our Thames sailing barge.

MFV Trawler *Greyfish* LT361

An all steel trawler the *Greyfish* was built by R. Dunston Ltd, Thorne, Yorkshire in 1961 for Huxley Fishing Company located in Suffolk. She came in at 160 tons and was registered to Lowestoft where I think the photograph was taken in August 1968. Whilst contracted out to the oil industry she ran aground and was wrecked near Lerwick in 1973.

Faversham. A harbour view

An interesting collection of wooden boats long before the age of those ubiquitous white plastic jobbies. We must assume our picture is Faversham as two of the boats bear the registration letter F indicating that Faversham, Kent is their 'home town'. The third boat is an interloper from London. They would all appear to be motor boats judging by the exhaust pipes sticking out clear of the superstructure. The crew of the *Faustulus* appear to be in deep conversation. The picture can be dated to the 1960s thanks to the Ford car parked up on the dockside in the extreme left of the picture.

A rather longer photographic excursion into the world of 1960s motorcycle sport.

Motorcycle sport, or any other sport for that matter, paid no part in your young authors life. At school football and cricket were things to be avoided at all costs. Then motorbikes, well initially a moped, and an apprenticeship at the local British Bath Works came along. As an aspiring metallurgical chemist, sounds good that, my immediate guv'nors, a Mr Sheehan and a Mr Jones were both keen motorcyclists. So in the midst of my railway period, 1963, armed to the teeth with a large format twin lens reflex camera I found my way in the company of Mr Sheehan and his fiancée on their elderly BSA Golden Flash sidecar outfit to, of all things, a motorcycle scramble at Pirbright, Surrey. It would also be my last. If I'd ever thought that the environs of the Bath Works foundry or even a steam loco sheds were dirty they had nothing on a motorcycle scramble. Being a dry day the amount of dust thrown up by the bikes was something to be seen to be believed. Clouds of the stuff. On coming home mother wondered where I'd been to. The same couldn't be said for a day out at a motorcycle sprint the following year. By then I had acquired a 35mm SLR camera and once again I was a passenger in a sidecar, this time with Mr Jones in his BSA Super Rocket. The sprint meeting was held at the now decommissioned 'airfield' of RAF Debden. Now that was something else, that I could do again. And eventually did. But little enthusiasm could be generated from these few excursions into motorcycle sport, even a speedway meeting with the rabble made little impression. At least Speedway seemed to treat spectators well; you could have a drink or even a meal whilst watching the racing. To me it was more a social event like greyhound racing so whilst four bikes going round and round in a dirt oval seemingly did a lot for some folk sadly it did little for me. Then my old mate Buster took me to a road race meeting at Brands Hatch. Easter 1965 that would be. If the sprinting caught my imagination then road racing fired it up. As for railways and shed bashing that had had its day. Either accompanying Buster in his old van or with the rabble on our bikes road race meetings were the business. London's Crystal Palace and Brands Hatch were our nearest circuits and back in the

Pirbright Scramble 1963.

Crystal Palace & Lydden circuits 1965
The top picture features a National meeting at Crystal Palace. Not short of a few spectators and close to the action. The lower picture is of a Club meeting at the newly opened Lydden circuit. The number of spectators could be counted on one hand. But the racing could just as fast and furious.

Brands Hatch 1967
Druids Hill Bend
With and without the grandstand.

The lower picture also shows the unsung heroes of any race meeting - the track marshalls!

1960s the old A20 to Brands would be heaving with thousands of bikes on race days. We even rode out to more distant outposts such as Lydden, Silverstone and Mallory Park. These latter two circuits along with Brands Hatch would stage International meetings especially following the Isle of Man TT races. These would be eagerly anticipated with Grand Prix 'Stars' riding exotic multi cylinder four and two stroke Italian and Japanese machinery. With no Grand Prix on the UK mainland racing enthusiasts had to make do with endless British single cylinder machines. Close racing it may have been but an International meeting would be excitement in itself. And in the quiet times between races you had any number of self appointed trackside experts for entertainment. With such excitements you tended to ignore the somewhat basic facilities, you parked up in a field to spend the day standing out in the open come rain or shine. Grub was limited to hot dogs, with or without onions. Or nothing at all. There was of course at extra cost the grandstand, which sounded grand but inevitably wasn't. Toilet facilities could be basic in the extreme. But despite the tens of thousands of spectators that went each year to the bigger race meetings there was, unlike football matches, never ever any trouble. Things could get a bit silly on the ride home though especially for us lot on London's South Circular Road.

During the inter-war and immediate post war years all forms of motor cycle sport boomed in the UK but as time passed by most faded away from the headlines. Scrambling was on the TV for a while as was I on one occasion but unfortunately being lapped by one Peter Butler in a production bike race. Still at least I was once on TV, and Peter was a man at the top of his game, I never was. Whilst I was to become involved in sprinting and road racing and these therefore get some coverage elsewhere in this book of mine both scrambling and speedway were very popular both before and after the Second World War. Even my mother who has no interest in motorcycles went to speedway meetings as a young woman. Scrambling was initially dominated by British lightweight two strokes and larger capacity four strokes bikes but as the 1960s passed by both European and Japanese bikes began to monopolise the sport and even that wonderfully quant English term 'scrambling' fell out of use the sport becoming known as Motocross. When it came to Speedway there was only one bike of choice and that was powered by the British built 500cc four stroke single cylinder ohc JAP. This engine was THE speedway engine for some forty years and when the company finally closed its doors in the early 1960s the JAP engine speedway bike slowly faded away over the following decade as riders changed to Czechoslovakian engined ESO and Jawa bikes.

Straight Line Sport - Sprinting

Man and machine against the clock. So it ever was. The sprinting of motorcycles goes back to the early days of motorcycling and was popular both before the Great War and the following inter-war years. Many clubs would organise sprints at all manner of venues from seaside town marinas to the grounds of stately homes and even factory sites. Even long sandy beaches weren't immune, provided the tide was out.

Sprint venues were either on the flat or run as hill climbs and could be either 'straight' or 'twisty' and would vary from a standing quarter-mile up to a half-mile, with some hill climbs being up to a mile long.

Following the Second World War and through the 1950s and early 1960s sprinting once again regained its pre-war popularity with many clubs able to organise events at former RAF airfields.

Whilst the majority of sprints were single lane events twin lanes were quite common, although in the nature of the sport the two competitors still rode against the clock and not each other. Put this way, when the rider got the thumbs up or the green light he had time to adjust his tackle and settle down before dropping the clutch. Traditionally the bike would be 'chocked and blocked' on the start line, that meaning being positioned correctly with a block then set against the rear wheel. The only way was forward.

Sprints or 'High Speed Trials' along the sea front were still to be found following the Second World War at such places as Weston-super-Mare and Hartlepool as well as the now well established Brighton venue. The Sunbeam Club commenced organising sprints at Ramsgate in 1956, this Club being famous for running the Gatwick Sprints in pre war years from 1931 until the beginning of hostilities.

With the number of varying clubs running sprint meetings through the 1950s, the National Sprint Association was formed in 1958 by enthusiasts to co-ordinate matters. As such the NSA started to run their own meetings from 1962 onwards, eventually becoming the dominant factor in straight line sport with riders competing in the prestigious NSA Championships as well as National and World record attempts.

Through this period big British bikes dominated sprinting, a 1000cc Vincent ridden by George Brown consistently ran the standing quarter mile in the low 10 seconds but it was another bike and rider that smashed the 10 second barrier and that was Alf Hagon on his 1300cc J.A.P. special in 1967.

But by the mid-1960s Drag racing, an import from those dastardly Americans, slowly took over the mantle from sprinting as the premier straight line sport.

Sprinting at Club level continues to remain popular primarily on former RAF airfields, whilst most of the seaside town sprints or 'High Speed Trials' had disappeared leaving Brighton as the last survivor in the long history of a sprint by the seaside.

A twin cylinder Triumph accelerates away along Debden's long runway the hanger forming an appropriate backdrop. The year is 1964 and some twenty years previous Debden was a fighter command airfield and would have a different tale to tell ....

George Brown and 'Super Nero' his 998cc Vincent

George Brown on his 1000cc Vincent 'Super Nero' blasts off from the start line at a Debden sprint meeting in 1964. Many sprinters would name their machines, the bikes then becoming as well known as their riders. George Brown worked for the Vincent company before starting up his own motorcycle business in the early 1950s retiring from road racing to concentrate on straight line sport. The event pictured is a twin lane affair the other rider being on a Norton International, the Sunbeam car pictured to the right is powering the timing lights. Being a warm and sunny day the timekeepers are sitting out in the open and literally taking the vapours. And by now must be totally deaf.

The start line…the only way is forward.

Fred Cooper on his 498cc Triumph 'Hermes' (top picture) on the start line at the Ramsgate sprint, sometime in the 1960s. Ear defenders anyone?. Charley Rous, 998cc Moto Vincent (middle picture) lines up to a somewhat over enthusiastically painted start line at a 1960s Debden meeting. Our start line man keeps a keen eye up the sprint line no doubt waiting for a clear runway. A last quick check round by our unknown sprinter (lower picture) as he waits for the off at a 1960's Ramsgate sprint. *Courtesy Vintage motor cycle sprint section and Nick Pettitt/Brian Sparrow collection.*

Ian Ashwell and 'Saturn' his 998cc Vincent

Two pictures of 'Saturn' Ian Ashwell's 998cc Vincent. The top picture features the bike 'naked' without its dustbin fairing at a1964 Debden meeting. Note the old crushed petrol can in use as a bike stand. What else?. The lower picture features a fully faired 'Saturn' blasting off from the start line at a Duxford sprint in the 1960s. At this time Ian Ashwell was a main contender in sprinting but sadly lost his life in an accident whilst riding 'Saturn' at the 1968 Brighton Speed Trials.

Bottom picture Courtesy Nick Pettitt/Brian Sparrow collection

Bill Bragg on 'Yellow Peril'

Bill Bragg, left, sitting on 'Yellow Peril' his 650cc Triumph. A self taught motorcycle engineer Bill Bragg took to sprinting following a serious motor cycle racing accident. 'Yellow Peril', would be transported to meetings on his motorcycle sidecar outfit, other bikes being pulled on a trailer. The distinctive fairing was believed to originate from a Second World War American fighter's drop tank. The other sprinter and machine remain unknown. Debden 1964

The passage of time.

The sprinter and the two bikes shown here remain a mystery. It's the 1964 Debden sprint meeting that I went to but already the event has slipped into history. The sprinter with his distinctive chequered helmet remains unknown. We are no wiser in the lower picture despite the bike's name being partially displayed across the dustbin fairing and having carburettors poking out at all angles. The car is a Standard Vanguard Phase III if it helps. May this be a lesson to us all to keep accurate records as to what we photograph.

Vintage Bikes and Velocettes

A pair of vintage machines or perhaps back in the 1960s just a pair of old bikes. Balancing on some old wooden boards is a 500cc Rudge Ulster alongside a 1000cc JAP Special. However, our little girl takes no interest as she has far more important things to attend to. An interesting moment in the affairs of sprinting (lower picture) as the timekeepers, top of picture, have all turned their attention to our Velocette rider returning from his run. Being a former timekeeper I suspect the reason being is that they failed to get his riding number first time around.

Big Beasts!

'Thor', Ernie Woods 1000cc JAP engine fitted in a Norton Featherbed frame at the Debden 1964 meeting. The bike was built by another sprinter Francis Williams in the early 1950s who sold it onto Ernie Woods by the end of that decade. However, it would be Ernie Woods that christened the bike 'Thor' and note the use of a decent bike stand, something not all that common in the 1960s. As an aside, this picture reminds the author that in photographing motorcycles you quickly become aware of men's fashions in the trouser department. Our picture above shows a twin engined Triumph dating to the 1980s. The photograph shows the bike's builder Derek Harmsworth warming up the rear tyre at a 1980s Bovingdon sprint meeting. However the bike was never to reach it's full potential and was eventually sold it still being campaigned today.

Lower picture courtesy Derek Harmsworth

Derek Harmsworth and his 500cc Triumph

A fine study of Derek Harmsworth on his 500cc Triumph at a Welsh sprint meeting in the early 1970s. Derek commenced sprinting in 1966 and by the 1980s was on top of his sport, holding many National Sprint Association and Auto Cycle Union Championships as well as National Speed records. Derek also held the World speed records in the 500cc sidecar class for standing start quarter mile, kilo and one mile. *(Courtesy Derek Harmsworth)*

Drag Racing and Santa Pod Raceway

By the 1970/80s Santa Pod featured a tower construction that spanned both lanes that gave race officials and timekeepers an excellent view down the track. This picture makes for an interesting comparison with the earlier photograph of the 1964 Debden sprint meeting. Although the picture above is out of time with the book being taken in 2002 the two bikes that are featured are both period 1960s machines. Unusually both bikes sport dustbin fairings which, although commonplace in the 1960s, had long fallen out of favour by the time this photograph was taken.

Whilst the rather gentlemanly affair of sprinting held sway in the UK, the American version of straight line sport, Drag racing, exploded on the home front in 1964.

Even in America Drag racing was a relatively young sport kicking off after the Second World War with the rise in unofficial car racing down a town's main drag, which to you and me would be the town's High street. Hence the American term drag racing. That would be those tearaways again, supposedly formerly WW2 types now bored with living. As the name implies two riders were not only running against the clock but also against each other. The first past the finishing line wins.

This means that trackside both riders position their bikes to a light beam and when they get the green … they GO.

The first event in the UK was in early 1964 at the former RAF base of Duxford and went under the title of the 'Big Go'. To me that conjures up something completely different …

This was followed by the first British International Drag Festival held over six meetings through September and October 1964, two of these meetings being held at Blackbushe, Surrey. The following year, 1965, the Second International Drag Festival was reduced to two meetings only, one again being held at Blackbushe. Both these festivals featured cars and bikes from both sides of the pond, the first Dragfest generating huge crowds of spectators. Sadly the British weather conspired against the second Dragfest with heavy rains doing their worst, the Blackbushe event I remember well having ridden down on my bike. The meeting started dry but when the rains came it became quickly apparent that Straight line sport in the wet is something entertaining for spectators but not to be recommended. Riding home I had my own little race with a sports car on a short section of dual carriageway prior to running into Camberley. I easily had him but we parted the best of company waving to each other, but then he was dry and no doubt warm whilst I was by then bloody cold and soaking wet.

Such was the interest generated by the two Drag Fests that the UK's first permanent Drag Strip opened the following year at Santa Pod Raceway, Bedfordshire, the first meeting being on Easter Monday, 11th April 1966.

It would be fitting that this American version of straight line sport kicked off at Santa Pod as under another name and a different time Santa Pod would have been known as Podington airfield and home to the United States Army Airforce 92nd Bombardment Group during the Second World War.

Whilst the Americans arrived at Podington shortly after the airfield opened in 1942, it was

September 1943 that the B17 Flying Fortresses arrived. By the time of their departure in July 1945 several hundred missions had been flown, it was for nothing that the 92nd was known as 'Fames favoured few'.

Many years later that could have equally applied to the fastest of the Drag racers.

Initially Drag racing at Santa Pod was the preserve of big British bikes. The big, but now somewhat dated, Vincent and J.A.P 'V' twins were campaigned along with more conventional Triumph or Norton parallel twins. As engine capacity limits were relaxed double engined Triumphs and Nortons became common.

Many riders of this period entered both sprint and drag race meetings until many of the former RAF airfields used for sprinting became untenable for the fastest machines. Straight line sport more than most attracted competitors who were also competent engineers and many bikes were built, stripped and tuned in the owners' garage or shed, others less skilled would be at a disadvantage no matter what 'back street bodgery' was indulged in.

With standing quarter times forever getting quicker by the mid 1970s the nine second barrier was finally smashed by Keith Parnell on a 750cc Triumph twin, at a time when Japanese bikes were starting to make their presence felt.

By the early 1980s it was all over for the British as Japanese bikes were fast becoming the competitors' natural choice of machinery. Time, in more sense than one, had moved on.

Rogue Et Noir 2 - more than a name

'Rogue Et Noir', the bike, came about in the early 1970's, a conventional 750cc Triumph based drag racer ridden by Keith Parnell of Lanner, Cornwall. By the summer of 1975 these two would go down in straight line sport history being the first to crack the nine seconds barrier at 8.93secs at 151mph for the standing quarter mile. But for drag racers time never stands still and 'Rogue' went on it's way less it's engine and 'Rogue Et Noir 2' was born incorporating some of the original bikes engine parts. However 'Rogue 2' was to be an innovative machine being one of the first of a new breed of rear engined drag racers, the engine being placed as near to the rear wheel as possible. The picture of 'Rogue 2' dates to 1976 but the show board propped up against the rear wheel is somewhat misleading, so we'll ignore it. So whilst 'Rogue 1' was written into the record books 'Rogue 2' place in history was to be something perhaps more profound being one of that last breed of Brirish drag bikes that took the final 'Hurrah'.

Photo courtesy Phil Steele

Road Racing - Part One.
Big British single cylinder jobs and all that.

1960s Short Circuit Aces

The 'King of Brands Hatch' Derek Minter (top picture) and 'The Master of Mallory' John Cooper. Both ride Manx Nortons.

A misnomer if ever there was one as road racing had been banned in the UK way back in the 1920s. For racing enthusiasts road racing, other than the Isle of Man, generally meant short circuit racing. And usually on a Tarmacadam surface.

Brands Hatch and Silverstone would be the best known examples today but many more circuits, or tracks, exist some such as Mallory and Cadwell having their origins in designated parkland. Many other circuits owe their existence to the Second World War being former military airfields, whilst before the war Brooklands was extremely well known to the British public.

Road racing was split into varying engine capacity classes as was scrambling and straight line sport, and these would generally be the 125cc, 250cc, 350cc, 500cc and over 500cc or unlimited Classes

These capacity classes would start to change as time went by. However, following on from the Second World War with the revival of road racing in the UK including the Isle of Man TT races and the European based World Championships, the premier classes would always be the 500cc and 350cc. For this reason they were known as the 'Senior' and 'Junior' Classes.

The machines that were the staple diet for competitors in those early post war years were the British 'over the counter' single cylinder overhead camshaft (ohc) four stroke 350cc and 500cc Manx Norton's the 350cc AJS 7R and the 500cc Matchless G50. These companies also entered Works teams on similar machines in the World Championship Grands Prix until they were outclassed by the 'one off' multi-cylinder Italian Works Gilera, Moto Guzzi and MV Agusta machines. Unable to compete against the Italians the British pulled out of Grand Prix racing in 1954, and with spiralling financial costs the majority of Italian companies followed suit in 1957 leaving only MV Agusta. This company then had a clear field in the Senior and Junior Classes until the Japanese four stroke Hondas started to compete in these classes in the mid 1960s.

Interestingly, the Norton company entered a road-based ohv parallel twin 500cc in the 1961 Isle of Man TT races, known as the 'Domiracer'. It took third place but any further development was discontinued as Norton's closed their race shop shortly after. Surprisingly the last year a British single cylinder machine won a Grand Prix was by a privateer, a private entry, as late as 1969.

For privateers the British singles would be the natural, and for the Senior Class the only choice of machine. A spectator at the 1970 TT races would find the Senior and Junior race start line

Manx Nortons

A trio of 350cc Manx Norton's with American rider Lance Weil heading off Chris Conn and Ray Pickrell into Druids Hill Bend, Brands Hatch. 9th October 1966.

packed with more four stroke single cylinder jobs than you could shake a stick at. But within a few years they would be gone, replaced in the main by screaming Yamaha two strokes. Although it would take another five years or so before Yamaha managed to take the Senior and Junior World Championships, motorbike racing had changed out of all recognition.

Back on the mainland to be a spectator at UK short circuit meetings during the 1960s the 350cc and 500cc events would be totally dominated by British four stroke singles, many of them 'breathed on' by highly experienced tuners. An International meeting would bring additional excitement with Grand Prix stars on multi-cylinder Italian and then Japanese Works machines. Occasionally, very occasionally, a local short circuit 'ace' on a British single would trounce the visiting Grand Prix star riding some exotic Works machinery. Most of the UK short circuits had their own local 'Aces'. Derek Minter was the 'King of Brands' whilst John Cooper was the 'Master of Mallory', both riders on Manx Nortons.

However, the writing was on the wall for the big singles when Norton, AJS and Matchless ceased manufacturing their racing machines and supplying spares in 1963. Up till then these reliable 'over the counter' machines gave, for the short circuit 'scratchier' and the Grand Prix 'privateer' alike, competitive machinery.

However, the British singles were to receive a extra lease of life when all the spare parts and tooling for the AJS and Matchless machines were purchased in 1966 by Colin Seeley, a sidecar racer, who not only continued to supply spares but produced his own racing bike, the 500cc Seeley powered by the former Matchless G50 engine. Likewise, John Tickle took on the spares etc. for the Manx Norton in 1969 ultimately producing his own version of the Manx which he manufactured into the 1970s.

The 1964 Earls Court Motorcycle Exhibition

Exhibited for the first time the Rickman Brothers 499cc Metisse G50 racing bike. With the Matchless company ceasing production of their G50 racer in 1963 some 170 G50 engines were supplied to the Rickman Brothers for incorporation into their own racing bike for 1965 season. Also included, for the first time, were disc front brakes.

In the 250cc 'Lightweight' Class, the single cylinder British two stoke Greeves Silverstone and Italian four stroke Aermacchi racing bikes had it their own way until the arrival of the Japanese machines in the early 1960s. Yamaha introduced their air cooled twin cylinder 'TD' series two stroke racers in 1962. These were originally based on their road bikes but continual development resulted in the water cooled 'TZ' series being introduced in 1973 by which time Yamaha had long dominated the 250cc Class.

With overbored, well possibly overbored, 250cc Yamahas proving themselves more than capable of competing in the 350cc Junior Class the introduction of the air cooled twin cylinder two stroke 350cc TR2 in 1969 saw the final death knell of the single cylinder four strokes. Yamaha then superseded this model in 1973 with the water cooled TZ2 version.

By the early 1970s the British stranglehold of the 500cc Senior Class in National and Club events was under threat. Overbored 350cc Yamahas were becoming common with Suzuki introducing their two stroke twin cylinder air cooled 500cc TR500 in 1967. Within two years Kawasaki followed on, unveiling their 500cc two stroke air cooled three cylinder H1. The Suzuki TR500 was later replaced by the more sophisticated four cylinder water cooled two stroke RG500 in 1974. The scream of two stroke engines had by now all but displaced the throaty roar of the British four stroke singles, they now being outclassed in both National and Club events. Save for the occasional canter by the more conservative competitor some respite came for the uncompetitive British bikes when single cylinder only classes were introduced in the mid 1970s. This was followed in the 1980s when Classic bike racing made its debut.

Meanwhile back in the 1960s, the 'Over 500cc or Unlimited Class' had a great appeal at both National and Club level due to an abundance of machinery available from stripped down road bikes such as the 650cc Norton twins and the Triton, a Triumph twin engine fitted into a Norton Featherbed frame

From the origins of the Unlimited Class came the Formula 750cc Class which made its debut in 1971 with the introduction of several UK Championships including the 750 Formula TT races in the Isle of Man. None of this was surprising as the large capacity 750cc road bike was the British manufacturer's last throw of the dice in the face of fierce Japanese competition.

British companies did extremely well in the first instance fielding Works teams with BSA/Triumph and Norton entering racing versions of their production road bikes, the three cylinder Rocket/ Trident and twin cylinder Commando. Triumph took the chequered flag in the first two years of the Isle of Man Formula 750 TT with Norton winning in 1973. Equally impressive results were obtained in the various homeland championships with John Cooper on a BSA 750cc three cylinder Rocket actually displacing Giacomo Agostini on the Italian Works 500cc MV from first place at an international event at Mallory Park.

But for BSA/Triumph and Norton financial troubles were to overcome them and the Works teams were soon disbanded and from 1974 onwards the Japanese two stroke Suzuki F750 took centre stage.

The Brits had gone.

Brands Hatch 1966

An interesting view of the Brands Hatch paddock 'warm up' area. Competitors would be initially called for over the paddocks tannoy system to assemble in the 'warm up' area prior to their particular event. On being given the OK from the paddock marshal all competitors would then run down 'en masse' through the tunnel which took them to the inside of the circuit and the start line. Behind the 'warm up' area but out of the picture is the notorious Paddock Hill bend and in the far distance can be seen the track leading up to Druids Hill bend which back then was set in the countryside. Today the warm up area has been swept away and whilst the Druids Hill bend remains the trees have succumbed to the M20 motorway which passes close by the circuit at this point.

Brands Hatch - 1966 & 1967 paddock shots.

International Motor Cycle Race of the South. October 1966

Two photographs taken in the paddock on the day. The 350cc Junior race, the first race of the day. was billed as the star event between World Champion Mike Hailwood on his Works 350cc six cylinder Honda and the 'young pretender' Giacomo Agostini on the Works 350cc three cylinder MV Agusta. With no motorcycle Grand Prix staged on the UK mainland it was not often that British race fans saw International GP stars on exotic Works machines. The photograph above features Mike Hailwood accelerating the 350cc Honda through the paddock warm up area for the tunnel that took riders under the track into the centre of the circuit and the start line. When it came to the race the fans were to be disappointed as the Honda engine failed a few hundred yards after the start leaving Agostini with an easy win over a whole pack of British singles. Whilst the bike no doubt survives Mike Hailwood was tragically killed in a road traffic accident in March 1981.

International Motor Cycle Race of the South. October 1966

The second picture shown here was taken during the morning of race day with Giacomo Agostini's mechanic Vittorio Carrano waiting to fill up the 350cc MV. The circuits 'petrol station' still exists today although it has been somewhat redressed over the years and now has more modern pumps. Note the cost of petrol per gallon and the somewhat critical look of the enthusiasts as they scrutinise Agostinis MV. Whilst the Junior race was a anti climax the 500cc Senior race was enlivened with two former Grand Prix 500cc four cylinder Gileras in the field. Some enthusiasts thought a rerun of the great days when MV and Gilera clashed might be expected. Sadly any challenge to Agostini and the MV failed to materialise the Gileras finishing mid field in a gaggle of British singles.

'King of Brands' Race Meeting 24th March 1967.

Two shots of competitors as they commence lining up in the paddock for the 'King of Brands' race to start. A good selection of Manx Nortons and Matchless G50s can be seen including (top picture) No 24 Neville Landrebe from New Zealand whose Matchless G50 sports disc front brakes and No 45 Percy Tait on the Works twin cylinder 500cc Triumph. A couple of riders are wearing jet style crash hats and several of the bikes still sport the full Peel 'Mountain Mile' fairings.

Derek Minter, The 'King of Brands'

Featured here are the 250cc two stroke Works Cotton Telstar (top picture) and the 500cc ohc single cylinder Seeley ridden by Derek Minter in 1966. The Cotton had a Villiers Starmaker engine which had been introduced in 1963 while the 500cc Matchless G50 engined Seeley appeared three years later. Minter usually rode Manx Nortons and at Brands Hatch always rode with race number eleven. For part of the 1966 season Minter competed on the 500cc Seeley, he retired from racing at the end of the following year..

Senior and Junior machines.

Reg Kirby's 350cc and 500cc Rickman Metisse machines (top picture) were powered by AJS 7R and 500cc Matchless G50 engines. The Rickman brothers had developed their own frames for road racing bikes and also pioneered the use of disc brakes in the sport, note the disc brake fitted to the 500cc machine. On this occasion the bikes were ridden by Bill Ivy. The lower picture illustrates two traditional Manx Nortons, a 350cc and 500cc these bikes being many competitors choice of raceware whilst the Ford Thames vans were the favoured means of 'race transport'.
Unforunately, the negative of the bottom picture has been damaged.

Road bikes to race tracks.

Two successful adaptions of road bikes, The Triumph factory developed their own racing bike (top picture) from their basic 500cc twin cylinder ohv roadster, the bike being ridden by Works rider Percy Tait. The lower picture is of Paul Dunstall's Dominator the engine being a 750cc road based ohv Norton engine fitted into a former Works Norton Domiracer lowboy frame. Over the years several riders rode for Paul Dunstall. Both the 500cc Triumph and the big Dunstall Dominator were successfully campaigned throughout the 1960s.

Engines and Frames.

This BSA Gold Star (top picture) sports a 350cc ohc Velocette KTT engine, a very odd combination, whilst the lower photograph is of a 1000cc Vincent engine shoehorned into a Norton featherbed frame. A combination not totally unheard of in racing circles of the 1950/60s.

A Japanese Enclave

A rare beast indeed, a former semi-Works twin cylinder 305cc Honda CR77. Not many of these machines escaped into dealerships let alone private hands. The owner/rider was Dave Simmonds who also rode the equally rare 125cc Tohatsu pictured alongside. The photograph was taken sometime in 1966 and by this time the Honda had understandably acquired a Norton Featherbed frame. This picture is a little taster of the rising sun, a Japanese enclave within the paddock. Behind the Honda and the Tohatsu are three 'over the counter' twin cylinder 125cc Honda CR 93 race bikes. These were still relatively early days for Japanese racing hardware and few examples would be seen around the paddock in those days but within a few years they would sweep all before them. So there you are a little something of what machines you would find around the paddock at a Brands Hatch meeting in the mid 1960s. Today (2017) all these bikes, British and Japanese, would now all be deemed as classic machines and no doubt be highly prized, highly polished and equally highly priced.

Road Racing - Part Two
Production Racing - when big British parallel twins ruled the day

A 1965 500 mile endurance race programme.
Courtesy John Durrant

Following the Second World War motorcycle races for standard production road bikes were introduced at the Isle of Man TT races. Known as the 'Clubman's Series', within a few years they were dominated by the single cylinder BSA Gold Star which continued to do so until the Series was abandoned in 1957.

The other major event for production road machines through this period was the yearly Nine Hour endurance races introduced at Thruxton in 1955 by the Southampton & District Motorcycle Club. These races were likewise dominated by BSA Gold Stars until they were also discontinued in 1957.For 1958 the Southampton Club introduced the 500 mile race and this event ran yearly till 1973, although not always at the Thruxton circuit.

From the late 1940s onwards all the major British manufacturers introduced large capacity 650cc ohv parallel twins with many of these companies entering their own bikes through their dealerships in prestigious events such as the 500 mile race.

Initially the Norton concern were successful with their 650cc Dominator SS but it would be the Triumph 650cc T120 Bonneville that went on to dominate not only the 500 Mile race but production racing through the 1960s.

By the mid 1950s the BSA group had taken over the Triumph concern which although it retained its own identity made the group the worlds largest manufacturer of motorcycles.

Nortons would return to the 500 mile race with some success in the early 1970s, with their upgraded 750cc parallel twin Commando. The 500 Miler was replaced by the Powerbike International endurance races for 1974.

Another famous endurance race for production machines was the 24 hour French Bol d'or whose history goes back to the 1920s. Following on from the Second World War the race was all but dominated by French riders but it was Norton machines that did the winning till the races ceased temporarily in 1961. With the races recommencing in 1969 the Japanese company of Honda initially took the chequered flag but the newly introduced three cylinder ohv 750cc Triumph T150 Trident won the following two years and on both occasions with English riders. From then on British machines were never to win endurance races again. The Japanese, mainly Honda, were to see to that.

It may be of some interest to say that during this period production bike races were started by kick-starting the things. Just prior to the start I, like many other riders, would suffer badly with nerves and of also fluffing the start, something that could hang heavy on a rider. If you failed to start the bike within the first few kicks you could be rapidly reduced to a state of utter despair. Many of the endurance races would be started 'Le Mans' style, the riders having to run across the track jump on the bike and crank it into life. All good fun.

On the UK club scene the BMCRC - British Motorcycling Racing Club - had included production races within its meetings for many years and by the 1960s had been joined by the Bantam Racing Club, British Formula Racing Club and the Southern 67 Club. All these clubs included production races, the championships of which were hotly contested.

Production bike racing - 1960s.

The flags down (top picture) and a production bike race literally kicks off at a Bantam Racing Club meeting at Snetterton in 1967. The lower picture offers a classic action shot of Charlie Vance on a 650cc Triumph T120 Bonneville ahead of the 650cc BSA A65 Spitfire of Clive Wall at Snetterton in 1967. The Triumph Bonneville is interesting as it has high level pipes.

Bottom Picture. Courtesy Clive Wall

Throughout this period British factories could give considerable support to Club production racing through their dealerships, providing the dealership had a rider capable of winning. A great variety of machines were always to be found in Club production races. However, as said, it would be the ubiquitous 650cc Triumph T120 Bonneville that would ultimately be the choice of most competitors, especially as the Triumph company offered factory race parts for its machines. The Thruxton Bonneville appeared in limited numbers from 1965, being the production racer version of the road bike.

Last throw of the British dice

Clive Wall rides a 750cc T150 Triumph Trident manufactured from 1968 to 1975.
Courtesy Clive Wall

It was also not uncommon to find production races now being included in National race meetings, Brands Hatch adding the Class into their programme in 1963. Such was the interest that a production race was included in the BMCRC Hutchinson 100 International race for 1965, Mike Hailwood taking the chequered flag on a Works 650cc A65 BSA Lightning Clubman. This model had been introduced by BSA that year as a potential production racer and was supplied with twin carburettors and close ratio gears. She was finished in gold trim with drop handlebars, rear set footrests and siamese exhausts. The following year, 1966, BSA took first place again but this time it was with the more powerful Works A65 Spitfire, whilst in 1967 the newly introduced and much publicised 750cc Norton Commando took first place.

Production racing was introduced for the Diamond Jubilee of the Isle of Man TT in 1967 and this event then ran for nine years although for the last two years of its existence it was reconfigured as a ten lap endurance race.

Both BSA and Triumph entered Works teams on A65 Spitfires and T120 Thruxton Bonnevilles with Triumph going on to win that year. A Dunstall Norton took first spot in 1968 but other than that Triumph then continued with their wining ways, the newly introduced three cylinder 750cc T150 Trident winning in 1969. BSA pulled out in the same year..

The Dunstall Norton was interesting. When Nortons closed down their race shop in 1963 Paul Dunstall, a former road racer turned business man, purchased the Works Norton twin cylinder Domiracers with all the spares and components. From this he eventually went to on to successfully supply his own racing and road going versions of the Norton till the late 1970s.

Nortons themselves were to make a welcome appearance at the production TT in 1969 with their Commando model, the factory then going on in the early 1970s to produce a limited number of purpose-built production racers. Whilst the Commando was a modern machine it was based around the well established but outdated 750cc ohv parallel twin engine. It has to be said that Honda introduced its overhead camshaft four cylinder CB750 model only two years later.

The 1970s were to be the Indian summer of British influence in production racing both in the Isle of Man TT races, long distance endurance racing and at home in Club events.

Whilst the Triumph Bonneville had been eclipsed by it's stable mate the three cylinder Trident, it would be the Norton Commando that at the start of the 1970s would become the club production racers machine of choice.

Whilst Works Triumph triples continued to dominate the production TT, the entry was fast going the way of Japanese and European machines. When Triumph pulled out after winning the 1975 event, the following and last year of the production TT British machines didn't even make a dozen entries.

Through the same period Japanese machines were beginning to make their presence felt at club meetings initially with 500cc machines such as the two stroke three cylinder Kawasaki and the twin cylinder T500 Suzuki. With the larger capacity Japanese machines becoming ever more popular, for the British bikes it was all over.

Sadly a sport once dominated by companies such as Triumph, BSA or Norton had collapsed as Japanese manufactures took over a diminishing UK motorcycle market leaving British companies reeling with poor management, mergers, strikes, political interference and ultimately having nothing new to offer. By the end of the decade those once great British motorbike empires had gone their factories empty, derelict or demolished.

Spitfires at Angels Five

Tony Smith leads Clive Wall out of the hairpin at Snetterton in 1967 both riding 650cc BSA A65 Spitfire's. Whilst Tony Smith is on a Works bike Clive Wall rides a standard production version. For those who are connoisseurs of BSA A65 Spitfires the detail differences between the two machines will be apparent.

The Japs are coming, the Japs are coming...............

Seemingly a somewhat innocuous picture of a chap on a touring motorbike. The event is the 1966 Brighton High Speed Trials, the rider is Allan Robinson and the bike is a twin cylinder double overhead camshaft 444cc Honda. Introduced to a somewhat surprised British public at the same event the previous year it acquired the nickname of the 'Black Bomber'. Later barred from entering the 500 mile race due to its exotic specification this bike was the first Japanese large capacity machine. Suzuki, Yamaha and Honda had by the mid 1960's made a name for themselves in the smaller capacity market.....but this was something different. Although not Hondas best seller the bike being discontinued in the early 1970's it could be said that the Black Bomber was the first shot over the bows to the established large capacity British motorcycle industry. Not that they took much interest.

British parallel twins. Triumph T120 650cc Bonneville

Following the Second World War the British motorcycle industry concentrated on single and twin cylinder pushrod operated over head valve (ohv) machines. The twin cylinder machines were of the parallel twin design which Triumphs introduced in 1937 with their very successful 500cc 'Speed Twin'. A 650cc version, the Thunderbird, was added in 1949 with a sports version the Tiger 110 being introduced in 1954. This gave way in 1959 to the upgraded 650cc T120 Bonneville fitted with twin carburettors. As with all twin cylinder models the engine and gearbox were of separate construction but were redesigned in 1963 as a single unit being then known as of 'unit construction' configuration.

Whilst the 750cc three cylinder ohv T150 Trident was introduced in 1968 the 650cc Bonneville remained in production till 1973 being superseded by the T140 750cc version. Despite restyling and other improvements production finally ceased in 1983 by which time production was in the hands of the Workers Co -operative at the old Triumph Meriden factory.

1960 T120 Bonneville of pre-unit construction.

The picture above shows a standard 'unit construction' production Bonneville adapted for production racing in the 1960s and fitted with Triumph competition Thruxton silencers but with non-standard clip on handlebars and headlamp brackets. On the following page we have a fine shot of John Hedger (top) powering his Bonneville along the start/finish straight at Snetterton in 1968 while Peter Butler (bottom) has two fingers on the clutch lever as he accelerates out of Bottom Bend, Brands Hatch in 1965. Note the straight handlebars and high level pipes.

British parallel twins. Triumph T120 650cc Bonneville

British parallel twins. Norton … From Dominator to Commando.

The Norton concern had a long history with single cylinder over head camshaft (ohc) machines from the road going sports based International to the famous racing Manx Norton. Their involvement with ohv parallel twins commenced with the introduction of the 500cc Dominator in 1949 the 600cc version being available in 1955 by which time the famous featherbed frame had been introduced. The 600cc Dominator was phased out with the introduction of the twin carburettor 650cc Dominator in 1961 which sported the new slim line featherbed frame. The 750cc single carburettor Atlas appeared in 1962 but both models had ceased production by 1967 the 750cc Atlas engine continuing in a newly introduced Commando model. This was very much a motorcycle of the 1970s and the vibration problems associated with the parallel twin engine were overcome with the engine and transmission being isolated from the bike itself by a sophisticated form of rubber mounting. Following Nortons return to competitive road racing in the early 1970s they introduced a fully equipped production racer version of their 750cc Commando. By 1973 an 850cc road Commando was introduced but financial problems within the company brought production to an end in 1977 finishing what was the most sophisticated of the archetypical British parallel twins.

The picture above is the author on his 750cc Norton Commando at Brands Hatch in 1975. The bike was a stock standard model dressed up in production racing clothes. Other than fitting the then revolutionary new transistorised ignition system the engine was in standard trim. Racing the bike for two seasons I did reasonably well on her finally retiring at the end of 1975 by which time big British bikes in production racing were in decline. Within a few years they would all be gone. Riding his 650cc Dominator Alan Smith (following page, top picture) takes a fast right hand bend at Snetterton in 1966 while the middle picture features Brian Davisons 650cc Dominator at Cadwell Park in 1967. In the lower picture Malcolm Button's attention is diverted at a 1968 Snetterton meeting whilst waiting on his Dominator for the production race to start. Grid positions were by ballot.

.Top and Middle pictures courtesy Carol Smith and Clive Wall

Alan Smith 1966

Malcolm Button 1968

British parallel twins. Norton 650cc Dominator.

British parallel twins. BSA… Rocket Gold Stars to Spitfires

Whilst BSA had the reputation for manufacturing 'bread and butter' bikes they certainly knew how to name them. BSA introduced their first parallel twin a 500cc A7 model in 1947 the 650cc A10 Golden Flash appearing two years later. The somewhat sportier A10 Road Rocket was introduced in 1954 being replaced by the rather similar Super Rocket in 1957. This model then ceased production in 1963 BSA having introduced their redesigned 650cc parallel twin, the A65 Star, the previous year. This model featured a totally new unit construction engine and gearbox. However before the A10 model bowed out in 1963 a limited number of Rocket Gold Star's were produced this being BSA's only true sports twin cylinder bike up to that date. The A65 Star was joined by, and another first for BSA, its twin carburettor stable mate the A65 Lightning in 1965. This model was also available in Clubmans form as a potential production racer but was produced in limited numbers as it was replaced by the A65 Spitfire in 1966. This was to become BSA's fastest ever parallel twin sporting many innovative features including twin Grand Prix carburettors. However it was to be short lived and ceased production in 1968. By the early 1970s the BSA group was in considerable financial difficulties with the BSA factory closing in 1973.

The picture above shows H Robertson on his 650cc BSA A10 Rocket Gold Star at Bottom Bend, Brands Hatch in 1965. Tony Smith, following page top picture, features on the works A65 Lightning Clubman at the 1965 Brands Hatch season opener in April 1965. The middle picture is of Len Reeds A65 Lightning taken in the paddock at Snetterton in early 1969, the clipons and headlamp brackets are again non standard while the silencers have been modified with 'flats' for enthusiastic cornering. The lower picture features Clive Wall at Snetterton in 1970 on the ex works A65 Spitfire, sponsored by Dick Smith of R H Smith M/C, West Drayton. Little is known of this machine other than she is believed to have been one of a trio entered by the BSA factory for the production bike race in the 1966 International Hutchinson 100 meeting at Silverstone. The race was won by John Cooper on one of these machines but what this bikes involvement was is not known other than R. H. Smith Motorcycles purchased it a few years later. Clive Wall campaigned the bike from 1969 to 1971 taking several highly contested Club Championships on the way. My interest in the machine was that I purchased it for the 1972 season but spent the year rebuilding it following throwing the bike down the road at my first race meeting. Such was the bikes disgust at my treatment of it that the engine called time on me at the end of the 1973 season, by which time BSA A65s had disappeared from the production racing scene. She now lives on peacefully in a motorcycle museum. Whilst many former period 'proddy' race bikes still remain the property of their owners no doubt many more have been sold on for small fortunes, their new owners being blissfully unaware of the old tale of the Irishmans shovel.

British parallel twins. BSA… Lightnings and Spitfires

Top and lower pictures courtesy BSA Group Magazine and Clive Wall

Meanwhile down in the forest . . .

Traction Engines

And that be traction engines. The four pictures shown here are taken from 'The Collection' so we have no clues as to the woody location or the date but further research plumps for the 1960s. Our photographer paid two visits and on his first trip *Titan* Reg, No. NM 340, top picture, was out of use. She was built in 1915 by Marshall & Sons of Gainsborough, Lincs. A plate on the engine informs us she is owned by a Mr Leith and a Mr Pearce of Camborne, Cornwall. Meanwhile in the lower picture another Marshall engine Reg, No. TA 3624 built in 1913 is clearly working under its own steam.

Traction Engines

On our photographer's second visit *Titan* was being steamed whilst a 1896 J & H McClaren engine Reg, No. BD 5448 was towing a somewhat bedraggled 1904 Burrell's of Thetford engine Reg, No. AF 3531 out of its tin shed. The name *Attraction* can be made out painted on the boiler.

At the time of the photographs being taken whether these traction engines were already preserved and guaranteed a future I do not know but what is certain is that they all survive today.

Life down on the Farm

Whitevine Farm, Nr. Crewkerne, Somerset

Whitevine Farm

Meeting up with Iris it was not long before we were holidaying with her country cousins the Oxenbury's at Whitevine Farm, near Crewkerne, Somerset, a family-run dairy farm of some 150 acres. The two pictures above date to June 1970, the previous page picture also dates from June 1970 and shows the farmhouse's 'east wing' with the long single story dairy parlour to its right. The old Ford lorry has its load of seven full steel milk churns ready to run down the track for collection. She is positioned in a downwards direction ready to bump start her as she never had a working battery. Note the washing out on the line, the hay rick and two old cast iron baths for drinking water. We follow the cows up the track, top picture, after milking, whilst the lower picture has Iris tying up the empty return churns following collection from a wooden stand positioned alongside the lane. With the farm not on mains electricity and milk production going from churns to bulk storage and handling the Oxenburys had to pull out of milking in 1973.

Whitevine Farm

Hay, dried grass that is, would be the most natural option for feeding cattle through the winter months. Through the summer grass would be allowed to dry then cut and baled. The top picture has Pip Oxenbury rueing (lining up) the hay on his David Brown Cropmaster with a side rake whilst I follow behind on the Fordson Major turning the hay over with a tedder to assist drying. Whilst this picture dates to July 1970 the lower picture taken some six years later and shows baling in progress with Phil Oxenbury working with a Ford Major 4000, Jones baler and bale sledge. Baling reached its peak during the 1970s with some 6500 manageable sized bales produced over the summer months to be stored in barns or in ricks.

Whitevine Farm

The physical hardships associated with hauling and handling bales gave way in the late 1970s to silage production and then large round bales. Straw, a by-product of wheat, was also baled during the summer months for winter bedding although not to same quantity as hay baling. In the top picture which dates to September 1985, Pip Oxenbury loads on the last few straw bales with the Ford Major 4000 watched over by dad Phil as the ladies do the stacking. The trailer tractor is their Massey Fergurson 165. Loads of both hay and straw would be hauled on considerably larger trailers being stacked eight bales high. Phil when in his seventies could still pitch fork a bale on to a trailer three bails high. In the lower picture a Lister elevator is put to good use loading straw bales onto the rick. This pre-dates the top picture by two years.

Whitevine Farm

Tractors, tractors, tractors. The top and middle pictures date to August 1993 with the author driving the Ford Major 4000, top picture, which by now has lost its cab whilst in the middle picture we have a International 674 with its load of hay and humans. No rush yet as Butch the farm dog still relishes the shade under the tractor. Drinking water for cattle was always an absolute necessity as the lower picture, taken in 1976, shows. Whitevines reservoir was the only water supply which one way or another found its way to a collection of old cast iron baths. Dozens of them were littered about the place. These cast iron baths I found of interest having done my time at the British Bath Works, Greenford, West London. By the mid 1970s the cast iron bath had already been declared obsolete in a modern world. Close Inspection could reveal a baths maker and one at least came from what was once considered the Bath Works most up to date moulding plant. Dated 1958 in less than twenty years it was relegated to a farm.

Whitevine Farm

We finish our little excursion down the farm looking at the other end of business. It's back to June 1970 and Phil Oxenbury waits on the David Brown Cropmaster, top picture, as Pip loads up the trailer with slurry scraped up from the yard. This was then shovelled out evenly across the fields. By 1973, see above, a reconditioned rotaspreader had been aquired and the term 'shit splatting' came into its own. On the shovels are Pip Oxenbury and the author. As time progressed a way of work changed from dairy to beef etc., with tractors becoming more sophisticated and just a little larger. Whilst the Oxenbury's sold up in 2016, Pip took his old Fordson 4000 tractor with him. Although the land is still being farmed the buildings themselves have since fallen out of use.

Whitevine Farm

A Class 33 drifts past Whitevine Farm with an Exeter bound train on a misty morning in April 1980. The farm's northern boundary was the old Southern Railway main line from London Waterloo and old Phil Oxenbury had many a tale of the railway's doings. First name terms would be had with the track gangers and platelayers. Tales would be retold over again from the day the mighty 'Devon Belle' needed a push start from a lowly tank engine following a signal check, to the day the Plymouth gin train caught fire with all the contents being lost to the flames. Our picture shows Number One child assisted by Megan the farm dog viewing the train's passing with the number of carriages always being counted off...seven...eight...and sometimes even nine. Clever dogs collies.

A Farmer's Day Out
The Great Dorset Steam Fair. 1970

The origins of the Great Dorset Steam Fair date back to the late 1960s when a small group of enthusiasts put on a bit of a do at Stourpane near Blandford, Dorset. The first real Fair was staged in 1969 and then again 1970 the year I took these pictures. By 1971 the Fair had again moved and flourishes today at the much enlarged site at Tarrant Hinton, Blandford Forum.

Fowlers at work

A ploughing competition gets underway with a Fowler ploughing engine in the top picture, whilst the middle picture shows the humble portable steam engine. This example was manufactured by Marshalls of Gainsborough, Lincs and dates to 1933. In the lower picture we have a Fowler convertible engine (i.e. could be made into a roller) having hauled up a supply of coal and water for the ploughing engine and now rests alongside an elderly cultivator.

Threshing machines at work.

These two pictures feature traction engines powering threshing machines. The crew of an unidentified traction engine, top picture, appear to be in deep discussion whilst the threshing machine is more in view in the lower picture with a 1920 Burrell engine Reg, No. YA 366. Of interest is the chap on the extreme left armed with his cine camera, tri-pod, and audio cassette player.

Wood sawing

A Garratt traction engine of 1918, Reg, No. BH 8009 is put to good use sawing logs. Iris and I visited the Fair with her country cousins who farmed near Crewkerne, Somerset. We escaped from the car park whilst they became trapped, resulting in us getting home to West London before they got back down the road apiece.

The South & South West - A Decade after Beeching

Southampton Terminus June 1977

Following on from our holidays during the 1970s with Iris's cousins in the West Country it wasn't long before we were trawling round the many former station and loco sheds sites closed during the previous decade or even before. So we kick off with Southampton Terminus which opened in 1840 serving the town with a further extension into the Docks themselves, see picture above with track on extreme left. A large Hotel 'The South Western' was then added alongside the station buildings with a glass canopy being added between the two buildings for the convenience of passengers. Originally named 'Southampton' the station was renamed 'Southampton Terminus' in 1923 by which time 'Southampton Central' station on the main through lines from Waterloo to Bournemouth had taken most of the traffic. With 'Central' becoming the town's main station and on the electrification of the main line in 1967 Terminus station closed completely. Whilst the Dock extension remains all other rail tracks were removed within a few years of closure the former trackbed being used for car parking. The Hotel had become offices following WW2 and the rear of that building can clearly be seen in the picture above. Both the former hotel and station buildings remain intact today as flats and as a casino. The glass canopy also remains but the platform area has long been cleared being utilised for both car parking and housing.

The Ocean Terminal, Southampton Docks 1984-1985

The Ocean Terminal opened in 1950 to serve passenger liners working the North Atlantic route including Cunard's *Queen Mary* and *Queen Elizabeth*. The terminal boasted the most luxurious of facilities for travellers and was rail connected with platforms both inside and outside of the two story building. The internal track had platforms on both sides to speed up both arrivals and departures. With the demise of the great ocean liners during the 1960s the Ocean Terminal was partly replaced in 1966 by the nearby combined passenger/freight Queen Elizabeth II Terminal. The Ocean Terminal closed in 1980 and was demolished three years later. The top picture dates to 1985 and shows, to the left, the former terminal's interior track with a single platform edge remaining *in situ*. The lower picture, left, dates to 1984 and shows the site of what would have been the magnificent Art Deco styled Ocean Terminal southern entrance. Note the terminal's interior track curving round in the foreground to rejoin the Doks's main running tracks. The lower picture, right, shows the Art Deco styled Ocean Terminals electricity transformer house which would have also provided public access via a bridge to the Ocean Terminal's viewing area.

Salisbury (GWRly) & Sutton Bingham June 1977 & July 1971

Salisbury's GWR station, as photographed in 1977, was the terminal of that company's line from Westbury. The station closed to passengers in 1932 but remained open to goods traffic and then as storage sidings till the early 1990s. The refurbished building remains in commercial use today fronting the new DMU depot.

Sutton Bingham station, lower picture, was located on the former SR Waterloo to Exeter main line west of Yeovil Junction. The station was reduced to an unstaffed halt in 1960 and closed completely in December 1962. The picture dates to July 1971 the line having being singled four years previously. Nothing now remains.

Chard Junction. Seaton Junction July 1976

Both Chard and Seaton Junction stations were located on the former Southern Railway's Waterloo to Exeter main line. The line west of Salisbury passed to the Western Region in 1963 with both stations closing in 1966. A branch line ran from Chard Junction station to Chard which closed to passengers in 1962. The picture, above, dates to the mid-1970s amd shows the site of the branch line bay platform. Today only the Up main station platform remains. Seaton Junction station was rebuilt in 1927 with four tracks including passing loops and a branch platform to Seaton positioned on the Down side. The photograph dates to July 1976 and despite the truncation of the Up loop and the, by then, repositioned telegraph poles on the old Down main very little has changed, presenting to the passing traveller a ghost station in the middle of nowhere.

West Bay and Bridport June 1973 & September 1976

The Bridport branch connected to the Great Western's Yeovil to Weymouth line at Maiden Newton. A later extension was made from Bridport to West Bay to serve the harbour but closed to passengers back in 1930 and goods traffic in 1962, the track being removed three years later. Goods traffic was withdrawn from Bridport in 1965 and the branch closed completely in 1975, having only remained open due to a subsidy from Dorset Council. Track removal commenced shortly after closure. Whilst West Bay station has survived the years and remains today as a café, Bridport station has not been so lucky the site having been redeveloped as a supermarket. Of the pictures, West Bay dates to June 1973 and Bridport to September 1976 and, as can been seen, my Iris has sadly long missed the last train.

Lyme Regis July 1970

The Lyme Regis branch joined the former Southern Railway main line at Axminster on the Waterloo to Exeter main line The branch was sharply curved in places resulting in three elderly Adams 4-4-2 radial tanks working the line until 1961. The branch was a victim of the Beeching Report losing its goods traffic in 1964 with complete closure the following year. The track was lifted in 1967. The site remained derelict for many years, the wooden station buildings being removed in 1979 for use elsewhere. The top photograph was taken in July 1970 with a Bradfords lorry on the trackbed whilst the lower picture dates from the mid 1970s. Nothing now remains of the station, the site being redeveloped into a small industrial estate and builders' merchants.

Exmouth August 1977

The rather grand Southern Railway station at Exmouth was the terminus for both the branch from Exeter and the line to Sidmouth Junction via Budleigh Salterton. Whilst the latter suffered the fate of the Beeching Report and closed in 1967 the Exeter branch still survives although a spur to Exmouth Docks closed in the same year. Major rationalisation took place in the early 1970s, the station being reduced from a four platform terminus to just one platform with a new small replacement station building opening in May 1976. The grand old station buildings and platforms were cleared in the early 1980s to make way for the A376 Marine Way. The pictures all date to August 1977.

Barnstaple Town c.1976

Barnstaple Town station was the first intermediate station on the Southern Railway's branch from Barnstaple Junction to Ilfracombe. Unlike the Junction station, Town was north of the River Taw and therefore the line crossed over the Taw by means of a distinctive curved steel girder bridge. Until 1935 the narrow gauge Lynton to Barnstaple Railway connected with the Ilfracombe branch at Barnstaple Town station. The Ilfracombe line was threatened with closure under the Beeching Report with goods traffic being withdrawn in 1964 followed by passenger traffic in 1970. Track lifting took place in 1975 with the girder railway bridge going in 1977. Town station survives as a restaurant, both photographs date to 1976 as the tracks have gone but the bridge hadn't.

Bude July 1971

Bude and Padstow were the two destinations of the branch that ran from Okehampton on the Southern Railway's North Devon main line from Waterloo to Plymouth.. The branch itself started at Meldon Junction just west of Okehampton. With the transfer of all former Southern lines west of Exeter to the Western Region in 1963, Bude lost its through connection to London Waterloo, being reduced to a local service only. Subject to closure in the Beeching Report, goods traffic ceased in 1964 with complete closure in 1966 and demolition and redevelopment to a housing estate in 1975. The photographs date to July 1971, and it seems some form of parcel service is still operating. The Austin A55 van in the picture is ours.

Padstow September 1976

Padstow was the other destination of the branch from Okehampton this line parting from the Bude line at Halwill Junction, a station once in the middle of nowhere. Padstow, like Bude, suffered a decline in both goods and summer passenger traffic and came under Western Region control in 1963, eventually losing its direct services to London (Waterloo). Subject to the Beeching Report, goods traffic was withdrawn in 1964 with passenger traffic ceasing in 1966. Padstow station actually closed the following year when the Bodmin connection ceased. The station remains intact, the buildings now being the offices of Padstow Town Council and part of the trackbed remains as a cycle path crossing Little Petherick Creek by the former railway three span iron bridge which fortunately was never dismantled.

Callington September 1975

Callington was the terminus of the Plymouth, Devonport & South Western Junction branch line which was originally, in part, a narrow gauge mineral railway. Callington station originally boasted a single track overall wooden canopy and connected with the L&SWR London (Waterloo) to Plymouth main line at Bere Alston. The PD&SWJR and L&SWR became part of the Southern Railway at the 1923 Grouping. Coming under control of the Western Region in 1963 and following the Beeching Report the old main line was singled and remained open only from Plymouth up to Bere Alston and then on to Gunnislake an intermediate station on the Callington branch. Nothing now remains of Callington station. The photographs date to September 1975 by which time the overall canopy had been demolished.

Bodmin General September 1976

Bodmin, later renamed Bodmin General in 1949, was the terminus station of the short GWR branch from Bodmin Road (later Parkway) on the former GWR Plymouth to Penzance main line. A further line then ran out from Bodmin General to connect with the Southern Railway at Boscarne Junction for the Wadebridge and Padstow line. Subject to the Beeching Report both lines including Bodmin General closed to passengers and goods in 1967 with china clay movements from nearby Wenfordbridge coming to an end in 1983. The photograph dates to September 1976 and whilst the station is closed and boarded up, china clay traffic is still in evidence. The branch from Bodmin Road (Parkway) to General with the short stub to Boscarne Junction reopened as a heritage line in 1986.

Radstock North . S&DJRly July 1976

With the Somerset & Dorset line subject to the Beeching Report, goods traffic at Radstock North ceased in 1964 with complete closure in March 1966. However, a short spur of the old line remained open at Radstock to service the local collieries and in 1970 the Somerset & Dorset Circle moved onto the site and Radstock North's future seemed secure. Sadly all coal traffic ceased in 1973 followed by the Trust moving out in 1976 being unable to secure the site from British Rail. All remaining track work was then quickly removed with the station and surrounding area being cleared by 1980. The top picture dates to July 1976, the lower picture taken at around the same time and shows the subway which ran under the main running lines at the west end of the station adjacent to the level crossings on the A367.

Bath (Green Park) early 1970s & September 1976

Opened in 1870 as Queen Square the station was the terminus of the Midland Railway (later LMSRly) ten mile branch from Mangotsfield station on their main line from the Midlands to Bristol. The company took care to build a grand façade to Queen Square which blended in with Bath's Georgian Architecture although it only boasted an arrival and a departure platform.
The Somerset & Dorset Joint Railway reached Bath in 1874 and had come to an agreement with the Midland Railway to use Queen Square as its Bath terminus. This connection would create considerable through traffic on the S&DJRly be it freight or summer passenger workings from the Midlands down to the south coast despite the time consuming train reversals at Queen Square.

The station was renamed Green Park in 1951. From 1958 the station came under the control of the Western Region and from then on much of the through traffic was routed away from the S&D line to such an extent that by 1963 the line was reduced to local traffic only. The Beeching Report recommended closure and the S&D line closed completely in March 1966. Passenger traffic on the old Midland line into Green Park also ceased in March 1966 with goods traffic remaining till 1971. Although utilised as a car park the station area became neglected and fell into disrepair till the 1980s when full restoration took place financed by Sainsburys the supermarket chain. The former station buildings are now used by various small retail establishments. The two photographs opposite date from the mid-1970s and the two above from July 1976, the top picture featuring Iris sitting on the boot of our 1968 Vauxhall Victor.

Evercreech Junction & Highbridge. S&DJRly Sept. 1976 & July 1977

Evercreech Junction station was the connection for the Burnham branch with the A371 road crossing the line just south of the station and was the location of the picture dated September 1976. The Down station buildings survive as a private residence the trackbed being infilled and put over to garden use. Highbridge station was the last intermediate station before Burnham with the branch line both crossing and connected to the former GWR main line. Although the S&D closed in March 1966 a short stub of the branch remained open until 1972 to serve both a local creamery and to bring in large quantities of concentrated fly ash for construction of the nearby M5. This resulted in the demolition of much of the station and by July 1977, the date of the photograph, only a single platform remained. The repositioned branch 'stub' was removed in the early 1980s the site now being overwhelmed with housing and a trading estate.

Yeovil Town & Hendford. July 1971 & July 1973

Yeovil Town station was on the GWR Yeovil Pen Mill to Taunton branch with a connection to the former Southern Railway at Yeovil Junction. Subject to the Beeching Report the line, including Town station, closed to passengers in 1966 and goods the following year. All track work had been removed just prior to the July 1971 photograph with demolition two years later. The site was then redeveloped into the Town car park which in turn was redeveloped some 25 years later into a leisure centre. Hendford station, lower picture dated July 1973, was the original station at Yeovil on the Taunton branch opening in 1853 and closing shortly after following the opening of Town station. A goods yard was located alongside the Brunel built station and whilst the trackbed remains as a pedestrian/cycle track the actual site has been redeveloped into a trading estate.

Langport West July 1973

Langport West was an intermediate station on the GWR branch from Yeovil to Taunton. Subject to the Beeching Report the branch closed to passengers in 1966 with goods going the following year. By the time of these photographs, July 1973, all track work had been removed and the station buildings demolished. The station site was eventually cleared and a small industrial estate now occupies the site although the road bridge featured in the picture still survives. The lower picture is of a small office situated in the goods yard which itself was set back from the station. Of interest the warehouse, extreme left, and the white building in the background are still extant.

Chard Central, Donyatt & Ilton halts. July 1976

Chard Central station, of Brunel design with a substantial single road canopy, was originally the terminus for the GWR branch from Taunton. The Southern Railway also had a branch from Chard Junction terminating in Chard at their Town station which closed to passengers in 1917 the line then running from Taunton to Chard Junction as a single entity. Chard Central was originally known as Chard Joint being later renamed as Chard and then in 1949 as Chard Central. The branch was closed to passengers in 1962 and completely in 1966, Chard Central station remains today as a retail outlet surrounded by a housing estate. The Ford Thames van at Chard is ours.

Donyatt and Ilton, pictured right, were intermediate halts on the GWR section of the branch being opened in 1928. Interestingly, whilst Donyatt was constructed of wooden railway sleepers Ilton was of concrete slabs. The photographs all date to July 1976, and once again Iris, at Ilton, has missed the last train home…again,

The Collection

Tiverton June 1971

Tiverton station was on the GWR Exe Valley branch which ran between Exeter (St Davids) and Dulverton. There was also a short branch from Tiverton to Tiverton Junction station on the former GWR main line. The Exe Valley line was closed to passengers in 1963 with goods going following year, the short branch from Tiverton to Tiverton Junction closing to passengers in 1964 with goods traffic lingering on till 1967. The two photographs were taken in June 1971. Demolition came some time later, the station site being redeveloped into part of the new A367 Great Western Way. The former station site was identified by the house standing middle distance in the lower June 1971 picture.

Three Cornish stations

Otterham station, top picture, is on the Southern Railway Halwill Junction to Padstow line which closed in 1966. The station was located in the most exposed section of the line hence the rather bleak look to the 1973 picture. The station remains as a private residence.

St Agnes station, middle picture, was on the GWR branch from Chasewater to Newquay. The branch closed in 1963 the photograph being taken in July 1979 when the site was being redeveloped into a small industrial estate. Surprisingly, the station building not only survives but has been completely restored.

Nancegollen station, lower picture, is on the GWR Helston branch which connected to the former GWR Penzance main line at Gwinear Road. The branch closed to passenger traffic in 1962 with goods going in 1964 and track lifting commencing the following year. The photograph was taken in September 1975 from a nearby road bridge and while this remains the station site has been redeveloped into a small industrial site.

Loco Sheds, Yeovil Town & Pen Mill June 1971 & July 1976

Yeovil Town loco shed, top picture, closed in 1965 one year prior to the closure of the adjacent Town station. Track lifting commenced shortly after closure the photograph being taken in June 1971. Within a few years the station and loco shed area were cleared becoming a large car park which in turn was redeveloped at the turn of the new century into a leisure centre. Yeovil Pen Mill loco shed, lower picture, was an original broad gauge wooden affair that closed in 1959. On a Home Counties railway trip in 1961 our coach driver parked up on the nearby A30 road bridge while a young volunteer was dispatched to check if anything was in. There wasn't. The old shed was demolished in the early 1960s and by the time of my July 1976 photograph only an inspection pit and a adjacent small brick built stores remained.

Taunton November 1976 & March 1984

A square built roundhouse dating to 1896 with a large corrugated repair shop being added in the early 1930s. The loco shed closed to steam in October 1964. The top picture dates to November 1976 the shed yards remaining in use as a diesel stabling point while the repair shop had been taken over by the civil engineers' department. Photographed from the old coaler ramp the loco shed itself had been reduced to little more than a shell but gave a superb view of the railway station beyond. The lower picture dates to March 1984 featuring the still intact coaling plant ramp. All these remaining structures were later cleared around the time that the civil engineers' dept moved out in the early 1990s. The former repair shop then lingered on in a derelict state till the whole site was cleared and levelled circa 2012.

Swanage & Radstock June 1979 & July 1976

Closed in January 1972 the Wareham to Swanage branch was then long in the hands of diesel electric multiple units. Steam had been dispensed with in 1966 the loco shed, pictured above, closing that year. The fortunes of the branch were to change in 1979 when preservation dawned its early beginnings being noted scattered around the old shed yard in June of that year. The loco shed and turntable were reinstated in 1985. Radstock loco shed, lower picture, closed in March 1966 and was once set to emulate Swanage with the Somerset & Dorset Railway Trust moving into the station and shed site in 1970. Sadly this was not to be the society moving out to Washford in 1976 the site being cleared for housing circa 1980. My photograph dates to July 1976 and features the preservation societies last act at Radstock in removing the loco sheds three way access point for further use at Washford.

Bridgwater (GWR) & Moretonhampstead July 1977 & Sept. 1976

The single road GWRly loco shed at Bridgwater, top picture, was originally part of the much larger carriage and wagon works which opened back in 1893. The Works closed in 1947 following a disastrous fire the buildings being demolished some time later leaving only the end bay as the loco shed. Closed in 1960 the building when photographed in July 1977 was in use as a garage by an aggregate company. The whole site was cleared during the mid-1990s, being eventually redeveloped into an industrial estate. Moretonhampstead loco shed, lower picture, closed back in 1947 but remained in use as a stabling point till the branch closed in 1964. Track removal commenced the following year and whilst the station was demolished the loco shed survived initially in use as a coal store. By the time of my photograph in September 1976 it was, and still is, in use as a garage for a road haulage company.

A Cornish holiday, an industrial past

Wheal Coates

Chapel Porth September 1973

'Wheal', a Cornish term for a mine.

Holidaying down to the West Country it wasn't long before Iris and I joined the multitudes heading further west down Cornwall way. These adventures started in the early 1970s and in those days it would be an epic drive down the old A30 without a hint of a duel carriageway other than the notorious Honiton by pass. Once into Cornwall it wasn't long before an old engine house with its stack would appear on the horizon.

Most would ignore such things and head straight for Newquay, sun, and surf. Well for that first holiday of ours, 1972 it was, whilst Newquay was our chosen destination we didn't have the sun and didn't do surfing. No wet suits in those days, you had to be brave. So thanks to your author we landed up in a Cornwall that not many tourists would ever see nor want to see - the old tin and copper mining areas where the desolate ruins of this long gone but once immense industry festered away. We even took a peek around St Austell at the strange world of the china clay industry. When that holiday was over I couldn't blame anyone if they never wanted to go to Cornwall with me ever

Cornish holiday.
Iris and our Ford Corsair parked along the old A30 with Scorrier Consuls in the background.
September 1975

again. But we did…
In a world way before the Internet was even thought of my thirst for knowledge on the subject was quenched by raiding the many bookshops that existed in those days. But even then information could be hard to find.

Copper and tin output in Cornwall reached its zenith during the 19th century the county being for a time the world's major producer of these metal ores before major foreign competition depressed the price. Cornwall was more intensively mined than anywhere else in the UK and at its peak there were countless mines in operation from giant concerns to those little more than a hole in the ground. For keeping mines free of water, hauling ore to the surface or for preparing or dressing the metal ore steam powered beam engines were put to work which were housed in purpose-built granite engine houses. At one stage hundreds, perhaps up to six hundred, of these engine houses proliferated throughout the mining areas of Cornwall. The largest or more successful of these mines such as Dolcoath, Levant and Botallack would in their day become household names.

The association of Cornwall with the tin trade stretches back to great antiquity initially by river streaming long before underground working commenced. Once mining started it would lead to the Cornish miners' unceasing battle against water. Cornish mines were very wet and as mines went deeper and deeper so the problem of

Popular Cornish Tourist Spots?
Blue Hills mine, Trevellas Combe, near St Agnes.
June 1972 and Poldice mine, St Day,
September 1976

keeping them dry intensified. Oddly enough those mines on Cornwall's western peninsular which worked under the sea would be the driest.

Whilst tin was always in demand, with the advent of the industrial revolution, copper eclipsed tin production reaching a peak during the early 1860s From the 1850s onwards huge copper reserves were found in Australia, America, and Chile and with older copper mines becoming exhausted and unable to compete production went into decline and by the 1880s copper mining was virtually at an end..

However Dolcoath a long established copper mine at Camborne but now near exhausted continued to prosper when large quantities of tin ore were found under its dwindling reserves of copper. This would lead to high expectations throughout Cornwall that deep tin was to be found under shallow copper and on that basis many investors, or adventurers as they were known, put their money into old or near exhausted copper mines. Not all succeeded and many investors lost their money on ventures that never had much hope of success. By the early 1870s there was an upsurge in tin prices with many mines being reopened but those great expectations were to be relatively short lived as by the mid 1870s Cornwall's tin output was challenged first by the Malayan states and then Australia. This resulted in tin prices crashing through the 1880s leaving only a handful of Cornish tin mines working by the 1890s. Fortunes, however, were yet again to be partly restored when at the dawn of the 20th century something of a revival occurred in the tin markets. Investors once again floated new ventures as old tin mines were restarted but once again by the beginning of the Great War there was little to show for it.

Following on from the Great War with increased tin output from abroad prices totally collapsed and for a period during the early 1920s not one mine was left working throughout Cornwall. Many remained on a care and maintenance basis their owners hoping for a turnaround in the industries fortunes. Whilst it was easy to close a mine down, it was a lot more difficult to reopen one. By the 1930s only three mines were at work, these being East Pool & Agar United and South Crofty at Pool, near Camborne and Geevor on the western peninsular near to St Just. These mines had over the years greatly enlarged their underground workings, or setts, by buying up and working closed mines that bordered them. In some cases this was a necessity as adjacent mines had to be kept free of water to maintain the parent companies own production. It was not unknown to break into the water filled workings of a long abandoned mine with tragic results.

The coming of World War Two bought some relief with Government subsidies to East Pool & Agar United. Time and money was also spent opening up old prospects but to no avail as tin output actually fell throughout the war years.

With the end of hostilities the Government subsidies' to East Pool & Agar United ceased and the mine was quickly abandoned. Despite the fluctuations of world tin prices and the political uncertainties of foreign tin producers in a post war world two new ventures in Cornwall, Mount Wellington and Wheal Pendarves commenced operations. Sadly both of these latter day prospects were to fail to be followed in 1990 by Geevor leaving South Crofty as the sole working mine in Cornwall. This was to continue until 1998 when even South Crofty finally closed and that as they say was that. Well in the case of South Crofty.....possibly...or possibly not.

New Ventures

Wheal Pendarves, Camborne, Sept 1975
and Mount Wellington, St Day,
September 1976

Engine Houses and Beam Engines

Wheal Peevor's engine houses, Scorrier. September 1973

Common to all engine houses during their working days would be the high pressure steam powered beam engine with its associated boiler house and stack. A rocking beam, or bob, as it was called in Cornwall would be balanced on the front or bob wall of the engine house while a piston rod from the steam engine would be attached to the inside end of the bob. The power of a steam engine would be reflected on its piston/cylinder diameter.

For de-watering mines, which in Cornwall could be very wet, large powerful pumping engines were generally required with steam engine cylinder diameters being in the region of 40 inch to 90 inch with one up to 100inch.

The engine house itself would be positioned adjacent to the shaft, the shaft itself being under the outer end of the bob. A succession of connected heavy wooden plunger rods and pumps effectively pumped water from the mine by the rocking of the beam. The power of these engines was immense working a bob which could weigh up to fifty tons at about eight strokes per minute with the deepest mines going down to 3000 feet. These great pumping engines, manufactured in Cornish foundries, were the centerpiece of any mine and took on great importance; the shaft that they worked being invariable named after a manager or other person of importance.

The 'Outdoor' end of a beam. Goonvean. September 1979

Smaller engines of around 20 inch to 30 inch cylinder diameter would be engaged in hauling ore to the surface and were known as Whim engines. Here the outer end of the bob would have a connecting rod fixed via a crank to a large rotating flywheel/drum assembly to which wire ropes were attached for the hauling of metal ore up the shaft which could be some distance from the engine house itself. Whim engines also powered rows of stamps which were used for crushing ore down to a manageable size prior to processing. It was also not unknown for winding and pumping engines to use the same shaft, the winding engine being positioned a short distance from the pumping engine.

By the end of the 20th century and now over 100 years since its peak tin and copper mining in Cornwall was mostly a memory. Due to their immense size and construction many former engine houses remained but now empty, derelict and open to the elements. It has been said that they will remain till the end of time itself. Of their beam engines only a handful survived the scrap man and are now secure in preservation. To find any surface buildings retaining a slate roof was a rarity and as for any remaining plant or machinery…well you could forget that, that scrap man had long been

Rusting Relics.
Derelict stamps at Blue Hills mine, June 1972. An old horizontal engine at South Crofty, June 1974. And a gently rusting kibble, September 1979.

and gone. In many instances a form of natural landscaping had taken place over the years leaving nothing but the empty engine house itself.

But it was those derelict engine houses that caught my imagination and drew me back time and again. You really could wander where you pleased amongst the ruined buildings, rough ground and old shafts. These were mostly fenced in, some adjacent to its engine house others partially hidden in undergrowth many being reduced to convenient rubbish tips. Some old shafts you would find still clean cut to the surface whilst others were dangerously falling away, so you soon learnt it was not advisable to get too near other than to throw in a large stone and count the seconds before a dull thud or splash was heard. But all this dereliction and decay was a far cry of how the mine would have appeared many years previous something that was beyond my comprehension other than could be glimpsed in old photographs.

Even engine houses themselves have diminished in numbers over the years several having been blown up during the last war for fear they be used as landmarks by the Luftwaffe.

As I understood it there were about three hundred engine houses still around by the late 1960s but one engine house known by myself to have been demolished in the early 1970s was Wheal Seton. This old mine closed back in 1890 and was situated on the western slopes of the shallow Tuckingmill valley at Tolvaddon just west of Pool. By the turn of the 19th century much of the eastern slopes of this valley were occupied by the substantial tin ore dressing floors of nearby East Pool & Agar United. Since the latter's closure in 1945 the whole area became an industrial wasteland. Along with the demolition of the old Wheal Seton engine house much of the more substantial long standing remains of the old ore dressing plant were cleared with some landscaping to improve things. Me, I'd prefer the industrial wasteland but then I don't live there.

Throughout the 1970s Cornwall remained our holiday destination and even with wet weather you could always see the sun shining 'over there'. Over the years we poked around many of the old mining areas in Cornwall but the following photographs act as a mere taster and concentrate on the old mines around Carn Brea and far out on the Western peninsular.

Right:
Since demolished.

Wheal Seton engine house and the substantial remains of the extensive ore treatment plant for East Pool & Agar United. Tolvaddon. September 1975

The Collection

Hayle - an industrial harbour

Through the 19th & 20th centuries Cornwall had many harbours serving the fishing, mining and the china clay industries.. Of these Hayle was extremely busy serving the mining districts of Camborne and Redruth with coal, timber and various other essential commodities. Despite the slow decline in the mining industry coal remained a major commodity due to the opening in 1910 of the nearby power station. Hayle remained a thriving industrial harbour right up to the 1960s when decline set in leading to its closure as a commercial harbour in the 1970s. The power station closed in 1977. Hayle at one time boasted two great foundries and engineering workshops these being Harveys and Copperhouse which were located in close proximity of each other. The owners and employees of Harveys and Copperhouse lived near to their factories and Hayle became a town of two parts. Both these great concerns competed against each other especially over rights to the harbour and waterways. They manufactured everything for the mining industry from complete beam engines to all manner of associated machinery. With the mining industry in decline Copperhouse closed its foundry in 1869 the company being eventually purchased by Harveys in 1875 which itself closed in 1903. It is said Hayle never really recovered from these closures. The picture comes from 'The Collection' and is dated to the early 1970s showing Harveys wharf retaining many of its original warehouses and still busy in all aspects of the metal trade, Today the wharf is disused and all of the old buildings have long been cleared. Likewise the power station has long gone,.

A view over Pool. September 1976

Looking south over Pool from the bob floor of the East Pool & Agar United 80 inch pumping engine on Taylors shaft. Being on holiday it is of course a wet dull and miserable day but through the mist can be seen the high ground of Carn Brea, some 700 feet above sea level. To the left of the picture is whim engine house of East Pool & Agar and way over to the right can be glimpsed the extensive workings of South Crofty. To the west of South Crofty are the scattered remains of Dolcoath and way over the horizon on the southern slopes of Carn Brea lay the village of Carnkie and the Basset mine group.

East Pool & Agar United
Sept 1976 & June 1972

Formed in 1896 when East Pool took over the adjacent Wheal Agar. A major tin producer following the Great War the mine was abandoned in 1945 and its engine houses which sat near to the old A30 road in Pool, near Camborne were mostly demolished. However two engine houses not only survived demolition but surprisingly retained their beam engines. The top picture features the 90 inch pumping engine on Taylors shaft opened up in 1924 replacing the old Wheal Agar pumping shaft which had collapsed in 1921. The engine came second hand and was the last engine house to be built in Cornwall. On closure of the mine the engine remained working to keep nearby South Crofty dry until replaced by electric pumps in 1954.

The lower picture is of the 30 inch whim just along the old A30 which worked Mitchells shaft. By the 1970s both engine houses were open to the public. The picture of the 90 inch on Taylors shaft dates to September 1976 whilst the 30 inch Whim on Mitchells dates to June 1972 since when a replacement boiler house has been built alongside the engine house.

South Crofty Sept 1973

Commenced initially as a copper producer and expanded throughout the 19th century. A new shaft, Cooks, was sunk at the beginning of the 20th century with work suspended till just prior to the Great War. A disastrous run of ground causing the collapse of the nearby Wheal Agar pumping shaft in 1921 prompted quick action. By 1922 a second-hand 90 inch engine was installed on Cooks shaft with, unusually, a concrete engine house. With Cooks shaft going down to around 2300 feet and loads on the engine forever increasing the fifty ton bob broke in December 1950 killing the engine man and totally wrecking the engine. From then on all further pumping was achieved with electric pumps. The two photographs both date to September 1973 and feature the mine itself and a close up view of the concrete engine house, its stack having been long cut back. Whilst the extensive steel winding headframe remains which itself replaced an earlier smaller version the concrete engine house was demolished during the 1980s.

South Crofty August 1972 & Sept 1979

Opened at the beginning of the last century Robinson's shaft's engine house contained a second hand 80 inch engine for de watering the mine. During the 1930s South Crofty was forever expanding taking over neighboring setts including the once mighty Dolcoath. The 80 inch engine finally ceased work in May 1955 being replaced by electric pumps and had the distinction of being the last Cornish beam engine working on a mine in Cornwall. By this time the engine was 101 years old and was presented by the company to the Cornish Engines Preservation Society. On refurbishing the engine house the upper part of the stack was found to be unsafe and was cut back. The top photograph takes in the engine house and associated mine buildings and dates to August 1972 whilst the lower picture dates to September 1979. During our holidays in Cornwall it was not possible to visit this engine house as it was still part of a working mine.

Dolcoath The Queen of Cornish mines. Sept 1976

Dolcoath sat next door to South Crofty. She became the most celebrated copper mine in Cornwall commencing around 1720. By the middle of the 19th century its reserves of copper were rapidly diminishing until deeper explorations found large quantities of tin under the copper. Tin was to be Dolcoath's savior and at its zenith employed around 1600 people and boasted some ten steam engines at work of which three were pumping engines. Principle of these was New Sump which originally contained a 76 inch engine which was later replaced by an 85 inch as the shaft deepened to 3300 feet. The deepest in all Cornwall. By 1911 a new winding shaft, Williams, was completed to the south of the sett and at 3000 feet deep it was worked by a steam powered wire wound traversing drum set on a short railway track. Not only was Williams a winding shaft electric pumps were located at the bottom for de watering the mine. By the 1890s tin output was in slow decline

but Dolcoath remained Cornwall's prime tin producer till the Great War. With the post war collapse of tin prices and despite cost cutting methods such as the introduction of many electric pumps replacing steam pumping engines Dolcoath closed in 1921 having been in production for some two hundred years. Its output over this period was some 80,000 tons of black tin and 350,000 tons of copper. As can be seen there is precious little left for such a once grand concern. Previous page, top, the old 1883 stone build air compressor house is the only building remaining in reasonable condition. The pitiful remains of New Sump pumping engine house can be seen, previous lower, whilst the picture above shows the more substantial remains of East shaft whim engine. Whilst the beam engine had been removed in the 1890s the building survived as it was converted in 1913 to an electrical substation. The lower picture above is the derelict Williams shaft winding house set some distance to the south on the lower slopes of Carn Brea.

The Basset Mines Group Sept. 1979

Whilst the mines north of Carn Brea stretched though the towns of Pool and Camborne the Basset mines were south of the highest point of Carn Brea set in the open countryside around the village of Carnkie. The Basset group was formed in 1896 from a merger of Wheal Basset and South Francis United. Whilst Wheal Basset was centered around Carnkie South Francis United was situated to the west of the village. But even these two concerns were in turn mergers of much smaller mines. The photograph dates to September 1979 and was taken from Carnkie Hill looking towards the lower slopes of Carn Brea. To the left of the photograph, can be seen the engine houses of the former 80 inch pumping and 30 inch whim of Lyles shaft whilst set some way up Carn Brea can be seen the substantial ruins of the old West Basset stamps and dressing floor with its associated engine house.

The Basset Mines Group   June 1974

The Basset mines were originally copper producers but by the latter part of the 19th century were producing more tin than copper. Again it was deep tin under shallow copper. Due to the way the Basset group came into being there were at Carnkie two separate sets of stamps and dressing floors opposite each other. The top picture shows the old West Basset dressing floors on the slopes of Carn Brea with its engine house which held a 40 inch rotary whim for powering 80 stamps (ore crushers). The lower picture which has sadly some negative damage is of the former Wheal Basset stamps located on the opposite side of the valley on Carnkie Hill. Of interest here were the two engine houses positioned side by side which both housed 30 inch rotating whims powering 96 stamps.

The Basset Mines Group July 1973

The South Francis United section of the Basset Group was situated to the west of Carnkie. The main shafts here were Marriotts and Pascoes with tin ore being transported by tramway to the ore crushers and dressing floors of West Basset. The top picture shows the extensive surface works around Marriotts shaft. The large cathedral like building in the centre held a most unusual compound pumping engine with inverted cylinders and a under bob while the building to the left held a horizontal winding engine The inset picture features both the 80 inch pumping (left) and 30 inch whim engine houses of Pascoes shaft with the lower picture of the 30 inch whim showing its ruined boiler house. The pumping engine on Pascoes shaft was totally destroyed by an explosion during the Great War and was quickly replaced by a new engine built 'up country' which became the last Cornish engine ever built. Both these shafts worked to a depth of some 2050 feet. With the falling price of tin the Basset group closed in 1918 and the mines abandoned leaving the remaining dumps being reworked during the Second World War.

Botallack Sept. 1973

An old tin mine whose history goes back into the mists of time. Located on Cornwall's western peninsular to the north of Cape Cornwall the engine houses of the Crowns section were remarkable being set low down on the rugged cliffs. These engine houses and shafts were visited by Royalty during the 1860s which led to Botallack becoming famous as the gentry willingly parted with their money to follow the Royal footsteps. The lower engine house held a 30 inch pumping engine which dates to the 1830s while the higher 24 inch whim engine house with its inclined shaft dates to the 1850s. The mine went down to a depth of some 1400 feet working up to a third of a mile under the sea bed. During the 1840s Botallack became a major copper producer but by the 1860s turned into one of the richest tin producers in Cornwall. However within a decade a fall in the price of tin caused Botallack to abandon the Crowns section in 1874 although the pumping engine continued working till 1895 when a disastrous underground flood from a nearby mine caused the mine to be totally abandoned. The photograph dates to September 1973.

Botallack Sept. 1975 & June 1973

Ten years after the 1895 closure with tin prices increasing Botallack was reopened the mine being dewatered, a new winding shaft sunk and surface facilities provided. The new shaft was named after a Mr Allen one of the directors. The nearby Wheal Owls which itself was an amalgamation of several smaller mines was also acquired. The top picture which dates to September 1975 shows, to the left, the fenced off Allens shaft whilst the stack from the horizontal winder remains *in situ.* In the lower picture taken two years earlier we see the Wheal Owls engine house that held a 36 inch pumping engine whilst in the background are the remains of the 32 inch whim engine house. Wheal Owls was abandoned in 1893 following a disastrous flood the sett being taken up by Botallack in 1906 although precious little work was done there.

Botallack Sept. 1975 & August 1999

Looking out over the sea from Allens shaft are the remains of the old arsenic calciners and stack photographed in September 1975. The mostly demolished brick labyrinths show where arsenic was deposited from the roasted ores and then physically removed. Nice work, if you can get it. The lower picture is again Allens shaft which at a depth of 1400 feet was the centre of the 1906 reworking. The venture was not a success and Botallack closed in 1914 for the second time. The metal headframe and winding shed photographed in August 1999 were erected over Allens shaft during the 1980s when Geevor reworked this section of Botallack due to high tin prices. Once again history repeated itself with tin prices collapsing and any further development work came to an end. The two engine houses of the Crowns section were restored by the Carn Brea Mining Society during the mid 1980s.

Botallack Sept. 1975

A walk along the cliff tops at Botallack takes you past the shattered wall of the 1906 period power house The Crowns section engine houses are way down the cliffs over on the left while the rough path takes you northwards through the torn up landscape towards Levant....

Levant Sept. 1975

A short walk along the cliff top track from Botallack takes you to Levant. Mining commenced here during the latter part of the 18th century for both copper and tin. In fact not only was Levant the greatest producer of tin and copper of all the mines in the Cornish western peninsular it was producing copper as late as 1910 becoming the last Cornish mine to do so. Levant worked down to around 2100 feet the workings stretching out up to a mile under the sea bed and at its shallowest a mere forty feet below the seabed itself. The photograph dates to September 1975 and shows the odd looking whim engine house which served Skip shaft and still contained, preserved, its 24 inch engine. Not that we could see it. To its right stands the empty engine house which once contained at 45 inch pumping engine

Levant August 1999

Levant suffered a major disaster in 1919 when 31 men were killed in an accidend at the end of their shift. After this tragic occurrence the lower levels were abandoned and the mine never really recovered and had been totally abandoned by 1930. The sett was eventually taken over by nearby Geevor and Skip shaft was reworked in the 1970s a new wooden headframe erected which can be seen in the previous page located between the whim and the derelict pumping engine house. Levant's surface remains extend some distance along the cliffs and present a scene of total dereliction. In the top picture a stack stands proud over the remains of the power and air compressor house and its associated buildings whilst the lower picture shows the crumbling remains of the four 1860s arsenic calciners.

Geevor Sept. 1975

Originally known as East Levant and then North Levant the mine was a tin producer from the early 19th century. With the falling price of tin the mine closed in 1895 and it was not until the turn of the century that prospecting restarted with an Australian company becoming involved in 1905. Geevor Tin Mines Ltd was formed in 1911 with Wethered shaft, named after one of the directors, being the main shaft till replaced by the more westward Victory shaft in 1919. It would be this shaft that the mine remained centered around. During the 1960s Geevor continued expanding seawards and the long closed Levant sett was aquired and de-watered. As late as the 1980s Geevor undertook prelimary work on the old Allens shaft at Botallack.

Geevor July 1973

No great granite engine houses ever graced Geevor Mines Ltd as the newly constituted company went for electric power from the very start de-watering the mine being achieved with underground pumps. The top picture features the headframe and wooden winding shed of Wethered shaft which was replaced by the Victory shaft in 1919 and eventually abandoned during the 1950s .The Victory shaft, lower picture, was eventually sunk down to 2100 feet including an inclined shaft put in during the 1970s which connected the workings of Geevor to Levant. The metal headgear of the Victory shaft replaced an earlier wooden version in 1954. Sadly Geevor could not withstand the global collapse of tin prices in 1990 and closed that year the pumps being turned off in May the following year. Geevor now lives on as a museum. But then again…

On the Clay

Out and about on the clay. The picture above is of an unidentified and long abandoned clay pit with its associated engine house whilst the picture opposite features a working clay pit at Goonvean. Both photographs date to September 1976.

The Cornish china clay industry dates back to the 18th century when the ability to produce fine white china, or porcelain, for the gentry was finally perfected. China clay, kaolin, is basically decomposed granite and once the ability to produce porcelain had been perfected many other commercial uses were explored and by the late 19th century the industry had rapidly expanded. As our holiday expeditions down Cornwall way in the 1970s suffered from the usual vagaries of the British weather we found ourselves sampling not only the delights of the long defunct mining industry but also the surrealistic world of the china clay industry around St Austell on the south Cornish coast.. This at the time was still a major industry in Cornwall and its effects could be witnessed miles away resembling to us some form of moonscape of great white circular pyramids. You could not miss them. Travelling in amongst them was something else, never had we encountered anything like it and soon understood why they were known locally as the Cornish Alps. Hensbarrow Downs, the area around St Austell would prove to have the largest deposits of china clay in the world the clay being extracted from the ground by the use of high pressure water jets. The extracted china clay would result in great pits which became deeper and larger as time went by whilst the resulting waste material went to form those great white spoil tips, the Cornish Alps. Less obvious to the public gaze were the deep clay pits themselves and to take a peep at them you had to use your initiative and sometimes wander where you shouldn't. If memory serves me right it was on one of these little excursions that we came across two engine houses complete with their long defunct beam engines still *in situ*. To find engine houses on the clay came as a surprise which apparently it shouldn't as the Cornish beam engine had long been put to good use in the china clay industry for pumping the slurry from the bottom of the pit to the surface. As the years passed

steam was eventually replaced by electric pumps with the last beam engine being stopped in the late 1950s. Once the china clay had been extracted from the slurry it would be pumped to local 'clay dries' for heating and drying prior to loading into railway wagons in either bulk form or bagged for transportation. With a modern centralised clay drying installation eventually opening at Par harbour most china clay was eventually pumped directly to this installation resulting in the majority of the old rail connected 'in house' clay dries being closed. From the dries at Par the china clay would be transported out by rail or road or shipped out from Par or Fowey harbours. In recent years the trade in china clay has considerably diminished with Par harbour now little used.

Greensplat & Goonvean
Sept. 1976

Greensplat's empty engine house, top picture, held the last working Cornish beam engine, a 30 inch, which ceased pumping in 1959. The engine was removed in 1972 and set up at the Poldark mine museum where she remains today working under compressed air. The old engine house itself was not so lucky being demolished by the china clay company in 2000.
The lower picture features a disused 50 inch pumping engine in its engine house at Goonvean clay pit near St Stephen. The engine was purchased second hand in 1910 and had a new beam fitted in 1928 this being the last beam to be produced for a Cornish engine. She stopped work circa 1955 and was removed for safe storage in 2008 whereupon the engine house was demolished. Both photographs date to September 1976.

Parkandillick Sept. 1976 & Sept. 1979

Two photographs of the engine house complete with its preserved 50 inch pumping engine on Parkendillick clay pit near St Stephen. Purchased second hand she was installed on site in 1912 and was retired circa 1955. Shortly after being retired the engine and its house were officially preserved by English China Clay Company. The engine can be run on compressed air but is not generally open to the public as the engine house remains on private property. The top picture dates to September 1976 whilst the lower picture which includes the circular settling tanks was taken three years later. Of interest in the above pictures and also at Goonvean are the surrounding waste tips which at the time were a natural part of the landscape. The car in the top picture is our 1968 Vauxhall Victor.

Courtesy Roger Winnen, Cornwall Railway Society

Former Clay Dries

Carbis Wharf, top picture, was one of the many coal fired and rail connected clay dries scattered around the china clay workings. These clay dries were situated at the end of a one mile siding which joined the St Blazey to Newquay line at Bugle. Over the passing years the rail traffic slowly dwindled away with the clay dries closing in 1989 being the last coal fired ones to do so. The chimneys in the background were part of the nearby brickworks. The photograph dates to August 1990 prior to the track being lifted in 1992. The lower picture is of the Wenford dries at St Breward on the Wenfordbridge branch on the Bodmin to Wadebridge line. This line totally closed in 1967 save the branch up to Wenford dries which closed in 1983. The dries themselves finally closed in 2002, the lower photograph being taken some ten years later. Whilst the old dries of Carbis Wharf have long since been refurbished as holiday lets Wenford dries remain derelict although there are plans to rebuild or convert them into luxury flats.

Clay Hoods and diesel locos, August 1984

The two photographs above were taken at Par station in August 1984. The locomotives, Class 37s, had been introduced on clay workings in the late 1970s replacing first generation diesel classes. The wooden four wheel wagons known as 'clay hoods' date to the mid 1950s and they follow on from Great Western designs. However the hoods themselves originate from the 1970s and comprise of tarpaulin sheets thrown over a central metal hoop. These came about to overcome continual water seepage problems that occurred with the original flat stretched tarpaulin covers. Clay hoods were always restricted to local trips within Cornwall and were gradually phased out of service finally going in early 1988. Both trains are heading eastwards for Fowey Docks reversing at Lostwithiel

Diesel locos & 'Tigers' May 1988

Another clay train photographed at Par station but some four years later in May 1988. Whilst the Class 37 diesel locomotives are still in charge the old wooden clay wagons have now given way to new build four wheel purpose built 'Tiger' clay wagons. The train, comprised of No.37673, nine Tigers and a box van, is running east on the main line and possibly originates from Parkandillack heading out of the county. The single box van behind the locomotive contains bagged china clay.

Charlestown - an early China Clay harbour May 1988

Located two miles to the south east of St Austell the small harbour at Charlestown opened in the late 18th century initially for the copper trade but subsequently for china clay. With no rail connections all china clay was delivered by road and loaded into boats via five retractable shoots. Charlestown harbour was eventually eclipsed by the larger and rail connected harbours of Par and Fowey. From the 1980s the china clay traffic at Charlestown went into decline as bulk freighters became too large for the harbour, the last load of china clay being shipped out in 2000. The photographs date to May 1988 when only three of the clay shoots remained .The boat featured in both pictures is the *Anna II* a former Belgium pilot tender built in the 1950s. It is unclear when she was sold off and arrived at Charlestown but at some time she became wrecked at Torpoint on the River Tamar where she still remains..

Pentewan - an early China Clay harbour Sept. 1976

Originally a small fishing harbour Pentewan was enlarged in the late 18th century and again in the 1820s for both fishing and the expanding china clay industry. Being some four miles from St Austell a tramway was laid to the harbour which was upgraded to a narrow gauge railway in 1829. The harbour reached its peak in the 1850s but its inconvenient location and continual silting problems coupled with the closure of the railway in 1918 sealed the harbours fate. With the last clay boat departing in 1929 and all commercial trading ceasing in 1940 the harbour's entrance shortly became silted over. The pictures date to September 1976, the top showing the silted up harbour entrance whilst the lower shows the water filled harbour with the remains of the wooden railway viaduct and track which ran alongside the dock face for loading china clay.

A Cornish 'Des Res' Sept. 1975 & Sept.1979

Whilst researching the china clay industry in St Austell on the Internet I came across a site detailing the local practise of selling off old railway carriages for cheap accommodation. Remembering that I had taken some photographs around St Austell of grounded carriages back in the 1970s I thought it might be interesting to include them. But on wanting to go back to the site it totally eluded me. Both photographs are of former Great Western Railway six wheelers and whilst the top picture, dated to September 1975, shows a good example with something of an extension the lower example, September 1979, is what estate agents may loosely describe as being in need of some updating. The girl in the top picture is my Iris whilst the owner, a lovely old lady, didn't fancy having her picture taken and has wandered off.

Cwm Marine Colliery and Ebbw Vale steel works. August 1977

South Wales   An Industrial Landscape.

Motoring up the Ebbw valley in the mist and rain one weekend in August 1977 Paul briefly pulls his old Ford Cortina over for me to grab a quick shot of Cwm Marine colliery. A few miles further up the valley I catch a quick picture of the steelworks at Ebbw Vale (Pictures opposite top & bottom) The inclement weather I had long associated with the South Wales valleys. Four of us, Peter Askey, John Durrant , myself and Paul Wells were reliving our old train spotting days doing the sights of old steam shed sites. This interest had kicked off a few years earlier and had somehow gained momentum culminating in this weekend away to South Wales. Paul was to be our chauffeur, well it was his car, and Paul loved to drive something which would test our mettle to the limit.

It was trainspotting back in the early sixties that took me to South Wales something that would also prove to be my introduction to the landscape of heavy industry. From steelworks and docks to the collieries and spoil tips of the valleys it was all a far cry from the suburbs of West London. And we weren't short of the odd factory or two

Those first trainspotting excursions were with the Home Counties Railway Club. travelling by train and then coach. It was also a fact that the sun never seemed to shine on the valleys. For me it was nothing but endless mist and rain which severely limited any attempts at photography with my cheap box camera. These trips always seemed to contain an element of morons. Not for me the hurling of childish abuse from our coach as we sped on our way or the singing of bawdy songs. Oh, the English abroad!

But going back to 1977 the steelworks of Ebbw Vale were already winding down, the blast furnaces already cold the story being told was that 'specialisation' was to be the future for Ebbw Vale. But the steelworks itself faced total closure. Seven years later the picture of Abercynon collieries headgear (left) was taken by myself in June 1984 whilst driving a new Ford Sierra from a local Ford dealer on the then relatively new high speed A470 expressway to my company's yard in Acton, West London. By this time my 'career' initially in the foundry trade then in the world of record pressing had taking a dive and I was 'resting' as a car delivery driver. Happy days though, a job with perks. Creative navigation took me on a slight detour up the valleys taking in a few collieries. Also the sun was shining. Unheard of. So it was I came across Ebbw Vale once more only to find no steelworks. Just a vacant plot. It wouldn't be long before the collieries went the same way. A decade later it seemed to me that the South Wales valleys had become another Cornwall but without the tourists. With mine shafts filled and surface buildings cleared there seemed to be little to show of an industry that once dominated the landscape. Even Cornwall still had its granite engine houses. Plenty of evergreen trees though. My photography around collieries was somewhat restrained due to the ongoing politics of the time. Not a time for happy snappers. Once previously I had managed to get myself and a new car delivery, a big Jaguar of all things, involved in the middle of a confrontation between striking miners and the police. Following the mass closures of collieries in the 1980s one deep mine remained working in South Wales and that finally closed in 2008 leaving only open cast mining which have in recent years reverted to rail haulage.

Cwm Marine & Abercynon colllieries June 1984

Cwm Marine was a deep mine, some 1250ft, sunk by the Ebbw Vale Iron & steel Co which commencing coal production in 1893. Coal mines were extremely hazardous and in March 1927 fifty two men died following a gas/coaldust explosion during a nightshift. By Nationisation in 1947 some 1500 men were employed and during the early 1980s new winding and coal handling systems were installed. Cwm Marine closed in March 1989. Abercynon colliery was sunk by the Dowlais Iron Company with coal production commencing in 1889 working to a depth of some 2250ft. Following Nationalisation in 1947 the winding head gear was painted bright blue which eventually became something of a landmark to motorists on the 1970s-built A470 duel carriageway which passed close by. At that time around 1000 men were still employed but by 1975 the mine was linked to the Lady Windsor colliery which then brought all coal to the surface. Closure came in 1988. Both photographs date to June 1984.

Merthyr Vale colliery June 1984

Merthyr Vale colliery was sunk in 1869 by the Nixon Navigation Coal Co with coal production commencing in 1875 working to a depth of approx 1600ft. At Nationalisation in 1947 some 1200 men were employed and by the 1960s the mine received considerable financial investment with some 600 miners still employed through the 1970s. The photograph dates to June 1984 and closure came in 1989. It was the spoil tips from Merthyr Vale colliery which slipped onto the village of Aberfan in October 1966 killing 144 people including many children whilst attending school. This would be the worst disaster in the entire history of coal mining in South Wales.

Open cast mining or working outcrops had been undertaken for centuries in the Welsh valleys but it would be by the mid 19th century that deep mining came into its own precipitated by the industrial revolution. Welsh coal was of high quality with demands from not only within the UK but from around the world. Just prior to the Great War some 230,000 men were employed across some 600 mines with 57 million tons being exported in 1913 alone, Through the inter war years many private owned collieries failed to mechanise whilst having to come up to the challenge of oil and overseas coal production. Following the Second World War the industry was nationalised in 1947 which led to increased investment and modernisation. However from the mid 1950s a programme of closures commenced and following the miners' strike of 1984/85 mass closures began.

Nantgarw July 1985 & Celynen North collieries June 1984

Nantgarw was sunk in 1910 by the Taylor Navigation Steam Co coal production commencing in 1915. At a depth of some 2550ft it would be the deepest coal mine in South Wales. Bad geological conditions would dog the mine and it ceased production in 1927. On eventually reopening in 1952 a new coking plant had been opened alongside whilst all the mines original surface buildings were replaced although the mine itself was now working at around half of its original depth. The mine was merged with the Windsor mine in 1974 but with output declining from the early 1980s onwards Nantgarw finally closed the year after my July 1985 photograph. Colynen North was sunk in 1913 by the Newport Coal Co with coal production commencing in 1916. During its last few years the mine was linked to the Oakdale colliery with all coal being raised to the surface at that mine. The photograph was taken in June 1984 and the complex closed in 1989.

Coal Trains June 1985
Pontypridd station and Severn Tunnel Junction marshalling yards

It's June 1985 and two Class 37s head on down south through Pontypridd station with a coal train. The eastern side of the station is disused following track rationalisation in 1974 due to the decline in both freight and passenger services. The A4058 which can be glimpsed to the left of the picture has since been upgraded to a duel carriage express way. At Severn Tunnel Junction marshalling yards we again see a Class 37 on a coal train waiting to head out to perhaps London or the Midlands. With the introduction of block freight trains and the dramatic reduction in industrial and coal output Severn Tunnel Junction yards closed in 1987. The site remained derelict till track removal in the 1990s then landscaping with part of the site redeveloped for the M4 motorway.

Coal trains January 1986 & July 1985 Llanwern Steelworks

Two pictures of Class 37s again, what else, on coal trains working, top, on the main line heading for Llanwern steelworks whilst the lower picture is of another coal train this time running into the steelworks itself. The top picture dates to January 1986 and would be one of my last photographs taken during my wanderings while delivering company cars whilst the lower picture dates to July 1985. The Llanwern steelworks totally dominated the skyline for some forty years till closure in 2001 of the 'heavy end' of steelmaking meaning the blast furnaces, coking plant, Bessemer converters etc. Starting my apprenticeship as a metallurgical chemist at Allied Ironfounders I went with my fellow day release college students to visit Llanwern steelworks. I have to say our own foundry seemed very small beer.

Llanwern Steelworks July 1985

Built by Richard Thomas & Baldwin construction commenced in 1959 with the plant coming on stream in 1961/62. Originally known as the Spencer steelworks it became known as Llanwern when nationalised becoming part of the British Steel Corporation. The plant was located on a greenfield site alongside the BR Western Region London to Cardiff main line just east of Newport. Whilst travelling on a train past the plant the rolling mills alone seemed to me to go on forever. The 'heavy end' of the business, steelmaking itself, ceased in 2001 this vast plant being demolished three years later. The picture dated to July 1985 shows Llanwern's three blast furnaces and as I remember it took a bit of time as I had to negotiate with some cows to get the best shot. Having a steelworks set in the countryside seemed somewhat incongruous but then Llanwern was a modern plant. Whilst the site remains mostly undeveloped some steel work does remain but a pale reflection of its former self.

Closed Railway stations - Dowlais Central & Tredegar August 1977

The closed station and loco shed photographs were all taken on our August 1977 trip. At a rather desolate Dowlais Central we look towards the buffer stops although the large engineering concern of Guest Keen formerly the Dowlais Iron Works was nearby. The station was on a short spur from Pant and closed back in 1950 although workmans' trains continued till 1960. Paul is seen to the right talking to a local man lamenting Dowlais' industrial past. The station building and goods shed survive today as the Dowlais visitor centre but with little to associate it with the buildings former past. Tredegar station, lower picture, was an intermediate station on the Sirhowy valley line from Nantybwch on the Merthyr line to Risca for Newport. The line north of Tredegar initially closed in the early 1960s to be followed by southerly connection to Risca. Whilst the station and nearby loco shed remained derelict for many years following closure they have since been demolished

Loco Sheds - Cardiff Radyr August 1977

Our weekend away in August 1977 took in twenty six loco shed sites across South Wales and armed with little more than a 1960s Loco Shed Directory and a great deal of enthusiasm some sites required a considerable degree of detection. All the pictures in this section date to this visit. Cardiff Radyr was a four road depot located alongside the freight yards. Radyr closed in July 1965 the depot then being leased out to Powell Duffryn as a wagon works in which capacity it was in use on our visit. The top picture gives a general view of the former shed whilst the lower shows the part demolished coaler. The wagon works closed in the mid 1980s due to the reduction in coal and freight traffic. The yards themselves were rationalised in the early 1990s and closed by the end of that decade. The derelict former loco shed was demolished cicla 2002/03. A large housing estate now occupies the site.

Loco Sheds - Severn Tunnel Junction & Pontypool Road
August 1977

Severn Tunnel Junction loco closed in October 1965 while Pontypool Road had gone six months earlier. The area around Severn Tunnel Junction was soon cleared while the depot itself became used for car storage until the 1970s. By the time of our visit, top picture, the cars had gone but some sort of business life still seems to be going on. The depot was later demolished the site remaining undeveloped. No housing estate.....yet. Amidst the undergrowth Pontypool Road's rubble filled inspection pits and turntable pit were still clearly visible. The disused gasometer forms a backdrop on the other side of the running lines from the loco shed. The foreground clearly shows the cast iron turntable pit retainers. The gasometer was dismantled in 2005 by which time the railway yards had been partially redeveloped with roads and retail outlets. One wonders what remains in amongst the undergrowth on the remaining part of the site.

Loco Sheds Aberbeeg & Tredegar August 1977

Aberbeeg loco closed in December 1964 whilst Tredegar closed as early as June 1960. Both these loco sheds stick in my memory from my first Club outing to South Wales in 1960. With our coach working its way down the valley Aberbeeg loco presented a grand sight set down in the valley with its lines of simmering tank engines. Tredegar had already closed and was empty. On our August 1977 trip Paul seemingly retraced the old coach route and the picture, top, was as I first remembered it only the old loco was now an iron foundry. At some time this company moved out and a much altered loco shed remains occupied by an engineering company in what is now a small industrial estate. Tredegar loco shed was adjacent to the railway station and both were in a state of total dereliction on our visit. This state of affairs remained until the 1980s when the whole site was cleared away prior to road improvements.

Loco Sheds - Dowlais (Cae Harris) & Abercynon August 1977

Dowlais (Cae Harris) and Abercynon loco sheds both closed at the end of 1964. Dowlais (Cae Harris) was the terminus for a short branch from Nelson and by the time of our 1977 visit the site had been cleared although the loco shed inspection pits were clearly visible. At the rear was an infilled turntable pit which on a damp day some seventeen years earlier was full of frogs. Never had I seen so many. The site today shows no evidence of its railway past while the landscape has changed out of all recognition the 'Heads of the Valleys' duel carriageway now passing behind. Although trackless Abercynon loco remained totally intact and in use as a foundry in which use it remained well into the 1980s. Despite 'improvements' to the building the former loco shed remains in commercial use today but devoid of any association to its railway past.

Newport Docks, Alexandra South Dock December 1984

Whilst 'at work' I managed to wander down Newport Docks way a few times back in the 1980s. The original Alexandra dock opened in 1875 being situated to the west of and parallel to the River Usk. By 1892 a second dock had opened to the south of the original the two docks being known as the North and South Alexandra docks respectively. They were connected by a 60ft. wide communication channel. Further extensions to the South Dock took place in 1907 and again in 1915 which allowed a lock to be put directly into the Bristol Channel. By then Newport's Alexandra dock were extremely large and had taken on an inverse L configuration the dock being able to handle the largest ships something which it can still do today,

A Class 08 shunter, top picture December 1984, with a load of imported steel wire runs alongside No 6 Warehouse, South Dock, whilst in the lower picture the Class 08 is pulling its load away from the quays between No 6 and No 5 Warehouses. If you look carefully at the lower picture you'll see that my chum Paul Wells is just about to have his carefully positioned photograph ruined by a small van passing closely by. This view today has changed dramatically as although the two warehouses still survive much larger warehouses have been built alongside with a new road running over the old railway tracks. Newport Docks still handles rail traffic, especially imported coal, although over the years the system has considerably contracted.

Newport Docks, Alexandra South Dock July 1985

Two pictures of the bulk carrier *Jupiter* berthed alongside No 5 Warehouse, South Dock, July 1985. Whilst No 6 Warehouse is hidden from view in the top picture the coal terminal at the western end of the quay can be seen to the far right of the picture. The lower picture reminds me of the two chaps on the quayside trying and failing to bump start their car. Whilst the South Dock warehouse capacity has expanded since the 1980s the number of quay side cranes have dramatically decreased. Newport Docks never seemed to me to be very busy compared to pictures taken of the docks in days long gone but of course by the 1980s ships were much larger and since then they are much larger still. And Newport Docks can still accommodate them.

Newport Docks, Alexandra South Dock July 1985

These pictures are taken in the original part of South Dock. The top photograph was taken near to the cut connecting the South to the North Dock. The lower picture is of No 3 Warehouse and in the foreground can be seen the wall of the disused East Lock which gave access to the River Usk. Ignoring the old tub *Anayissog II* the top picture is interesting as a ship is berthed on the docks inner quays to the right in the picture, these inner quays originally handled the vast amount of coal traffic from the valleys. The backdrop is dominated by the three chimneys of Uskmouth A and B power stations. Originally both coal fired Uskmouth A's two chimneys can be seen centre and right. Built in the 1950s it closed in the 1990s and was demolished in 2002. Uskmouth B's chimney, extreme left, was built in the 1960s and now runs on bio mass fuels.

Newport Docks, Coal Terminal October 1985

This page features the coal import terminal located at the far western end of the South Dock. Coal exports ceased in 1964 up to which time Newport's Alexandra Dock had been one of largest coal exporters with some twenty coal hoists and their associated sidings located around the docks inner (town side) quays. All rail connections for the docks were at East Mendalgief Junction but by the 1980s only the eastern side (River Usk) quays were still rail connected. Coal imports commenced in the early 1980s by which time the inner quays had been redeveloped for other commercial uses. I was lucky on this particular day in October 1985 as a ship had recently berthed and was being unloaded whilst a train of empty coal wagons was being run down to the coal terminal for loading. The contraction of the docks railway system can clearly be seen in the top left picture.

Newport Docks. Internal breakdown crane December 1984

On one of my runs through Newport and detouring down to the docks I chanced to come across a breakdown train partly obscured behind some sheds adjacent to the North dock. Whilst I managed to photograph the breakdown crane I have to say that it's not the best of pictures of the associated carriage which was tucked in behind a disobliging large shed. The breakdown train was an internal user being restricted to working within the docks itself. The diesel engined crane was manufactured by Thomas Smith & Sons the jib bearing the legend 'Smith Rodney' whilst the carriage was a shabby 1938 third class GWR Collett carrying the internal user number W071342. The picture dates to December 1984. It is possible that they have both escaped into preservation

Cardiff Docks   October 1985

My early memories of Cardiff docks date to the early 1960s and are somewhat limited to East Dock loco shed. Unofficial access was made through either East or West Bute Docks. I don't remember much in the way of shipping, other than dockside clutter and endless railway tracks and sidings. East Dock shed took some finding. Our picture dates to October 1985 and is of Cardiff's largest dock, the Queen Alexandra. Note the liquid bulk terminal in the left background and the warehouses to the right which are all still *in situ*. The docks main lock is obscured from view. The history of Cardiff docks goes back to the Bute Docks. West Bute opened in 1839 and the East Bute dock some twenty years later. A lack of development within Cardiff docks led to the opening of Penarth and Barry Docks and as a result of this Cardiff Docks finally expanded opening Roath dock in 1887 followed the Queen Alexandra dock in 1907. And near all of this would be concentrated on one major export, coal. By the early 20th century coal hoists and miles of associated railway sidings covered vast swathes of the docklsnds area.

Cardiff Docks.
Queen Alexandra Dock
October 1985 & January 1986

Two views of the Queen Alexandra dock the top picture being a somewhat moody shot taken near to Compass swing bridge of a deserted Empire Wharf while across the water is the South quay which runs the entire length of the dock. The warehouses along Empire wharf and the South quay are now long gone. The lower picture was taken January 1986 along Bells wharf on the North quay the rail tracks being long out of use. By the Great War Cardiff docks was second only to Barry Docks in coal exports but these declined through the inter war years and matters failed to improve following the Second World War. Coal exports ceased in 1964 with West Bute dock closing that year and East Bute dock six years later the West Bute dock having been filled in. This area became derelict for many years redevelopment commencing in the late 1980s the area having now been totally transformed with housing, commercial outlets with some remaining industry.

Cardiff Docks, Compass Bridge January 1986 & June 1985

A motorcyclist crosses over Compass road and rail swing bridge which crosses the connection cut between the Queen Alexandra and Roath docks in January 1986. Until the opening of this connection cut all shipping using Roath dock came via the Roath Basin locks. The giant silos that form the backdrop to Compass bridge have since been demolished. The lower photograph taken in June 1985 is taken from Compass bridge itself and is of the Queen Alexandra docks Bells wharf which appears to be handling scrap and aggregates. The contraction of Cardiff docks following the closure and later redevelopment of the Bute docks leaves the Queen Alexandra and Roath docks in commercial use today.

Cardiff Docks   Roath Dock October 1985

Roath dock opened in 1887 to cope with ever increasing demand, ships originally accessing the dock through Roath basin sea lock. The top picture is of the Chevron oil berth located at the far eastern end of Roath dock which serviced a large liquid bulk terminal. The imposing edifice in the background is the old Spillers flour mill building and even this is a mere shadow of its once former self. Built in the 1930s it was demolished in the 1990s. The lower picture is off Pontoon Berth at the western end of Roath dock with, on the left of the picture, the communication cut leading to Roath Basin. These photographs date to October 1985.

Cardiff Docks Roath Basin June 1985

Roath Basin, June 1985. The top picture is of Britannia quay whilst the lower picture is of Junction dock which originally connected Roath Basin to the entrance of the Bute docks. Of interest the boat is the *MV Bowqueen* a suction dredger built in 1963 which finished her days in Madera before being scrapped in Portugal. With the closure of the Bute docks the connection to Roath Basin was filled in as can be seen in the foreground leaving the old lock gates *in situ*. Roath Basin fell out of commercial use some time after this photograph was taken the dockside having now been totally redeveloped with offices and hotels while the old Roath Basin sea locks are no longer in use.

Cardiff Docks - A railway reminder October 1984

Our solitary signal would seem to indicate that a train is due but you would have a very long wait, and as for the nearby water crane well that wouldn't have seen a steam engine for some twenty years or more. The location is at the eastern end of Roath dock near to the large liquid bulk terminal this line now being the only rail access into the docks today. The derelict remains of Roath Dock North East signal box which describes its location perfectly well. The trackwork around Roath dock had already been considerably cut back hence the closure of the signal box, the photograph being taken, if I remember correctly, from a new access road. The ship in the background was, I believe, laid up.

Cardiff Docks - A railway reminder October 1984

A atmospheric shot of a single remaining railway line somewhere within Cardiff Docks, location now forgotten.. October 1985

Further wanderings around Barry

Being away with the motorbikes all things railways faded away till I took my then new girlfriend Iris for a day out by the sea. To Barry Island. A sort of English Southend on Sea. Funfairs and all that.
It had actually been an island once, well at high tide. But with the arrival of the docks in the late 1880s all that changed and a direct rail connection to the island in the mid 1890s brought the tourist trade. And if some seventy years later there were some old rusty steam locomotives there then I quite forgot to mention it to Iris. The poor girl even wore a skirt. Oh dear. Still she took it quite well. The following year, 1969, the lady wore jeans. Too much excitement can overheat a lady so Iris decided to give Barry and its steam locomotives a miss, so from 1970 onwards Barry became a bit of a lads day out. By this time well over 200 steam locomotives had arrived and whilst many had already been disposed off scrapping had already ceased back in 1965 resulting in a vast scrap yard known to one and all as 'Barry dump'.
Those were also the days when railways still ran excursion trains using anything from old Mark 1 stock to diesel multiple units. For us it became a pilgrimage right through the 1970s. The top picture, taken in May 1971, is us whizzing past Barry Docks station which still retains its old large wooden Great Western Railway station nameboards. The top middle picture dates to August 1970 and sees us rumbling over Barry Islands metal viaduct looking eastwards over the West Pond site with the oil terminal and No 1 dock in the distance. The once extensive sidings here originally extended under our viaduct terminating at Barry Island's old harbour but these were lifted just short of the viaduct around the time steam locomotives began to be stored there. For us we are near to the end of a long exhausting train ride in a crowded DMU. The lower middle and bottom pictures were both taken in May 1971 with a DMU crossing over the viaduct having just pulled out of Barry Island station whilst the bottom picture shows the beginnings of commercial redevelopment on the site. This was to be somewhat short-lived as nothing now remains of this 1970s redevelopment. The lads jolly days out with British Rail petered out by the end of the seventies. My own last visit to Barry was a little later in 1984 courtesy of Lex Vehicle Leasing on a car collection job. By 1990 the yards were empty.

Barry Dump - West Pond June 1969

The West Pond site was so called because from the opening of Barry Docks it was just that, a large water filled pond that was eventually drained and infilled for commercial redevelopment following the Second World War. This resulting vast area of rough flat ground stretched from No.1 dock and the oil terminal westwards to Barry Island's branch railway causeway and viaduct the many sidings alongside the West Pond site being the ones used to store the steam locomotives. The West Pond site itself was later leased by Woodhams and used by them for the scrapping of rolling stock and further locomotive storage. Looking west in our June 1969 picture the railway viaduct can just be seen in the background with the high ground and escarpment of Barry Island to the left of the picture. One can only speculate as to how those residents whose houses so high up overlooking this incredible graveyard of steam viewed it all. A room with a view? It often crosses my mind if any of the residents or anyone else ever took any photographs from up there because if they did I've never seen any. But back down by the railway viaduct we along with everybody else would gain entry to the rows of rusting steam locomotives via the open spaces of the nearby spacious coach park. With the last loco departing in the early 1990s the whole West Pond site was eventually cleared including all the old storage sidings home for so many years to those old steam locomotives. The West Pond now waits redevelopment no doubt into the inevitable housing estate.

Barry Dump - West Pond August 1971 & November 1976

Two photographs looking over the West Pond site but in opposite directions. Standing on top of a loco boiler can have its moments but then I was much younger and fitter in those days. Taken in August 1971 and ignoring the Great Western locomotives we take a look north to Barry town in the far background. Meanwhile the lower picture dates to November 1976 looking towards the escarpment of Barry Island itself. The rebuilt West County and Standard 9F make unusual bed fellows but note the lack of tenders as by this time many had been sold off for commercial use. The scrapping of locomotives here had ceased in 1965 with I believe much of it going as raw material to European steelworks. But for us lot it really was one great playground for grown ups.

Barry dump - Upper yard May 1971

By 1964 the West Pond site was rapidly filling up with steam locomotives so a second dump was commenced in what became known as the upper yards. These were to the east of the West Pond site and stretched from the main running lines over to the disused goods shed and docks pump house near to No 1 dock. A fascinating area in which to wander amongst the debrie of docklands with steam locomotives scattered everywhere including the inclined ramps of disused dockside coal hoists. For me the upper yards had considerably more photographic appeal than the West Pond site. However if loco numbers were your game and with Great Western types having long lost their cast number plates we soon learnt that coupling rods told their own story carrying the loco's number. These we assumed to be correct despite finding so many other numbers having been crossed out, coupling rods like locomotive boilers tended to move around a bit.

Barry Dump - Upper Yard August 1970 & June 1969

Two pictures both nearer to the main running lines east of Barry station. The top picture taken in August 1970 is of a Great Western Hall Class locomotive whilst the lower picture taken in June 1969 shows the top end of a line up of Great Western types dumped nearby. Whilst the derelict steam engines have long gone Barry town remains and today part of the warehouse in the top picture and the terraced houses of Broad Street that feature in the background of the lower picture still exist although the row of concrete garages have gone. The actual locations have been lost for all time to a new Barry, a medical centre now features where the top picture was taken whilst a housing estate now sits where our line up of old Great Western locomotives once lurked

Barry Dump - The old pump house May 1971

Of all the industrial, dockyard and railway buildings scattered around the upper yards none was more prominent than the square tapered brick chimney of the last remaining docks hydraulic pump house. Three were built their hydraulic pumps powering the dockside coal hoists, lock gates, swing bridges and cranes. This particular pump house had closed back in the mid 1950s so by the time we started our wanderings the building was derelict as was also the nearby goods shed and much else around the western end of No 1 dock. Despite all my visits to Barry I failed to photograph any of the coal hoists or dockside clutter and on looking back can only assume that I was obsessed by the steam locomotives. Barry Docks ultimately comprised of two main docks and were for a time the largest coal exporters in South Wales with 25 coal hoists backed up with over one hundred miles of sidings. Coal exports prior to the Great War could be measured in millions of tons but this declined considerably in the inter war years and finally ceased in the early 1970s the last coal hoist being demolished in the early 1980s. The top two pictures both date to May 1971, and show the former entrance to the demolished loco works and the disused goods shed.. The lower picture and the next few pages feature the pump house and whilst the chimney alone is evident in the above picture this is something that was pure chance as I was trying to photograph the cat. The pump house along with the old goods shed have now become unlikely survivors in a redeveloped landscape although somebody cared enough for the pump house as it became a listed building in the 1990s. In recent years the building has been refurbished into commercial outlets whilst the goods shed has become the terminal for the Barry Tourist Railway and the Rail Centre. Other than these two survivors the whole upper yards as I knew them have been swept away and in a way gentrification has come to the old docks, the area now being known as the water front.

Barry Dump - The old pump house August 1970

Two views taken in August 1970 from the eastern end of the West Pond locomotive dump looking towards Barry town and part of the upper yards area. The pump house features in both pictures with the goods shed to the left in the top picture whilst a motley collection of small huts feature in the lower picture. Locomotives can be just made out on the high ground behind the pump house while amongst those locomotives in front of the pump house is the North British Warship Class No.D601 being visible in both pictures. It has to be said this locomotive seemed to spend much of its time at Barry being shunted from one location to another.

Barry Dump - The old pump house August 1971 & Sept. 1984

Two more views but this time fourteen years apart, the top picture taken in August 1971 whilst the lower is September 1984, the undergrowth having grown somewhat in the intervening years. A solitary West County No.34092 formerly 'City of Wells' features in the top picture along with some brake vans with a long line of newly arrived wagons. The lower picture manages a lonesome Presflo cement wagon while close inspection of the pump house reveals it is starting to show the ravages of time.

Barry Dump - The old pump house

August 1970 & Early 1974

Two views of the pump house but this time both taken from the high ground north of the building. The top picture was taken in a southerly direction and we glimpse the oil terminal and the West Pond loco dump with the escarpment of Barry Island in the far background. The locomotives in both pictures are all Great Western.

S & DJRly Class 7Fs August 1970 & August 1972

It was not my intention to include any individual pictures of steam loco's but the top picture is the only one that I took at Barry with an actual boat in it. Not the best of pictures of a boat but a boat nevertheless. The loco itself is former S & DJRly No 53808 and the date is August 1970 and she has already been purchased for preservation actually departing from Barry some two months later.. Some modern day enthusiasts might well have preferred the loco behind, the North British Warship, to have survived. As I sorted through for a picture to go with the above there seemed nothing more appropriate than sister locomotive No 53809 as seen in the upper yards in August 1972. She would depart from Barry in December 1975.

Railway Cranes May 1971 & August 1972

Wandering around Barry dump over the years I can only remember coming across two old railway cranes both of them being dumped around the upper yards and both feature on this page. The top picture is of a LM&SRly steam powered example the photograph dating to May 1971 As there seems to be plenty of loose coal thrown about I wonder if it was actually used within Barry Docks. The lower picture features a manually operated lightweight maintenance example photographed in August 1972 By chance perusing through a copy of Brian Hadley's book 'Graveyard of steam' a picture of this crane appears suitably daubed 'SOLD SWANAGE RLY SOCIETY'. The Swanage Railway indeed owns such a crane so I suppose that it must be this one.

Barry Dump - So wot's all this then? August & May 1971

Somewhere up in the wastelands of the upper yards a temporary wooden platform has been knocked up with wagons being run up to platform level with another at track level. It would look as if the contents of the wagons at platform level are being discharged into the wagons below using wheelbarrows. There seems to be plenty of scrap wood about and, in the top picture, a row of wagon wheels further up the yard perhaps indicates that old wagons are being disposed of. Whatever is happening the top picture is dated to August 1971 whilst the lower picture was taken three months earlier.

Barry Dump - wagons for scrap May 1971 & December 1976

One of the reasons why the steam locomotives lingered for year after year was Woodhams appetite for scrapping wagons. This was mainly centered around the West Pond site where these photographs were taken. The top picture dates to May 1971 showing a line of condemned low sided wagons being loaded up with scrap wagon axles. No doubt these would be moved off site using either a loco or possibly a tractor. To my knowledge Woodhams never owned or used a yard locomotive. The pump house can be seen in the far background whilst the oil drums in the foreground remind me of another book that I once published. Meanwhile in the lower picture taken in December 1976 another four wooden vans are meeting their end.

Barry Dump - Miscellaneous August 1972 & November 1979

The scrap remains of a wagon, August 1972, are now reduced to a heap on the West Pond site adjacent to the oil storage yards near to No 1 dock. In the lower picture taken in November 1979 Barry Island's escarpment forms prominent background to a part cut up brake tender again in the West Pond site. Introduced in the mid 1960s and coupled to the front of the train locomotive they gave additional braking capacity to diesel locomotives whilst hauling unfitted - loose coupled - freights. Many, as in this example, utilised redundant LNER bogie sets. Mainly used in the North East they were discontinued in the mid 1980s along with the end of loose coupled freights.

Barry Dump - Miscellaneous September 1984

Cement wagons and milk tankers. September 1984. The Presflo dry bulk cement wagon, top picture, awaits scrapping in the West Pond site the former Barry loco shed can being glimpsed in the background. Supplied between 1955 and 1963 they were withdrawn from service during the 1980s. The six wheel milk tanker, lower picture, numbered DW 3014 has finished its days in the Departmental fleet, note the legend 'not to be used for milk'. Introduced in the early 1930s they replaced the original four wheeled design. They continued in production until the 1950s and remained in revenue earning service till the early 1980s. Photographed in the West Pond she sits close up to the escarpment of Barry Island itself.

Barry Dump - Miscellaneous September 1984

Parcel vans, a British Railways 4 wheeled covered carriage truck, top picture, and a Siphon G the origins of which go back to the Great Western Railway. Both photographs date to September 1984. The CCT was introduced in the mid 1950s for local parcel services and whilst all were still in service at the beginning of the 1980s they had gone by the end of that decade. Meanwhile the Siphon G van can trace its history back to transporting milk prior to the Great War with production finally coming to an end in the 1950s by which time they were used for parcel and newspaper traffic. They remained in revenue earning service till the early 1980s with many then working on in departmental use. Both photographs were taken in the West Pool sidings the lower picture showing some of the new factory units/warehouses put up in the 1970s but now long gone.

Barry dump - Miscellaneous August 1971 & September 1984

Brake vans. Toads and Pillboxes, slang for former Great Western and Southern Railway brake vans. The top picture is of a Great Western 20 ton 'Toad' with its typical large cabin and veranda introduced back in the late 1890s and manufactured in various guises till the 1950s. Meanwhile in the lower picture we see a 25 ton Southern Railway 'Pillbox' brake van so called due its small cabin and veranda. Introduced in 1928 they remained in production till the early days of British Railways. Following the lifting of the compulsory use of brake vans to fitted freights in 1968 many vans then found alternative use in Departmental stock.. Our two examples on the West Pond site are both ex-Department vans, being DW17409 and DS 55124.

Barry Dump - Fellow travellers and other matters

Iris, June 1969

Peter, May 1971

John, August 1970

Brassiere on motion

We wander from Barry to Swansea

Swansea Docks - Kings Dock Junction March 1986

Taken from the A483 Fabian Way dual carriageway in March 1986 we overlook Swansea's Kings Dock Junction and signal box with Kings Dock in the background. The signal box, always manned by dock personnel, stands to the left of the many sidings which service the remaining Kings Dock coal hoists. The history of Swansea Docks goes back to the 1850s with the opening of the North and South Docks to facilitate the metals and coal trade. Both were located to the west of Swansea's River Tawe. With escalating levels of trade larger docks were required and these opened to the east of the Tawe, the first being the Prince of Wales dock in 1881 followed by Kings Dock in 1908. While coal was always one of Swansea docks major exports it became the first to adapt to the oil trade with the Queens dock opening in 1920 to take advantage of the UK's first oil refinery at nearby Llandarcy. Whilst the coal trade reached its peak by World War II oil became the dominant factor by the 1950s followed by the petro chemical business in the 1970s. Through this period up to five tankers at a time could be seen lined up alongside the Queens Dock oil terminals. With the passing of time the original docks west of the Tawe became obsolete the North dock closing in 1930 then being filled in whilst the South dock closed in 1971 to be redeveloped into a boating marina during the 1980s. The Prince of Wales dock ceased to be a commercial dock at that time and is now also undergoing redevelopment and gentrification. Following years of winding down the Llandarcy oil refinery and then the nearby BP petro chemical plant both closed causing Queens dock to become redundant. Kings Dock now remains Swansea's only commercial dock.

Barry Dump - Fellow travellers and other things (see previous page)

Just a few people pictures and other things. Iris clutches our sandwiches for a tender lunch, note the thermos flask. John Durrant stands between a pair of flat top book ends whilst Peter Askey ponders the meaning of life in the shattered remains of Barry Works. Only Paul Wells could have photographed what I now term 'Brassiere on Motion'. Something I had long forgotten. A discarded or mislaid brassiere. In a scrap yard. Whatever, but Paul saw the art in everything. Not much art in a picture of us four taken in November 1975 but a picture that I have managed to sneak into every book I have published so far. However I have gone one step further and have included by comparison a 'now' picture of us lot taken in September 2017 now in old age. Sadly Paul Wells died in 1988 following a road traffic accident and his place is taken by fellow 1960s train spotter and motorcyclist Geoff Ward. On this occasion we are standing alongside another former Barry resident flat top No 34081 *91 Squadron* at Wansford loco shed on the Nene Valley Railway. Thanks here go to the lads down the loco sheds who took the time to let us do our little bit of photographic nostalgia. Bottom right: 1971 Author in a chimey, well someone had to do it!

Swansea Docks. Kings Dock Junction and coal hoist sidings
March 1986

The A483 Fabian Way road bridge and Kings Dock signal box feature in the top picture with a Class 08 shunter heading off eastwards to the nearby Burrows sidings which still catered for wagonload traffic. The coal trains, hauled by Class 37s, comprised of unfitted 21 ton MDO wagons working down from the South Wales valleys the coal itself being exported to Ireland. The lower picture was taken near to the signal box and shows both the arrival and departure coal sidings these being known locally as the Tin and Violet sidings. Train loads of coal would collect in the inclined Tin sidings which ran up to the coal hoists as seen to the left of the picture. Wagons would then be shunted up to the hoists one at a time for unloading then returning by gravity to the Violet sidings, middle of picture, for making up empty trains for return working. Both pictures date to March 1986

Swansea Docks. Kings Dock coal hoists May 1984 & March 1986

Swansea was a major coal exporter and by the Great War 26 coal hoists were at work ten in the old docks, nine in the Prince of Wales and seven in Kings Dock. As coal exports went into decline South Docks coal hoists were scrapped in the 1950s with the Prince of Wales examples going in the mid 1960s. By the start of the 1980s only four remained working in Kings Dock. The top picture dated May 1984 shows Kings Dock looking westwards with half a dozen dockside cranes huddled up for company and three coal hoists, the nearest one then being out of use. The lower picture dated March 1986 shows the remaining two coal hoists. In the foreground only the railway connecting bridge retaining wall remians of the recently demolished third coal hoist. Swansea's coal hoists were the last examples working in South Wales. None survive.

Swansea Docks. Kings Dock coal hoists March 1986

With a chance run down to the docks I was lucky enough to witness a coal hoist at work loading the MV *Arklow Glen*. What I didn't realise was that within a year it would all be history as by February 1987 Swansea Docks had exported its last boat load of Welsh coal. All 520 tons of it. Within months the last two coal hoists had been demolished Kings Dock Junction signal box would shortly follow and the Tin and Violet sidings torn up. Many of the 21ton coal wagons were cut up on site. The view from Fabian bridge in 2016 is now one of waste ground with a single rail track running to Kings Dock where imported coal is now handled this being just one of the many commodities handled by Swansea Docks today.

Swansea Docks 'A' Shed Wharf March 1986

With the *MV Irini* berthed alongside Kings Dock 'A' Shed two of Swansea Docks tugs the *MV Herculaneum* and *MV Alexandra* lay berthed alongside 'C' quay. Both tugs were built in 1963 and both were sold on in the late 1990s, and whilst the *Herculaneum* departed for Greece being renamed the *Christos VIII* the *Alexandra* only managed to travel as far as Rochester, Kent where she was recently broken up. The lower picture, taken on No 4 wharf Kings Dock along from the coal hoists is of an electro-hydraulic crane grab. Sometimes referred to as an orange peel grab they are used for waste, mixed scrap, pig iron, rocks and some aggregates. Both photographs were taken in March 1986.

Swansea Docks. *MV Aberavon* & *PS Wingfield Castle*
May 1984 & March 1986

Berthed in the Prince of Wales Dock is the four crane mud dredger *Aberavon*, top picture dated May 1984. Built in 1969 by Ferguson Shipbuilders, Glasgow she worked clearing channels on the River Tawe. Sold on in 1991 to a Madeira company, she was eventually scrapped in 2006. Meanwhile the *PS Wingfield Castle*, lower picture, looks a sorry site having arrived at Swansea Docks in 1982 to become a floating restaurant. However being too large to pass the South docks locks she remained derelict at Swansea till purchased by Hartlepool museum and departed Swansea shortly after this photograph was taken in May 1986. The *PS Wingfield Castle* was built in 1934 by William Gray, Hartlepool for the L&NERly Hull to New Holland service till she was decommissioned in 1974 with the opening of the Humber suspension bridge. She has now been fully restored.

Swansea Docks - Miscellaneous May 1984

In amongst the many sidings around Swansea Docks I came across these two interesting items of old rolling stock. The top picture features a long wheelbase tool van which was located near to the Kings Dock signal box and used, I think, either as a store or even a bothy. The step ladders gives the clue to the old wagon being a permanent fixture, the windows were possibly added at the time. The location of the old four wheel wooden van, possibly of LMS origin, I cannot remember other than being in a siding along with condemned wagons. Both photographs date to May 1984.

Danygraig May 1984

Danygraig loco shed opened in 1896 by the Rhondda & Swansea Bay railway. All the photographs at Danygraig date to May 1984 the substantial stone building still being in original condition. The building comprised of a four road locomotive running shed seen to the left of the picture a now roofless two road repair shop and to its right an also roofless three road carriage and wagon repair shop. The central loco repair shop had an elevated roof which housed an overhead crane, the building itself being finished off with distinctive white corner stones. Along with Swansea East Dock shed Danygraig supplied locomotives for shunting duties in Swansea Docks. With the demise of steam working in the docks Danygraig become a diesel depot in January 1960 finally closing in March 1964 its allocation transferred to Landore depot. Danygraig then became a wagon works till sold off for commercial use in the late 1970s.

Danygraig May 1984

I must stake my claim to a little nostalgia when it comes to Danygraig loco shed. From my earliest trainspotting days I would look spellbound at the pictures in my Ian Allen ABC's spotters books of little saddle tanks outside the unmistakeable saw cut roof of Danygraig loco shed. By the time I managed to get there in October 1960 care of the Home Counties Railway Club the little saddle tanks had gone and I was presented with a handful of various diesel shunters. The two pictures feature the old locomotive repair shop, the top picture viewed from outside the rear of the building with the stone water tank. The lower picture taken from just inside the front entrance reveals the old rail tracks still *in situ* despite the old repair shops adaption for handling bulk hydrochloric acid.

Danygraig May 1984

The top picture features the former loco running shed looking towards the back of the building. Much still remains of its past, the roof is original and whilst all the front doors have gone three still remain at the rear. Two types of smoke troughs can still be seen although only one actual road and inspection pit remains. This part of the building seems to be used as a general store. The lower picture is of the former carriage and wagon works. The doors all remain intact as do the rails although the inspection pits have obviously been long filled in. The building still remains in use today (2016) as a chemical warehouse/distribution centre and whilst the running shed has been reroofed it still retains its distinctive saw tooth appearance. The rest of the building remains roofless the former repair shop having been considerably cut down in height and the former carriage & wagon works having also lost its sawtooth roof pattern.

Danygraig May 1984

Whilst the saw tooth roof pattern of the former loco shed remains the little saddle tanks which gave way to the diesel shunters have in turn given way to, of all things, great articulated road trailer tankers carrying hydrochloric acid. Well it makes for a change. The photograph was taken at the rear of the shed and through the window of my lease company's car a Ford Sierra, Reg, No. A971VUH. To us she was by then a ferry car so I had run several drivers over to South Wales for new vehicle collections. She appears a few pages back outside the old repair shop and also made the front cover of my previous book 'Diesels, Depots & Oil Drums' parked alongside to a Class 47 at Landore depot. The Ford Sierra was a good 'bread and butter' car in its day and like the Class 47 would now be viewed as a classic.

Margam steelworks March 1986

The production of iron from iron ore had become well established in and around the South Wales valleys but with the innovation of steelmaking in the mid 19th century and the decline in local iron ores the iron works gradually moved to the coast to take advantage of imported ores. With the introduction of commercial steelmaking came the advent of the integrated iron and steel works. Port Talbot's association with steelmaking began around 1902 with the Port Talbot steelworks. This concern imported iron ores and eventually became part of the nearby Margam integrated iron and steel works which opened on the site of a former copper works just after the Great War. A new deep water harbour was provided to facilitate the efficient discharge of imported iron ores with two blast furnaces, Nos. 1 & 2, located nearby. A third blast furnace, No 3, was built alongside the original two being commissioned in the early 1940s. Following the Second World War a massive expansion in steel production and processing began with two additional blast furnaces No 4 & No 5 coming on stream in 1956 and 1959. This huge extension to the Margam site became known as the Abbey Works whilst at the same time the original Port Talbot works finally closed completely in 1961 and was demolished within a few years the site being redeveloped into an industrial estate. By the 1970s Margam's three original blast furnaces were mostly out of commission with No 1 blast furnace being demolished by 1983 and No 2 going during the early 1990s. However No 3 blast furnace was retained as a 'stand by' for many years and despite being campaigned during 1991 was finally demolished c 2005/6. By this time much of Margams original 1920s steelmaking and processing plant had long gone. Our photograph, dated to March 1986, shows the M4 in the foreground with the Talbot Memorial Park and the St Theodore church in the middle distance with Nos. 4 & 5 working blast furnaces to the left with the defunct Nos. 2 & 3 blast furnaces and ancillary plant to the right. No 1 blast furnace had, as already stated, already been demolished.

Margam Steelworks March 1986

Two photographs feature the defunct No 2 & No 3 blast furnaces. The top picture features Incline Row with its local primary school and a dog taking its owner for a walk. Save the dog and his owner Incline Row remains little altered today (2016) which cannot be said for the industrial backdrop over the rooftops. As said the blast furnaces have now gone as has the giant iron ore transporter unloader which ran along an adjacent deep water dock just behind the blast furnaces. The lower picture is a close up of Nos. 2 & 3 blast furnaces including its extensive ancillary plant taken through what remained of a somewhat rusty dilapidated fence. Today (2016) nothing remains the area having been totally cleared although the new A4241 Harbour Way runs partway through the site.

Margam Steelworks March 1986

Well we've had some pictures of closed railway stations so how about a closed bus terminal. The one pictured above was located just opposite Margam's defunct blast furnaces with the former GWRly main line running in between. When this part of the steelworks was working this bus terminal would have been extremely busy during shift changes. Sadly all is now quiet with nobody to read the indecipherable graffiti. Today (2016) the bus terminal has been swept away replaced by a car park with the new A4241 Harbour Road running part way through the site.

Margam Steelworks March 1986

Last two pictures of Margam's blast furnaces taken again in March 1986 and both from Prince Street which runs parallel to the railway. The top picture features the defunct No2 & No3 blast furnaces and whilst these have long gone the houses remain as before. The lower picture is again taken in Prince Street but up close to steel fencing along the former GWRly main line and at a different angle showing No4 & No5 blast furnaces of the latter day Abbey Works. Of interest blast furnaces had a hearth diameter of some 25ft and could work a melt campaign of some 15 years or so between relining. I have pondered if the chipped GWR cast iron warning sign ever survived. A small housing estate has been built on the open land alongside the railway thus obscuring nearly all of the railway from Prince Street itself.

Neyland & Fishguard June 1984

We look down onto what was once Neyland harbour and its railway terminus which connected to the Carmarthen to Fishguard main line some miles to the north of the town. The railway came to Neyland in 1856 the harbour becoming the main ferry point to Ireland until upstaged by Fishguard in 1906 from which time it became something of a backwater. The railway closed completely in June 1964 the site being redeveloped into a marina on the occasion of our - Paul and myself - visit in June 1984. Little remained of the railway on our visit other than traces of dockside rail tracks and the stumps of the former harbours wooden pontoon. We end our picture journey around South Wales with Fishguard's North breakwater which when built in 1906 would have witnessed until the Great War the comings and goings of Cunards four funnel transatlantic liners. The breakwater was still rail connected at the time of our visit and don't you just love that large wooden sign. Deltics OK then.

South Wales Excursion

Once or twice through the 1970s we would enjoy Western Class diesel haulage on our South Wales adventures to Barry dump. These lads days out came cheap with rail excursions being regularly advertised in our local paper and run at vastly reduced fares. A bargain and no mistake. If suitable rolling stock was at a premium then DMUs would suffice otherwise it would be tired worn out early Mark I carriage stock which despite the age gave some degree of comfort. Come December 1976 this would be our last jaunt pulled by a Western Class diesel hydraulic. No 1013 *Western Ranger* was the loco and the photograph was taken on a cold wet Cardiff General station for our return run. With the steam heat on at least the compartment stock was snug and warm. This particular excursion was from Paddington, well Ealing Broadway for us, to Cardiff travelling on down to Barry Island by local DMU. The day for us finished as usual at The Feathers pub adjacent to Ealing Broadway station. For *Western Ranger* her days were numbered being withdrawn a few months later in February 1977 following pulling the Western Tribute enthusiasts special on the 26th February in company with fellow locomotive No 1023 *Western Fusilier*. This I photographed from Jacobs Ladder footbridge West Ealing whilst in a somewhat second hand condition having recently suffered some crushed vertebra and broken bones in an industrial accident. God, was I keen.

Blue Diesels - Part One

Bristol Bath Road August 1976

As a railway enthusiast the Western Class diesel hydraulics had passed me by, my interest waned about a year after the last few came into service and by the time it returned they had all but gone. However for my old school chum Mike Woodhouse they formed a large part of his working life seeing them up close and personal as an engineer fitter at Plymouth Laira depot. Mike was a professional railwayman and part of his time covered the period when diesel hydraulics still ruled supreme. Life was never to be easy for the men of Laira as when the Westerns went they still had the joy of the Class 50s to contend with . . . But as an engineer Mike had a passion for both classes and when opportunities allowed he captured them on film during their last few months in service. Here I am lucky enough to reproduce a selection of his Western Class diesel locomotive pictures taken 'on shed' during the end of their short but eventful lives. By the way I apologise for referring to loco's as 'she', Mike has told me off before about this as railwaymen never referred to locomotives as such. I suspect they called them other things . . .

By the beginning of 1976 some thirty odd Class 52 Western diesel locomotives remained in service. Twelve months later only seven remained and on the 26th February 1977 following an order from on high the last five survivors Nos. 1010/13/23/41 & 48 were withdrawn '*en bloc*'. The Western Region's long association with diesel hydraulic traction had come to an end. Whilst withdrawals had commenced in early 1973 and was complete in February 1977 the Westerns did linger. Ignoring those of the Class that escaped into preservation Swindon Works despatched them all the last of the Class being cut up in June 1979 The picture above features D1022 *Western Sentinel* sporting slight near side front end damage in the shed yard at Bristol Bath Road depot during August 1976.

Mike Woodhouse Augusr 1980
Photo: S Crowther

Bristol Bath Road   Jan.1977 & August 1976

Western Class loco No 1023 *Western Fusiler,* top picture, outside the maintenance depot in January 1977. She along with No 1013 *Western Ranger* worked the 'Western Tribute' special on Saturday 26th February 1977 and on return to Paddington they both worked light engines back to Laira depot where they were withdrawn. The following day No 1023 was once again despatched light engine but this time to Swindon Works. No 1015 *Western Champion*, lower picture, photographed inside the servicing depot, August 1976, displays her train reporting blinds set to 1015 the loco's number. When the locomotive train reporting codes were discontinued in 1976 the official order was for all loco blinds to be reset at '0000'. However some of Laira's depot staff had other ideas and unofficially commenced displaying the actual loco number. No 1015 was withdrawn in December 1976 but both this loco and 1023 escaped into preservation.

Bristol Bath Road August 1976

Another shot of Western Class No 1022 *Western Sentinel* at Bath Road again in August 1976 but this time positioned between the servicing depot, right, and the former steam age workshops now refurbished as the heavy maintenance/lifting shed. Note that the Class 50 No.50040 alongside has also had its reporting blinds suitably reset to 5040. *Western Sentinel* was withdrawn from Old Oak Common in January 1977 remaining in store there till May 1977 when she was hauled to Swindon Works being scrapped there in December 1978.

Bristol Bath Road August 1976

Two close up shots of No 1001 *Western Pathfinder* and No 1005 *Western Venturer* taken at the rear of Bath Road depot during August 1976. *Western Pathfinder* was otherwise known as the Carpet Cleaner by engine crews and fitters alike. Get it - no - Oh well never mind. She was withdrawn from Plymouth Laira in October 1976 following suffering crash damage then hauled up to Swindon Works in January 1977 and cut up the following August. Meanwhile *Western Venturer* was withdrawn the following month in November 1976 being hauled to Swindon Works in January 1977 and cut up in June. Unlike some of the class at Swindon Works both locomotives didn't linger that long.

Bristol Bath Road July 1976

An unusual picture of No 1072 *Western Glory* having something of a rest at Bath Road depot. She had been withdrawn at Plymouth Laira in October 1976 and following emptying out all fuel and water was towed up to Bath Road for use in trials using commercial air bags to re right her. Apparently these trials took place in late 1976 and although successful were never proceeded with. She moved on to Swindon Works in January 1977 being cut up during April. The lower picture taken in July 1976 features No 1051 *Western Ambassador* sitting on the Bath Road turntable which was retained following conversion to a diesel depot in the early 1960s. She was one of those Westerns which were re painted at Laira depot during the 1970s causing considerably friction with Swindon Works at that time. She was withdrawn from Laira in September 1976 and cut up at Swindon Works in August 1977.

Bristol Bath Road February 1976

Located at the rear of Bath Road depot the turntable backed onto the River Avon and the Bristol St Philips Marsh avoiding lines which spanned the river over a large girder bridge which can be seen in the photo's background. On this occasion in February 1976 Mike caught No 1036 *Western Emperor* being turned and this locomotive was slightly unusual in having its nameplates positioned slightly higher than all other members of the class. Withdrawn in November 1976 she was despatched to Swindon Works from Laira that month being cut up in February 1977.

Westbury August 1976

Westbury diesel depot opened in the late 1950s for servicing DMUs later taking on diesel locomotives which worked the many aggregate trains from the Mendip quarries. Many Westerns finished their days on these workings and several examples are shown here. Both photographs were taken out in Westbury's depot yards during August 1976 the top picture featuring No.1009 *Western Invader* and No.1048 *Western Lady* whilst the lower picture shows No.1036 *Western Emperor* and No.1070 *Western Gauntlet.* Whilst Nos.1009/36/70 were withdrawn in late 1976 No.1048 lingered on till January 1977. Other than No.1048 which was preserved all the others were cut up at Swindon Works.

Sold on for scrap December 1976 & September 1974

Two pictures of withdrawn Westerns whilst on route to Swindon Works for scrapping. The top picture features No.1071 formerly Western Renown which having failed with a seized final drive in December 1976 was removed from its train and dumped in the depot yards at Taunton. She was withdrawn shortly after and was hauled to Swindon Works in February 1977 being scrapped in November 1978. Despite the poor quality of the lower picture it is of interest as Mike has captured Western No.1070 *Western Gauntlet* hauling a scrap train of three other Westerns Nos.1014/62/73 passing through Bristol Temple Mills station in September 1974.

Newton Abbot January 1977

Stabled alongside Newton Abbot station one weekend in January 1977 No.1013 *Western Ranger* is on pw duties and only weeks away from withdrawal and ultimate preservation. During the end of its service career *Western Ranger* worked many specials displaying white buffers and regalia with red nameplates and thus acquired the nickname the Fairground Engine amongst railwaymen.
The former Newton Abbot locomotive workshops feature in the background and they still remain today in commercial use. Opened in 1892 they were totally modernised for handling diesel traction in the early 1960s. Following Plymouth Laira taking over responsibility for all diesel locomotive maintenance Newton Abbot workshops closed in 1970. However the old Works were to see some use again as the day following the withdrawal of the last Westerns Nos.1010/13/41/48 were towed to and stored inside a then locked Newton Abbot Works. The last two Nos.1041/48 departed in June 1978 having escaped into preservation.

Plymouth Laira September 1976

It's a sunny Saturday afternoon in September 1976 and No.1070 *Western Gauntlet* having been serviced is now ready for the road and sits outside the depot next to the depot's 45ton steam breakdown crane. No.1070 was the last locomotive to be serviced that shift so two of the maintenance crew take a break one fitter having his feet up in the cab, note his boots, whilst the other has his nose in the day's papers. Withdrawn in December 1976 *Western Gauntlet* remained dumped at Laira till March 1977 when she was hauled off to Swindon Works being one of the last of the Class to be scrapped in May 1979.

Plymouth Laira September 1976

A close up view of two Westerns, top picture, No.1013 *Western Ranger* and No.1015 *Western Champion* poking their noses out of the servicing shed one Saturday in September 1976. You could say *Western Ranger* is displaying her white buffers. The chap walking along between the locomotives is one of the depots 'turners' and is seemingly unaware of Mike taking his picture. Depot 'turners' would pick up locomotives from the incoming yards following the train crews having signed off. They would then run the locos round to the servicing shed for refuelling etc prior to setting them in the departure sidings for their next turn of duty. The lower photograph was taken on the same day and this time features No. 1048 *Western Lady* displaying some bodyside damage along with No. 1015 *Western Champion.*

Plymouth Laira

A somewhat second hand looking No 1022 *Western Sentinel* resides in the workshops following a engine room fire, her roof panels being scattered around on the high level decking. We have no date for this photograph. The lower picture is perhaps one not witnessed by many railway enthusiasts and features some name and number plates removed from withdrawn Westerns and placed into safe storage. Well perhaps not that safe as Mike managed to secure a photograph just before they were securely wrapped in old sacking for despatch by train to Paddington for collection by BR 'Collectors Corner' at Euston. We have no date for this picture but it must be around early 1976. Although only worth a fraction of today's prices they still had considerable value and 'unofficially acquiring' any plates would be at your peril.

Plymouth Laira   September 1976

Mike took these photographs of Nos.1013 *Western Ranger* & 1048 *Western Lady* coming 'on shed' from their booked duties during the back end of a morning shift during September 1976. His vantage point was Laira depot's locomotive incoming roads situated alongside the servicing shed which within a few years would be demolished to make way for the HSTs.

Plymouth Laira No.1015 *Western Champion*

There she sits.
Work stained in September 1976 with peeling paintwork but still radiating power and beauty.
Nothing more you can say really.

Plymouth Laira September 1976

During September 1976 Iris and I were on holiday in Cornwall where I undertook a few railway incursions the first being an unofficial wander around Laira's old steam shed site. We had no knowledge that Mike was working at Laira at that time as we had long lost contact with him, however we now think he was on the night shift. Away from the modern 1960s stylistic diesel depot the remnants of the demolished steam shed were reduced to storing rolling stock Dumped on one of the old shed's four roads were, pictured above, Nos.1037, 1043 & 1021 whilst on another road were Nos.1034, 1049 & 1063. Most had been withdrawn through the spring and summer of 1976 and were despatched to Swindon Works a few weeks following my visit. All, save No.1021, had been cut up by February 1977. With Iris now exasperated I pulled over on the A374 Embankment Road to take a quick picture of the depot and as luck would have it caught No.1068 *Western Reliance* coming in onto shed.

Penzance September 1976

My second railway incursion on that holiday was to the old steam shed at Penzance which held two Western's No.1028 *Western Hussar* and, as photographed, No.1051 *Western Ambassador*. The shed itself had only a few months to go before final closure the building being demolished shortly after. In the lower picture a section of old iron piping was being pulled out from the nearby pump house which had, as I remember, already been demolished. *Western Ambassador* itself was only days away from withdrawal following an electrical fire and soon found itself at Swindon Works being cut up in August 1977. The top photograph catches the end of a railway era, whilst in the lower picture it was also time up for Triumph Toledo cars which had ceased production that year.

Swindon Works April 1977

With the demise of the Westerns a tour around Swindon Works was on the cards. But having recently suffered a serious industrial accident I was somewhat fragile so come April 1977 my old mate Paul Wells took me in his old Ford Cortina. Sadly for me the old car's suspension coupled with Pauls high speed cornering didn't quite do me any favours. Somewhat the worse for wear I arrived to find Western's quietly rusting away in every corner save No.1015 which had found herself on 'gate guardian' duties. No.1033, lower picture, was withdrawn in September 1976 being put to use at Plymouth Laira on steam heating carriage stock. On our tour around the Works she was dumped along the northern perimeter wall of 'A' shop which looks if the place has had something of a clear out judging by the piles of junk scattered about. While No.1033 was cut up in May 1979 No 1015 went on to live another day.

Swindon Works April 1977

With some twenty five Westerns scattered around the Works yards or quietly rusting away in various corners two rows of Westerns had been assembled within the Works and were radiating out from 'A' shop into the old sleeper yards. Nos.1012/25/64/57 & 28, top picture, still manage an impressive line up whilst the other row, lower picture, consists of Nos.1011/34/63/21 & 05. Interestingly six of the above lasted into 1979 with No.1028 being one of the last two scrapped in June of that year.

Swindon Works April 1977

One Western class locomotive that did not linger following withdrawal in November 1976 was No. 1054. A Laira engine she was despatched to Swindon Works two months following withdrawal and was cut up just after our April tour around the Works. Swindon Works certainly never disposed of the Westerns in any particular order and whilst the first arrived in late 1973 the last, an engineless No.1009, arrived in May 1977. Several spent two years or more dumped in the yards while No.1011 was hauled to Swindon Works from Laira in November 1975 and wasn't finally cut up till January 1979. The lower picture shows a batch of retrieved Western Class Maybach MD655 engines possibly going on for re sale with one Western at least No.1009 having her engines removed at Laira for sale as mobile generators.

Swindon Works August 1977

Our Swindon Works tour in April 1977 produced no Westerns or for that matter any other locomotives being scrapped with 'C' Shop itself being reduced to cutting up wagons. Four months later in August 1977 Mike Woodhouse was at Swindon in a professional capacity and on this occasion several Westerns were being scrapped including Nos.1003 and 1063 which are photographed here. In both pictures Swindon Works 'A' Shop appears in the near background and whilst 'C' Shop was still active cutting up locomotives most of the original dump and associated sidings had been lifted.

Swindon Works - the end of an era
Western Class No.1041 *Western Prince* - April 1980

Western Prince was the second from last to leave and photographed in April 1980 a few months before she departed. She was in store at the old Newton Abbot workshops following withdrawal in February 1977 till purchased for preservation and hauled up to Swindon Works in June 1978. The last Western to depart from Swindon Works was No.1015 *Western Champion* (opposite page) which was withdrawn from Laira in December 1976 and hauled to Swindon the following month for scrapping but instead found herself on Works 'gate guardian' duties around the turntable. By August 1979 she was the last 'unclaimed' Western left at Swindon and a 11th hour bid for preservation saved her from being scrapped. She was purchased by the Diesel Traction Group in 1980 and photographed by myself in November 1985, leaving Swindon Works in 1990 by which time 'A' Shop had already been demolished.

Western Class No. 1015 *Western Champion*   November 1985

Blue Diesels Part Two

The Deltics, Belle Isle and The Ladykillers
February 1981

Belle Isle - Copenhagen Tunnels

Deltic Class No.55015 *Tulyar* runs light engine out of the southern portals of the Copenhagen tunnels working down from Finsbury Park TMD to Kings Cross station. We did not have long to wait for her determined return. By the 1980s the centre two tracks were the up/down fast with the western tracks, left in the picture, being the up/down slow. With track rationalisation underway the old eastern track bed, right, would soon be totally lifted. Come February 1981 Paul Wells and myself decided that to photograph the Deltics in action we had better get a move on as they were now reduced to secondary duties. None too soon as within a year they had all gone. Our planned soiree was to be at Belle Isle a location a mile north of Kings Cross station between the northern portals of the Kings Cross Gasworks tunnels and the southern portals of the Copenhagen tunnels. Even the name sounds evocative, in steam days it was truly atmospheric. Belle Isle I knew well from the big screen. The Ladykillers, a mid 1950s period colour film from Ealing Studious all set to a backdrop of steam trains and those Copenhagen Tunnels whose distinctive parapets became a major part of the film set itself.

Belle Isle North London line & York Way, Copenhagen viaduct

HST Set No.254 024, top picture powers its way through Belle Isle on the down fast lines. Most prominent in the picture is the North London line bridge crossing over the ECML from which the lower picture was taken in October 1984. Looking down to the left are the northern portals of the Gasworks tunnels and a multitude of tracks running under the 16 arch York Way Copenhagen viaduct five of which lead to Kings Cross Goods depot which can be seen in the far background. Several of these tracks have already been lifted as has the short branch line that features in the bottom right of both pictures which ran under the North London line to the Caledonian Road coal depot. This curious line features in part in The Ladykillers film as does the North London line set high above passing over express trains belching steam and smoke far below.

Belle Isle - The Ladykillers film and the Caledonian Road coal depot.

The short branch line referred to in the previous page ran on an increasing gradient under the North London line and parallel to the ECML up to a distant headshunt. From here a spur deviated away crossing behind the southern parapets of the Copenhagen tunnels to the Caledonian Road coal depot located on the opposite side of the ECML. This coal depot spur would feature in The Ladykillers film and pass directly to the rear of one Mrs Wilberforce's house, albeit a full size film prop. The 'house' itself was a quant detached twin gabled affair that bore little resemblance to the terraced housing down Frederica Street where our 'house' formed a cul-de-sac. Mrs Wilberforce was an elderly sweet and somewhat eccentric lady who would become the central character in The Ladykillers film becoming the landlady to a band of oddball criminals thinking them to be classical musicians. The criminals prize, a £60,000 van hoist with an unsuspecting Mrs Wilberforce being the main player. The three photographs all date to February 1981 and show what remained of the branch. In the top picture we see the brick incline curving away from York Way with a single track running underneath the branch to Kings Cross goods. The middle picture was taken slightly further along the branch and here we see the connecting spur to the North London line curving away under the branch. Copemhagen viaduct features in the background. The lower picture is a copy of a print, the photograph being taken by Paul looking back up the branch towards the North London line bridge and the Copenhagen tunnels. The Caledonian Road coal depot closed in 1967 with all the trackwork being lifted in the early 1970s. Around this time the area around Frederica Street and the Caledonian Road coal depot was cleared and redeveloped for housing and has now changed out of all recognition.

Belle Isle - HSTs

HST set No.254026, top picture, accelerates out of the northern portals of Gasworks tunnel on a down express with in the foreground the remains of the Goods & Mineral Junction signal box. Meanwhile HST Set No.254004, lower picture, just about disappears through the southern portals of the Copenhagen tunnels. Poking about behind the parapets of these tunnels we could find no trace of the short line that ran behind the Copenhagen tunnels over the ECML to the Caledonian coal yard. A builder's yard occupied most of the old film set site whilst a large crude detached building, as seen above and in other pictures, sits approximately on the site of Mrs. Wilberforce's 'house'.

Belle Isle - Classes 25 & 31

In steam days the up/down slow lines were the goods lines which ran into the large and sprawling Kings Cross goods depot and locomotive sheds. From the 1950s onwards traditional loose coupled goods traffic had rapidly declined but the York Way freightliner terminal opened in the mid 1960s as well as an aggregate terminal, part of which was on the site of the former loco sheds. Class 25 No.25176, top picture, is working past Copenhagen Junction into the still active goods depot whilst the lower picture features Class 31 No.31189 on a pw train. The brick arches of the Copenhagen viaduct make for an interesting backdrop along with the disused Caledonian Road coal depot branch curving away on a rising gradient towards the right of the picture.

Belle Isle - Class 31s

Class 31 No.31225 pulls away from York Way, Copenhagen viaduct on a parcels train passing a stationary Class 37 No.37051 on a train of empty 21ton aggregate hoppers. Meanwhile another Class 31 No.31423, lower picture, is caught running on the slow down lines approaching the southern portals of the Copenhagen tunnel with a Cambridge bound train.

Belle Isle Class 37

Having picked up an empty return working of 21ton hoppers Class 37 No.37051, top picture, is held on signals waiting for the road. The lower picture was taken later during the day as I have by now wandered high up along the disused Caledonian Road coal depot branch. I think No.37051 had been waiting for me as she moved off shortly after I had walked over to the former branch having stopped short at the bridge for the North London connecting spur. The remains of the Goods & Mineral Junction signal box which closed back in 1976 sit alongside. Paul can be seen further down the old trackbed having walked across the old bridge girders something I did not have the courage to do. My excuse for this lack of determination was that it was only four years since my last accidental flying stunt and I was in no rush to have another go at it.

Belle Isle Class 37

Our Class 37 No.37051 finally has the road and rumbles past just below me.

Belle Isle - Class 37

Another Class 37, this one being No.37097 bursts into the daylight with its train load of 21ton aggregate hoppers after running through the Copenhagen tunnels and commences crossing over the junction to the Kings Cross York Way freight terminal. It's not the best of photographs what with all the overhead electric clutter but then I didn't know the train was coming till it did. By the time I photographed No.37097 again she had discharged her load and was running light engine back to Finsbury Park TMD.

Belle Isle - Class 46

Running light engine from Finsbury Park TMD Class 46 No.46036, top picture, takes the up fast line to Kings Cross station to be within an hour or so working back with a parcels train. Our Class 46 and its parcel train, lower picture, are now on the down fast line which is the middle tunnel bore. Of the three tunnels the central bore was the original dating to 1850 with the western bore, right in picture, being added in 1877 and a further addition, the eastern bore, in 1886. Of interest are the remains of the Goods & Mineral junction signal box and the concrete processing plant which dates to the mid 1960s and is still operating today.

Belle Isle - Class 46

Two photographs of Class 46 No.46052 taken, once again, high up from the old disused Caledonian Road coal depot branch line. Our Class 46, top picture, is caught running into Kings Cross goods depot under the North London line bridge. If memory serves me we didn't have long to wait before she returned, lower picture, on a parcels train. Sadly I was a second too late on the shutter as the loco slips behind the remains of the old signal box. Note the coaching stock on this train, these would have been coaches taken out of service for various reasons and marshalled into the parcel train for moving forwards to Doncaster.

Belle Isle - Class 47s

Two pictures of Class 47s on down semi fast trains. No.47415, top picture, works hard on the incline out of the Gasworks tunnels with the Copenhagen viaduct as a backdrop behind which the railway yards extended over to the St. Pancras Midland main line. Today (2018), other than the ECML, all else has gone, indeed a blue tube containing the EuroStar line now crosses the ECML at this point. In the lower picture an unidentified Class 47 approaches the Copenhagen tunnels, today (2018) these same tunnel portals and embankments have taken on a neglected air with foliage extending down to the trackbed itself. Above the tunnels much has changed. Whilst the 1960s housing remains the commercial buildings and yards have been redeveloped and now stretch down to the tunnel portals themselves.

Belle Isle - Class 55 No.55009 *Alycidon*

Our little Saturday sojourn to Belle Isle to catch the Deltics was viewed a success photographing six Deltics in about four hours, the day only being marred by Paul's insistence in wanting kebabs for lunch something which would come back to haunt us later that evening. The picture features of No.55009 *Alycidon* emerging out of the Copenhagen tunnels with the up 10.45am semi fast ex York

Belle Isle - Class 55 No.55011 *The Royal Northumberland Fusiliers*

No. 55011 *The Royal Northumberland Fusiliers* storms out of the Gasworks tunnel incline with the down 12.05pm semi fast to Hull. The Gasworks tunnels although not long were steeply inclined at both ends to pass under the Regents canal.

Belle Isle - Class 55 No.55015 *Tulyar*

An imposing shot of No.55015 *Tulyar* on the down 12.20pm semi fast to York. Storming out of the Gasworks tunnel incline with the power full on she fills the sky with clouds of two stroke exhaust fumes.

Belle Isle - Class 55 No.55015 *Tulyar*

Another shot of No.55015 *Tulyar* as she passes me by having just run under the North London line bridge managing to totally smother me with dense clouds of two stroke exhaust. Not that it bothered me. The white painted loco cabs tells us she is a Finsbury Park locomotive.

Belle Isle - Class 55 No.55016 *Gordon Highlander*

No.55016 *Gordon Highlander* on the up 12.34am semi fast from Hull drifts past and within minutes will be arriving at Kings Cross station - on time.

Belle Isle - Class 55 No.55022 *Royal Scots Grey*

The last Deltic to be seen that day was No.55022 *Royal Scots Grey* passing under the North London line bridge on full song working the down 14.05pm semi fast to York. Paul and I found Belle Isle a fascinating location and for us not a day too late as the Deltics were all eventually to be based at York for the trans-Pennine services. Gresley's streamliners might well be long gone from Kings Cross and Belle Isle but for me the Deltics under full throttle were a close run thing and still a magnificent sight and something to behold.

Blue Diesels - Part Three
Trains past my office window

It was my old mate Paul Wells who got me in as a driver at Lex Vehicle Leasing, their office and compound being at Acton alongside the Paddington main line and the connecting spur to the North London line. This was 1984 and for the next two years or so driving cars became not so much a job but more an extended holiday with pay. The railways figured highly in this job and both Paul and myself took advantage of this, as drivers I think the management always wondered exactly where we were. No mobiles in those days. Then the management got their own back. Paul got the sack for being involved in an accident somewhere where he shouldn't have been and someone thought I would be better employed in the office. My 'promotion' to the office had me in charge of the 'loan fleet', in house cars used to cover for customers vehicles when off the road. Run on a card index system my day was generally spent with a telephone glued to my ear. Or taking train pictures. Nobody in the office ever queried this, I fancy that they just thought I was slightly eccentric. The top and lower pictures feature Class 56s on Bardon aggregate trains returning empty from Thorney Hill, Staines to Bardon Hill, Leicestershire. The middle picture is of a Class 37 just passing under the busy A40 Western Avenue the garage opposite being our drivers' first port of call for fuel when delivering cars. The Bardon trains were supplying aggregate for the Heathrow extension. These two pictures date to September 1986 whilst the Class 37 picture was taken two months earlier. The large Volvo 240 estate car seen in the bottom picture was one of our regular Loan fleet vehicles and always very popular amongst the country yuppie and Lovejoy types The two chaps on the right in the top picture are doing a PDI check on a new delivery prior to running it on to the customer..

View from an office Window

Top Picture. Another Bardon empties train heading up to Acton Wells junction on the North London line. On this occasion we have two Class 31s Nos.31121 & 31113 in Railfreight and BR blue livery. October 1986. Middle Picture. More interesting is Class 33 No.33008 *Eastleigh* repainted in 1960s green livery working a track inspection train, the coach to the left being the General Manager's saloon. November 1986. Lower Picture. Double headed Class 37s Nos.37238 & 37054 approaching the A40 Western Avenue overbridge with a train of empty Yeoman wagons returning to Merehead. February 1987.

View from an office window

Top Picture. With a silver roof this could only be a Stratford Class 47 this example being No.47054 working a Thameshaven to Langley oil train, the Volvo 240 estate meanwhile awaits its new owner. Poor thing. September 1986.

Middle Picture. An unknown Class 47 hauling an aggregate train of twenty ton open wagons. Suitable rolling stock must have been in short supply. These old wagons would be withdrawn from revenue service by the early 1990s. August 1986.

Lower Picture. Class 56 No.56101 on a Yeoman empties passing an unknown Class 47 on a Paddington bound empty newspaper train. Two Vauxhall Cavaliers, a saloon and a hatchback, can be seen amongst other cars in the compound. February 1987

View from an office window

Class 50 No.50025 *Invincible* works an empty Penzance sleeper train to Wembley carriage yards for servicing. August 1986. Middle Picture. A Class 73 electro-diesel No.73114 hurries past on the main line with an Acton to Northfleet 'Blue Circle' cement train. Cars include Ford Sierras, Vauxhall Cavaliers and a Golf GTi. Nice bit of tin ware that. August 1986. Lower Picture. Another empty sleeper working, this time hauled by Class 50 No.50014 *Warspite*. Note that the compound is now empty the company having moved out to a new site at South Ruislip. May 1987. Revisiting the site in recent years the compound was still in some use. Whilst our garage remains. the office from where I took so many photographs and the garage over the A40 Western Avenue had gone.

Lost and Derelict Places - London

The railway lands north of Kings Cross

The Granary Goods Depot, February 1981

Fish & Coal Offices, February 1981

Plimsoll Viaduct & original coal drops, February 1981

Save for its great terminal stations London's once intensive railway infrastructure has now been largely swept away. Back in the world of the 1980s much of this still survived and I was fortunate enough to at least catch a glimpse of a world largely gone by. The vast goods yards north west of Kings Cross station are now referred to as 'the railway lands north of Kings Cross' a term not come across back in the 1970/80s. The top picture taken from Goods Way features the 1852 build goods depot known as the Granary. By the mid 1930s the depot was adapted for outgoing goods only but with falling traffic levels during the late 1960s it became used for storage or warehousing. Our picture shows part of the building in use by National carriers. Goods Way then curves away in a northwest direction and passes the now derelict Fish & Coal offices, middle picture, a view which looks southwards the building taking in the contours of the Regent Canal just behind. Note Paul taking a photograph standing by my Vauxhall VX4/90 car. The lower picture taken a further few hundred yards northwards along Goods Way looks eastwards at two diagonally opposing rows of long split level warehouses having been originally built as coal drops. Known originally as the Eastern (left) and Western (right) coal drops the latter had become derelict by the 1980s. Planned redevelopment of goods yards north west of Kings Cross commenced in 1996 the area becoming known as Kings Cross Central and as such the Granary, Fish & coal offices and the original coal drops have all been retained and will eventually sit in a more gentrified or even beautified landscape.

London, the railway lands north of Kings Cross

The former Eastern and Western coal drops viewed from both the east and west, top & middle pictures. Built between 1852 and 1860 they were superseded in the 1890s by the nearby and more advanced Plimsoll coal drops. These were located on the opposite bank of the Regents canal along Camley Street. Rail access was made via the Plimsoll viaduct a ramp which ran up between the original coal drops leading to a short bridge which spanned the canal to the Plimsoll coal drops. This ramp alone remains and can be seen in both pictures the rails having been long lifted and partially converted to road use. With coal traffic ceasing in the early 1970s the Plimsoll drops were demolished in 1983/84. The old Ebonite factory chimney, top picture, can be seen in the middle distance was a local landmark for many years till demolished in 1983. Once past the original coal drops Goods Way gives way to a service road and in the lower picture we look southwards towards the 1898 build Western goods depot erected alongside the Western coal drops. From the mid 1930s onwards the depot was used for incoming goods only but from the 1970s onwards was used for warehousing. The building was demolished circa 2005. The five gas holders that feature in the middle picture make for an impressive backdrop and they remained in service till decommissioned in 2000 being dismantled by 2011. Three of these gas holders plus another one will be eventually be re-erected in the regenerated Kings Cross Central site and will eventually sit near to the original coal drops.

Original west & east coal drops, February 1981

The Plimsoll viaduct. August 1985

Western Goods Depot, August 1985

London, the railway lands north of Kings Cross

Picture A October 1984

Picture B   January 1976

Picture C   February 1981

The service road which continues on from Goods Way runs in a north-ish direction parallel to the St. Pancras main line on its western side opposite the 1960s freightliner yards before curving eastwards by a concrete batching plant and then runs up a walled incline to join York Way on the Copenhagen viaduct. The top picture (A) takes a southern view looking down the service road taking in the end of the Long Shed and part of the old loco shed site, middle left of picture. Turning east past the end of the Long Shed, we then join York Way as seen in the middle picture (B). The Long Shed features prominently in this picture along with the rail connected aggregate terminal's large hopper which features to the far left of the picture behind the long shed. Also visible are rail sidings with PCA wagons alongside three pneumatically fed dry cement silos to the right of the picture. A parcel train can be seen in the Long Shed. The lower picture (C) features the aggregate hopper which was situated in the old loco shed yards near to the site of the turntable. York Way and the Copenhagen viaduct can be seen in the left background of this picture along with the long closed York Road underground station. This building still remains but not so the Copenhagen viaduct which with the removal of the railway in its entirety was demolished circa 2008 with a new realigned York Way gradually falling away to the rail level that it replaced. The area was transformed.

February 1981

June 1977

London, the railway lands north of Kings Cross

Two panoramic views from York Way looking across the old Kings Cross freightliner yards (top left picture) and the aggregate terminal. Such photographs would have not been possible in the 1960s due to the proliferation of old railway buildings and the high walls of York Way. By the 1980s the old railway buildings had gone and York Ways high brick walls had either been demolished or considerably cut back. Kings Cross Freightliner yards which opened in 1965 are partially visible to the left of the above left picture with a Class 08 shunter at work. The former loco shed occupied the middle ground where now stands a large aggregate hopper to the right. The picture above right was taken further around so that the aggregate hopper is now to the left whilst the long shed features in this picture with parcel stock alongside. The service road runs unseen in the far background from left to right in both pictures and its rising incline can be made out in the extreme right of the top right picture. Loose coupled goods traffic had dwindled away by the late 1960s the freightliner yards closed in 1986 with the aggregate and concrete terminals being relocated and all remaining commercial busineses cleared by the early 2000s ready for future redevelopment. Other than the term 'railway lands' there is nothing remotely railway in the planned gentrification of Kings Cross Central.

London, Paddington Goods Depot

To those regular travellers who used Paddington station the goods depot located to the north west of the main running lines was something that could not be missed on the final approaches to the station. To passing passengers and from the platform ends it presented a long high outer brick wall topped with a roof line of angled cladding which almost extended to Westbourne Bridge which spanned the main running lines. Unlike Kings Cross goods depot Paddington goods was visible to the travelling public and like Kings Cross and other goods depots around London's terminal stations it was considerably larger than their passenger station counterparts.

Top:
October 1985

Middle:
July 1977

Left:
February 1986

London, the demolition of Paddington Goods Depot, March 1986

Picture A

Picture B

Picture C

The six pictures of Paddington Goods Depot were taken during March 1986 whilst I was on a driving job into West London. I simply drove into the site, you could in those days. The top picture (A), is taken inside the site looking east at the rear of the 1907 office building. Demolition of the building had just commenced and the outer facade had been totally covered in sheeting to protect the passing public. So we have a picture of its rear. The single story reception office can be seen in the extreme right of the picture. The middle picture (B), is viewed westwards with my good self standing outside the reception office looking into the shattered remains of the goods depot itself. The lower picture (C), is a similar view with an access ramp for road transport note the old rail in use as a wheel guard on the ramp. Also note the high outer retaining brick wall extreme left in both pictures. The top picture (D) on the next page is again taken from outside the reception office looking at the weighbridge and office. By the time of my visit approximately half the depot has been demolished and of interest is the A40 Westway flyover in the background. The middle picture (E) on the next page, is looking westwards towards Westbourne Bridge with this part of the depot having been razed to the ground. Again the A40 Westway can be seen to the right of the picture. The lower picture (F) on the next page shows the same view but looking east with the Westbourne Bridge behind me. To the left of the picture can be seen some of Paddingtons old industrial past.

London, the demolition of Paddington Goods Depot, March 1986

Picture D

Picture E

Picture F

The history of Paddington Goods Depot goes back to the opening of the Great Western Railway in 1838, the first passenger terminal station at Paddington being a temporary affair located on the goods depot site. On completion of the present day station in 1854 the original terminus was torn down and replaced by a purpose built wooden goods depot with a large brick built office block being added at its western end in 1907. This goods shed was in turn demolished in 1925 being replaced by a large 18 road seven gabled steel framed affair which was finally completed in 1932. From the 1950s onwards loose coupled goods traffic levels declined and Paddington goods depot closed in 1975. From then on the yards were used for various commercial purposes the depot remaining derelict till demolition in 1986 resulting in its outer facing wall to the main running lines being drastically reduced in height. This totally changed the environs of Paddington station opening up the area allowing the 1970 build A40 Westway flyover to be clearly seen. The former goods depot site was then put to various commercial uses including handling aggregates till the planned regeneration of the site commenced as the Paddington Central Complex in 1998 with redevelopment commencing in 2000. Today (2017) little remains of Paddington goods other than a few shattered remains of the former outer brick wall, the A40 Westway having once again disappeared behind 21st century architecture.

London, Battersea
Stewarts Lane loco shed

July 1977

Having already visited Stewarts Lane loco shed once before in this book we have moved on a few years. Closed to steam in 1963 and mostly roofless by 1967 the site continued to eke out an existence as storage yards for the CM & EE dept with a small part of the loco shed remaining as a diesel depot. The top picture was taken from a southern electric, sorry EMU, in July 1977 as we rattled over the site taking in the roof of the diesel depot, extreme left, the few remaining but now open roads of the loco shed with the water tank and eastern shed wall and offices on the extreme right. The old large DECCA building looks down over Stewarts Lanes now reduced circumstances all set to a backdrop of the local gas holder and Battersea power station which at that time was still working. The few sidings, middle picture, alongside the diesel depot held on this occasion a internal water tank wagon which isn't all that exciting so a few words about the old depository or DECCA building which features behind might be appropriate. This building has over the years appeared as a backdrop to many famous steam locomotives and could almost be said to be part of Stewarts Lane itself. Opened in 1903 it was built as a furniture depository by Hampton & Sons furniture makers and dealers. The building was large enough to survive a direct hit during the Second World War which took out one end of the building. This was later rebuilt to its original style. The Decca electronics & music company then occupied the building from 1956 till 1980 since when it was converted into self storage units. Whilst the large concrete coaling plant had long gone coal was still to be found at Stewarts Lane albeit in somewhat smaller quantities showing steam's continuing presence with two steam powered breakdown cranes, lower picture. Being the winter of 1986 I fancy the wooden pallets were for firing up a crane's cold boiler and not for a warming bonfire. The breakdown crane itself is ADRR 96510 one of the last steam working examples working on British Rail, see next page.

November 1983

October 1986

London, Battersea - Stewarts Lane loco shed November 1983

Stewarts Lane in November 1983 provided two steam powered breakdown cranes Nos.ADRR 95225 and ADRR 95201. Both were out in the shed yards and whilst one would be in steam the other would be held as an operational spare. The top picture features ADRR 95225 with that old Decca building as a backdrop. It is possible that this crane spent its working life at Stewarts Lane. Both were built by Ransom & Rapier for the Southern Railway in 1926 with a 36 ton lift capacity. Whilst ADRR 95225 was withdrawn in March 1986 and scrapped three years later ADRR 95201 held out another six months before escaping into preservation the following year. On withdrawal they were replaced by another two steam cranes Nos.ADRR 95209 & 95210, see previous page, and these were the last steam breakdown cranes in operation being withdrawn in 1988. ADRR 95209 was scrapped in 2010 whilst ADRR 95210 likewise escaped into preservation.

London, Battersea Park loco shed

June 1977

Despite having closed way back in 1934 I was vaguely aware of this loco shed having once noticed a complete roundhouse roof after crossing over the River Thames out of Victoria station. This was located on the opposite side to Battersea power station. Time and patience in various bookshops produced results, the loco shed originally comprised of three covered interconnected circular roundhouses built in stages from 1869 to 1889 being tucked away in a tight site alongside one of the railway viaducts serving Victoria station. So it wasn't long before some of us were heading south of the Thames again this time motoring over Chelsea Bridge and down Queensway Road alongside Battersea Goods Depot high brick walls which ran opposite to Battersea Park itself. We were rewarded to find, especially after some forty years since closure, all three still in existence. Well, sort of. Two of the old roundhouses were built on the west or the up side of Victoria station's main running lines and both were being used by National Carriers as their road transport depot. The three pictures on this page show the southerly of the two roundhouses and as can be seen most of the building has been demolished leaving just a section of the old loco sheds circular retaining wall. A vehicle inspection shed had been erected on the actual turntable site The two top views are looking north towards the River Thames and Victoria station whilst the lower picture takes a southern and closer view of the locomotive entrance point which can also be seen to the left in the middle picture. The gasholder of Battersea Park gasworks certainly takes centre stage.

June 1977

August 1979

London, Battersea Park loco shed June 1977

The second of these two roundhouses was located adjacent to the first alongside the up main running lines and remained totally intact and in use as a covered garage as can be seen in the two pictures on this page. The top picture takes a southern view with a single disused siding remaining in the foreground. This roundhouse originally had two locomotive entrances next to each other but as can be seen whilst one remains the other, to the left, has been bricked in. Dominating the old roundhouse in this picture is the gas holder of Battersea Park gasworks a structure which is shortly due to be demolished (2017) the site to be redeveloped for housing. The lower picture was taken through one of the roundhouses dirty windows and a set of rail tracks are still evident leading from the shed's entrance. Both roundhouses were demolished in 1986 the site being eventually redeveloped into futuristic multi story apartments known as 'The Bridge' and 'Chelsea Bridge Flats' etc. With today's new technology at your finger tips a somewhat futuristic Battersea Park unfolds before my eyes which makes me feel somewhat past my time.

London, Battersea Park loco shed

The third roundhouse of the group was built alongside the eastern or the down main running lines and was interconnected to the other two roundhouses through the railway viaduct itself. Not a true roundhouse but built with long elongated side walls it was by the time of our visit roofless and seemed to be in use as a builders' yard. The top picture looks westwards with the shed wall extending to the railway viaduct which has a Class 33 crossing over with a PW train. The middle and lower pictures show the roofless shell of the former loco shed both being taken from moving trains crossing over the viaducts. The tracks that feature in the lower picture ran under the brick viaduct which we have just passed over and would have once been connected both to the other roundhouses and Battersea wharf and goods depot which, sadly, we failed to investigate on our visits. The lower picture also takes in Lambeth goods depot which just peeps into view on the extreme left of the picture behind the railway viaduct. This roundhouse outlasted the other two by a few years the site now being occupied by the Battersea Dogs & Cats home whilst the brick built railway viaduct which features so prominently in the lower picture has been replaced by a more modern concrete structure.

August 1979

July 1977

March 1985

Battersea Power Station March 1985

Battersea Power Station opened in the mid-1930s being somewhat smaller than the iconic building that we know today sporting just two chimneys, then doubled to four with the opening of a second adjacent plant in the mid 1950s. The lower picture features the power station's wharf and cranes and some part of the associated coal handling systems. Colliers would be unloaded, the coal then being directed either to the boiler house via the enclosed belt systems viewed in the background, or to a huge 70,000 ton holding coal bunker. The bunker's overhead crane system can be seen to the right of the photograph. On closure in 1983 the power station building along with its wharf and cranes became listed buildings. Sadly this did not extend to the vast coal handling systems which were therefore scrapped during the 1990s resulting in the power station site taking on a somewhat sanitised appearance bearing little resemblance to its working days.

South Lambeth Goods Depot & Kirtling Wharf March 1985

On taking a train out of Victoria station and then shortly rumbling over the River Thames Battersea Power station would loom large in your sight. Tucked in behind the power station would be South Lambeth Goods depot, top picture, which was surprisingly of Great Western Railway origin. Opened in 1913 and further expanded in the 1920s with the rundown in freight traffic following WW2 the depot closed circa 1970. Overshadowed by the gasometer of Battersea Park Gas Works the buildings remained derelict till demolished in the late 1980s.The lower picture features Kirtling wharf which since the 1960s had been used by a concrete batching plant for handling marine dredged aggregates. These were then fed to the plant by a system of overhead conveyor belts. The plant closed 2015/16 and has since been dismantled. Moored alongside is the *MV Bowtrader* a single pump dredger which was sold off in 1993 and finally scrapped in Belgium circa 2014. Behind Kirtling wharf is Battersea Power Station's own wharf.

London. Feltham & Temple Mills marshalling yards.

Both Feltham, top picture, and Temple Mills marshalling yards worked on the 'hump' principle of sorting loose coupled freight trains. The top picture taken in April 1976 shows Feltham's now derelict clock-mounted control tower which oversaw all freight movements throughout the yards. Feltham 'hump' yard became fully operational by 1921 being one of the most technically advanced yards at that time. With the decline of loose coupled freight Feltham yards closed in 1969 leaving most of the site as wasteland today. Meanwhile in the lower picture which dates to November 1984 the remains of Temple Mills control tower shouts 1960s at you as the old yards were completely modernised to the 'hump' configuration in the late 1950s. Traffic levels dwindled away through the 1970s 'hump' working ceased in 1982 leaving the yards to eke out an existence till they finally closed in 1988 with track lifting taking place two years later. From then on the old yards became a forlorn wilderness till redevelopment commenced in 2001.

London. Bricklayers Arms loco shed. December 1983

By 1983 only one derelict steam depot site remained in London and that was Bricklayers Arms in south east London. Closed to steam back in 1962 the loco depot was flanked by goods sheds on either side the whole site being on a short branch line little more than a mile long. Following closure of the loco shed the repair shop lingered till 1969 the goods depot closed in 1977 and with the cessation of parcel traffic in 1981 the branch closed forever. The loco depot itself comprised of the four road St. Patrick shed a rather long former carriage shed. Adjacent to this and positioned around the turntable were the eight road Old shed, a large 1930s-build repair shop and the four road New Shed, a roofless semi derelict ruin being a victim of the Blitz. By the time of the branch closure the Old Shed had been long demolished but the shed roads remained available for storage as did the now roofless St. Patrick shed. By December 1983, the date of the photographs, all the trackwork along the branch had been lifted. The top picture looks north towards the Old Shed site with the skeletal remains of the goods shed alongside and the large repair shop in the background. The roofless St. Patrick shed features in the middle picture, its carriage shed heritage clearly showing, whilst the lower picture is taken from outside the repair shop looking south towards the Dunton Road bridge. The turntable would shortly escape into preservation. The repair shop existed for several years but eventually the whole site was redeveloped as a trading estate. Using modern mapping technology nothing had escaped the bulldozer even the Dunton Road bridge, a favourite for trainspotters, having being swept away by the developers. A new road, Mandela Way, has been laid through the middle of old site. The railway at Bricklayers Arms has gone.

London. Rotherhithe & West India Dock May 1985

Little more than a stones throw from Bricklayers Arms was Clarence Wharf, Rotherhithe. top picture. Opened in, the 1880s for the supply of coal to Rotherhithe gas works on the latter's closure in 1959 the wharf was then utilised by a local aggregates concern supplying marine dredged sand and gravel. Operations here ceased in 1992 since when the wharf was shortened and restored to a somewhat sanitised condition in keeping with the now regenerated residential area. Meanwhile West India Docks, lower picture, just north of the Thames comprised of three main docks and by the time of this photograph had been closed for five years. Containerisation and other factors bought about their decline from the 1960s onwards, regeneration commenced from the 1990s and today the docks are now much reduced in size and are better known as Canary Wharf. The docks sole occupant on the day of my visit was the *CS John W Mackay* a commercial cable layer built on the Tyne in 1922 and laid up in 1977 for possible preservation. Sadly she was scrapped in 1994.

London. Bow Creek, River Lea, Canning Town. January 1985

Both pictures show the industrial concerns that cluttered Bow Creek as photographed from the old Leamouth Road. The River Lea takes on a 360 degree course at Bow Creek, the top picture looking downstream to the River Thames whilst the lower picture takes a view looking upstream into North London. Jubilee Wharf's two mid 1930s belfast roofed timber warehouses, top picture, are surrounded by stacks of wooden crates, silos, a tracked crane and, with the tide out, three beached lighters. The lower picture continues on the same theme, various hoppers, silos and conveyer systems and several dock cranes. Note the boat tucked away up in the heavily silted dock something which seems to be an issue on this curve of the creek. A distinctive block of high rise flats captures the backdrop along with a couple of gas holders. Today the flats remain but nothing else other than dear old Bow Creek itself now surrounded by open spaces, and new roads.

London. Stratford Market station March 1983

Stratford Market station was located on the old L& NERly branch that ran from Palace Gates to North Woolwich. Stratford Market station closed back in 1957 due to its proximity to Stratford (Low Level) station which can be glimpsed in the top picture which was taken from Stratford High Street just opposite the closed Market station. The line would be electrified in 1985 becoming part of the third rail North London line with final closure coming in 2006. The middle picture looks at another DMU on a up train just running under the former station buildings, the platform stairways having long gone. Four tracks ran along this section of line those nearest the camera being for goods traffic only. The lower picture sees another up train passing Stratford Market station's degraded platforms which were finally removed in the 1990s. My photograph was taken from the former LNERly printing works which finally closed in 1951 These views were to change rapidly, the goods lines becoming the trackbed of the Jubilee line extension whilst the North Woolwich line was absorbed into the Docklands Light Railway. Whilst new platforms were installed the station buildings were refurbished for commercial use with an entrance on its western side to gain access to the platforms below.

London. Stratford Market sidings September 1983

Just to the south west of the long closed Stratford Market station was, and still is, a large building that housed the GERly and then the L&NERly print works. Built in 1893 the building was sandwiched between the North Woolwich running lines to the east and Burford Road. Closed in 1951 the building was at some time refurbished for commercial letting and for a short time in the 1980s I worked in one of its many units commissioning a gramophone record pressing plant. Interesting days. Further down Burford Road were the Stratford Market goods sidings which had closed by 1983 but retained by the CM & EE Dept. until 1988 when the site was redeveloped into the Jubilee Line's new train depot. The top picture features a bogie bolster with a load of electricial mast supports and a good view of the former print works. One of the former goods depot's warehouses features in the middle picture with a former Southern Railway 25 ton 'Queen Mary' brake van. Many old coaches converted by the CM & EE Dept. for overhead electrification work were present in the sidings including a former LMS coach, lower picture, bearing the legend. 'Electrification. Euston to Glasgow'.

London. River Thames. October 1984

If memory serves me right this photograph was taken from the Woolwich ferry looking westwards up the River Thames with the newly commissioned Thames barrier taking centre stage to the industrial backdrop of the Greenwich peninsular. The two large gas holders are of the East Greenwich gas works which ceased gas production in 1976. One gas holder remains to this day the other being demolished in 1985. The single chimney of Blackwall Point power station also features in the photograph which had already been decommissioned back in 1981 the site being cleared in 1987. In the foreground of the photograph are a few remaining lighters once a common feature on the Thames and the docks. Back in the 1950s some 5000 lighters were in use but on the closure of the docks most were scrapped with a few living on being converted to house boats etc.

London Royal Group of Docks. October 1984

The Royal Group of Docks, East London, consisted of three docks, the Royal Victoria, Royal Albert and the King George V constructed between 1850 and 1921. The docks suffered badly during the Blitz and despite something of resurgence through the 1950s the docks declined thereafter closing in 1981 due in part to containerisation. The two pictures opposite, looking in a westerly direction, are of the King George V and the Royal Albert docks taken three years after closure. The King George V dock, opposite left, was the smallest and last of the three docks being constructed to the south and parallel to the Royal Albert dock. Whilst some activity seems evident the three ships are laid up and out of use as is the large and impressive CWS flour mill, middle distance, which is actually set in the more westerly Royal Victoria dock. The mill was demolished in the 1990s. The Royal Albert dock, opposite right, is devoid of any shipping the land between the two docks being redeveloped into the single runway London City Airport which opened in 1987. By this time the dockside cranes, transit sheds and warehouses had been mostly cleared from both docks. Regeneration commenced from the 1990s onwards introducing commercial and retail busineses to the docks. Whilst not a single dockside crane survived several stretches of the former quay-side rail tracks remain, now only to be seen using modern mapping technology.

King George V Dock

Royal Albert Dock

London. Royal Group of Docks. October 1984

Two pictures taken at the eastern end of the King George V dock from Woolwich Manor Road girder bridge. The top picture looks over to the southern quay and shows some of the now derelict and fenced off pontoons which ran along this quay allowing ships to discharge their loads directly into barges and lighters moored on both sides of each ship Two empty lighters can be seen in the foreground one bearing the name 'Survive'. I wonder if it did. A group of surviving dockside cranes, lower picture, huddle up for company along the north quay, note also the different styles of warehousing in the two pictures.

London. Royal Group of Docks. October 1984

The Royal Victoria Dock's empty warehouses feature in the top picture's long focus view. Looking westwards we take in the two chimneys of the Blackwall Power Station which was located on the north bank of the Thames opposite Blackwall Point power station. Built after the Second World War it was converted to oil in the early 1970s but was closed in 1984 and was demolished four years later. The middle and lower pictures take in J. Ranks impressive Premier flour mill along with its loading wharf and grain elevators. Situated along the Victoria Dock's southern quay there was at one time three great flour mills working along this quay. Both the two lower photographs were taken from the Silvertown flyover with a long focus lens. The flyover itself was opened in 1934 being the first one ever built in this country. Whilst the now cleared wharf remains the flour mill itself was demolished in the 1990s, the site now taken over by housing with restored dockside cranes gracing the waterfront.

Lost and Derelict Places - West Midlands

Birmingham - Moor Street station. November 1983

Moor Street was opened by the Great Western Railway in 1909 due to overcapacity at nearby Snow Hill. The company's main line station in Birmingham was Snow Hill where problems arose by being approached from the south through a 635yd tunnel. This resulted in limited capacity for handling local traffic. Moor Street was a terminal station built alongside the Great Western's main running lines and adjacent to the southern end of the Snow Hill tunnel itself. With the downgrading of the old GWRly main line Moor Street became an isolated terminus in 1968 with the closure of the tunnel and the lifting of the through tracks. With the resurgence of rail traffic in the Birmingham area during the 1980s the former Great Western line was partially reopened in 1987 with new through stations being provided at Snow Hill and Moor Street, the old terminal station closing at the same time. The newly opened Moor Street being a through station was provided with its own entrance, the platforms being adjacent to the old terminal station. Through the 1990s the old terminal station buildings and platforms became derelict its disconnected trackbed becoming heavily overgrown despite the fact the station had become a Grade 2 listed. Due to the efforts of local volunteers the old station was refurbished with the booking office actually being reopened in 2002 for passenger use, the 1980s effort being demolished. Once again history was to repeat itself and with Snow Hill again suffering from overcapacity the old terminus was reconnected to the main line and reopened in 2010 being refurbished in true 1930s GWRly style. Whilst the first generation DMUs have long gone so has most of the Moor Street backdrop with only the white building to the right of the picture remaining. Of Moor Street station all has been restored.

Birmingham - Snow Hill station. February 1977

Snow Hill was Birmingham's old Great Western Railway main line station on its London Paddington to Shrewsbury, North Wales and Birkenhead routes. Rebuilt between 1907 and 1912 Snow Hill rivalled the LM&SRly's New Street station until the electrification of that line in 1967. This resulted in the old Great Western route being downgraded with Snow Hill losing its through services. The station then lingered on till closure in March 1972. The photograph above was taken from Birmingham North signal box and from this vantage point we look over the northern end of Snow Hill station. The two through platforms were long enough to hold two complete express trains and bay platforms were positioned either side for local services. The imposing former hotel and booking hall facade were located at the southern end of the station and were demolished in 1969 the same year track lifting began. And all this four years before the station was actually closed.

Birmingham - Snow Hill station. February 1977

The top picture again looks at the northern end of the old station but this time at rail level whilst the lower picture was taken on the western side of the station at the southern end of Livery Street. Here we take a peek through an old iron entrance gate at all that remained of the booking hall area which once boasted a large glass and steel overall roof holding a considerable number of separate ticket windows all faced off with carrara ware stone. Even now it amazes me how you could just gain access into derelict sites in those days with little in the way of fencing for the inquisitive enthusiast. On this particular cold and misty day my old mate Peter Askey and I just wandered into what was a totally deserted and derelict Snow Hill station.

Birmingham - Snow Hill station. February 1977

The old station buildings pictured here form a backdrop to Birmingham Queensway's 'History of Snow Hill' mural located down Snow Hill itself on the eastern side of the station. Crafted in 1969 during the redevelopment of Birminghams city centre at three hundred feet long and twenty feet high it was an impressive structure. I only managed to include a small part of the mural in my photograph, however I did manage to catch a West Midlands bus. What the artist choose to depict was quite fitting, namely Isambard Kingdom Brunel a Great Western Railway 'Castle' Class locomotive and very effective it looked too. Following closure Snow Hill station became a large convenient covered car park but as can be seen in the lead picture an eyesore set in a modern 1970s landscape. All things change and later redevelopments to the Queensway area in the 21st century saw the mural sadly destroyed in 2007 the area now over run with new roads.

Birmingham - Snow Hill station. February 1977

From the south the main running lines entered Snow Hill station through a tunnel which explained why the hotel above was somewhat shortlived being converted into offices. The top picture looks north into the old station from the trackbed whilst the lower photograph takes the opposite view. Due to the restriction that the tunnel imposed no southern bay platforms existed for local traffic these being provided at Moor Street station located at the southern end of the tunnel. Whilst through trains ceased in March 1967 all southern bound trains ceased in April 1968 when the tunnel closed. The lower picture certainly conjures up my own memories of Snow Hill. Arriving from Paddington on a express with fifty odd other trainspotters on a Club outing it was a mad scrabble up that wide stairway just taking in the huge wooden 'Brockhouse' board above our heads before boarding our waiting coach in Livery Street. That's about all I remember of Snow Hill.

Birmingham - Snow Hill February 1977

Three pictures take in a northern view. The top picture features the through running lines which have been partially infilled with an access ramp for car parking on the former trackbed as well as the platforms. Parking up amongst vandalised and burnt out buildings no doubt gave customers a great sense of security, the parking attendant having possibly plied his trade from an old caravan unless this is the home to the demolition men. The middle picture was taken down on the trackbed of the former through lines, the photograph being framed by the trainshed roof which along with the platform canopies has had all its sheet glass removed. It is no surprise that all the stations signage has gone. The lower picture is from the Livery Street side bay platform from which Snow Hill's last train service ran being a single railcar to Wolverhampton Low Level. Operating during rush hours only from May 1969 till closure, this earned Snow Hill the tag of the largest unstaffed halt in the country. Demolition of the station proper commenced around the time of our visit with all buildings being cleared by 1980 although the platforms themselves remained relatively intact for another five years or so being finally cleared for the new Snow Hill station.

Wolverhampton - Low Level station. May 1985

Wolverhampton Low Level station was on the Great Western Railways through route from London Paddington and Birmingham to Shrewsbury, North Wales and Birkenhead. The main station frontage, as photographed, was located on the downside and originally incorporated a train shed roof till removed in 1933/34. The station became known as the lower level as the nearby former LM&SRly station was at a higher level thus becoming known as the High Level station.. With the ongoing electrification work on the former LM&SRly West Coast route all passenger traffic was diverted through Wolverhampton Low Level from 1963 to 1967. This ceased in March 1967 when the electrification was complete and the old GWRly route was run down leaving only the rush hour local service to Birmingham Snow Hill which was withdrawn in March 1972. By this time the station had been put to use as a major parcel depot, this itself coming to an end in June 1981 with all connections to the railway ceasing in 1986 when the Divisional Engineering Department moved out. During this period the 1850s main downside station buildings were Grade 2 listed.

Wolverhampton - Low Level station. May 1985

Sun Street road bridge from which the top picture was taken was located just south of the station and viewed to the south overlooks to the right the tunnel portals and former trackbed of the old Great Western main line which had been lifted back in the early 1970s.The remaining tracks curve round underneath the bridge into the Low Level station, the line itself being of LM&SRly origin from Walsall. A short spur of this line, off picture, ran into the nearby Wednesbury Road goods depot, lower picture, which was located just to the north east of the Low Level station. Opened in the 1880s the depot closed in the 1960s due to the reorganisation of all goods operations to the newly developed Bescot yards. On closure the depot deteriorated until sold in 1988 for commercial use in which it remained till the mid 1990s when once again the building fell into disuse but this time was subsequentially demolished. The site is now occupied by the Royal Mail sorting office

Wolverhampton - Low Level station May 1985

The two pictures feature the southern end of the station, the top picture being taken from the Sun Street road bridge. Although the Low Level station closed to passenger traffic in March 1972 it remained busy having become a major parcel depot back in April 1970. All parcel traffic then worked into the station's southern end via the former LM&SRly Walsall line resulting in that end of the station retaining all its original trackwork. On closure of the parcel depot in June 1981 the station was used for storing rolling stock but as the years pasted neglect set in as can be seen in the two pictures. Through the 1990s the station became totally derelict but redevelopment of the site commenced circa 2005 with the Sun Street road bridge being demolished and replaced with a new section of road which cut across the long disused rail tracks. With redevelopment proceeding apace all remaining trackwork was lifted shortly after.

Wolverhampton - Low Level station. May 1985

Whilst the southern aspect of the station remained relatively intact for many years, track lifting at the northern end of the station commenced shortly after the cessation of through services. On becoming a major parcel depot in 1970 all remaining station trackwork at its northern end, save one track along the up platform, was lifted and the trackbed concreted over forming a hardstanding for vans and lorries. The top and middle pictures show the northern end of the now derelict station four years after closure of the parcel depot. Don't know how the old bus arrived as there was nobody about to ask. The lower picture shows the old trackbed leading northwards from the station and now occupied by a car scrap yard, it is interesting to note that whilst British cars are positioned to the left foreign cars are to the right. In the days when you could rummage around scrap yards by yourself this could save you a lot of time. Redevelopment of the old Low Level station commenced circa 2005. The listed station buildings and part of the down platforms being regenerated into a banqueting and conference venue with a large hotel being added to its northern end in 2008. The up platforms and buildings were cleared to make way for a housing development the former station trackbed now forming a garden area being edged off by the down platform. Even the footbridge has been retained giving access across the site. Once again my own memories of Wolverhampton Low Level were again with the Home Counties Railway Club, this time on an overnight trip to Liverpool. 'King' hauled from Paddington we pulled into Low Level station during the dead of night to stumble out on a cold misty and dimly lit platform to watch our 'King' coming off to be replaced by a 'Castle'. Not that I was interested, having 'copped' all my 'Kings' and 'Castles'.

Birmingham - Tyseley Loco Shed October 1976

Tyseley was the Great Western Railway's only locomotive shed in the Birmingham area being a brick built double roundhouse with a large repair shop added to the front of the loco sheds eastern end. Tyseley closed to steam in November 1966 by which time the eastern roundhouse and repair shop had been demolished the site being redeveloped into a diesel depot which remains today. The western roundhouse was demolished in 1968 by which time Patrick Whitehouse was on site having leased the old coaling stage to house his preserved steam locomotives. With the clearance of the western roundhouse its turntable was fortunately preserved so this and the coaling stage were to form the basis of the Birmingham Steam Museum The photograph of the preserved turntable was taken in October 1976 looking towards the back of the former roundhouse with most of the radiating inspection pit roads having been filled in and covered over to give hardstanding for storing Land Rovers from the nearby British Leyland Solihull plant. By the early 1990s all of these radiating roads had been recovered and put to good use storing museum stock.

Wolverhampton - Stafford Road Loco Shed October 1976

Stafford Road was one of two Great Western Railway loco sheds in the Wolverhampton area, and also the site of the companies large railway Works. The original small Works which dated to the early 1850s occupied land to the east of Stafford Road which then expanded in the early 1860s to its western side. The eastern side housed a single locomotive roundhouse which had expanded to three roundhouses by the mid 1870s. Stafford Road, and I remember it well, was a somewhat mean narrow main road separating the two sites with high walls on both sides and bore more of a resemblance to a prison. The 1860s Works were considerably expanded during the early 1930s whilst on the eastern side of Stafford Road additional dead end straight loco sheds were utilised from some of the original 1850 works buildings leaving only the erecting shop and stores. By the 1950s the loco sheds had become dilapidated with the two 1870s-build roundhouses being mainly disused having in part lost their roofs. Closure came in September 1963 with demolition of the site leaving, for reasons unknown, the former 1850s erecting shop which dominates the two 1976 pictures. The top picture looks west with Stafford Road running behind the derelict building which on its right can be seen, I think, an old air raid shelter. The lower picture looks north taken from the former roundhouses whose turntable and inspection pits were still detectable despite being roughly filled in and covered in foliage. The old high walls of Stafford Road can be glimpsed to the left in both pictures but within four years of these photographs being taken all had been swept away Stafford Road becoming a wide open duel carriageway with industrial estates on both the former main Works and loco shed sites.

Manchester - Victoria station October 1984

It could be said that Manchester Victoria station doesn't quite fit into the 'Lost & Derelict' part of this book. The station is anything but lost, but back in the 1980s the place wasn't exactly derelict but it was certainly the most dilapidated main line station that you could wish to find. Victoria station was something else. The picture above was taken in October 1984 from the eastern end of through platform 11 with a Class 31 No.31171 trundling eastwards running light engine and dwarfed by Victoria station's substantial but now cut back train shed. This once covered the whole station but suffered heavily from bombing during the Manchester blitz of 1940. That part of the train shed which covered the through five running lines as seen in the foreground of the above picture was subsequently removed following the war and never replaced. With the running down of Victoria station through the 1980/90s in favour of nearby Piccadilly station Victoria was drastically reduced in size and much of what you see in the picture above was demolished and cleared to became the Manchester Arena.

Manchester - Victoria station. May 1984

Two photographs taken at the western end of platform 11 featuring the West Junction signal box. The top picture looks east as a Newcastle bound Trans Pennine service comes in hauled by a Class 47 No.47440 whilst the lower picture takes a western view and features the signal box with Class 47 No.47051 acting as spare/relief. Platform 11 is of interest as it was at one time some 2200 feet in length making it the longest platform in the country being linked to the nearby Manchester Exchange station. Before Exchange station closed in 1969 platform 11 could accommodate three trains at any one time. By the 1980s much of the enclosed box structure canopy that once connected the two stations remained intact as can be seen in both pictures.

Manchester - Victoria station. October 1984

Working a Liverpool bound Trans Pennine service Class 45 No.45171 waits awhile at the eastern end of Victoria stations platform 12. With the contraction of Victoria station this service was withdrawn in 1989 in favour of Piccadilly station. Separated by five open through tracks from platform 11 this part of the station consisted of through platforms 12 to 17 being covered by the remaining portion of the train shed. In redeveloping a newer and smaller Victoria station these platforms were closed and the site totally demolished in the early 1990s being replaced by two new through platforms on the site of the former open through tracks. The Manchester Arena when built not only occupied this part of the old station site but extended over the newly built through platforms. The only thing even remotely modern on Victoria station in the 1980s was a small bright eatery installed at the eastern end of platform 12 which somehow seemed to intrude in its grim and dirty surroundings.

Manchester - Victoria station May & October 1984

Within six years these two views of Victoria station would be gone for ever, to be demolished and the site cleared for redevelopment into the Manchester Arena. The top picture was taken at the western end of platform 12 during May 1984 looking westwards towards West Junction signal box with the extended platform 11 to the left of the picture. Manchester Victoria station in the 1980s was not only distressingly dirty diesel but also took you straight back to the days of steam. The lower picture was taken at the western end of the station in October 1984 looking east with a Swindon built first generation DMU standing on platform 13 with a local service. You may note the rain is coming down in buckets something not totally unknown to me on my visits up Manchester way.

Manchester - Victoria station   May 1985 & May 1984

We finish at Manchester Victoria with some pictures featuring the terminal platforms 1 to 10 which were on the south east side of the main line platforms. The terminal stations train shed backed onto the graceful stone built 1909 station facade but at some stage British Railways had covered the train sheds frontage and south side with crude corrugated sheeting giving the terminal more the look of a run down goods depot. This was not helped by the trackbed between disused platforms 1 & 2 being roughly infilled with rubble. The top picture was taken on platform 5 during May 1985 with a first generation DMU and parcels unit still in overall blue livery. The inside of the 1909 facade is clearly visible The lower picture was taken the previous year from platform 10 and looks over to the train shed with first generation DMUs on platforms 7 and 8 and a two car DMU unit pulling out of platform 6.

Manchester - Victoria station. May 1984 & September 1983

Two photographs of parcel trains on platform 9. The top picture is of Class 25 No.25176 during May 1984 whilst the lower picture features Class 40 No.40197 in September 1983. Redevelopment of the terminus station was undertaken in the early 1990s and other than platforms 9 & 10 all the remainder were cleared and replaced in part with the Manchester Metrolink light rail system the remaining area being adapted for car parking. The train shed roof was cut back at the same time and renovated but by 2013 was dismantled and replaced two years later with a futuristic new 'L' shaped roof which in turn complemented the Manchester Arena. Victoria station is now a thoroughly modern affair which blends in well with its original 1909 facade but is a much different station from the one that I knew back in the mid 1980s.

Manchester - Central station. May 1984

With the contraction of our railways through the 1960s Manchester was not unlike most cities at that time and lost two of its main stations with Exchange and Central both going in 1969. Central was a large terminus affair and its traffic had suffered badly following the electrification of the west coast main line in 1966. By 1968 the last express services were diverted away to Piccadilly station and following closure Central became a car park in 1972. Over the next few years the train shed slowly deteriorated whilst the outside platforms and canopies were left to decay. Greater Manchester Council purchased the site in 1978 redeveloping the old station into the GMEX exhibition centre which opened in 1986. The three photographs are all taken from the 'buffer stops' end so to speak and date to May 1984 whilst redevelopment was underway. The top picture shows Central's train roof featuring its clock which wasn't working and I don't suppose had for many years whilst the Great Northern Railway's warehouse, middle picture, featured to the right of the station entrance. Closed in 1954 the warehouse also became a car park in which use it remained till the mid 1990s when it was redeveloped into a leisure and retail complex opening in 1999. The picture shows the edge of Central station's trainshed, left of the picture, whilst a wire fence partly obstructs the photograph. The building remains today but it would be impossible to photograph it from the same vantage point as a large modern building has popped up in between. The lower picture takes a peep inside the train shed with work well advanced exposing the station's undercroft, whether this was being infilled or not I do not know.

Manchester - Belle Vue loco shed and a mystery. October 1980

Not short of a pallet or two or even the odd oildrum the old steam shed at Belle Vue, top picture, still has its uses. Oildrums of course get everywhere. A former LM&SRly single roundhouse it lost its traditional high pitched roof in the late 1940s in favour of the flat concrete variety hence the 'built in' smoke troughs. Belle Vue closed early, in April 1956. A difficult photograph to take balancing on a pile of pallets through a broken window the picture shows the shed's back wall to the right, the turntable would have been on the extreme left. The site remains in commercial use although the shed was demolished circa 2012 although fragments of wall still remain as does the old fitting shop at the rear. The lower picture is now a mystery. That's my good self standing by Paul's Ford Cortina Mk3 but the Manchester location is now lost on me. How we came across the place I haven't a clue but at first glance we thought it might have been a loco shed. But it can't have been, or could it. Any takers?.

Manchester - Manchester Ship Canal. May 1985

Manchester Docks were served by the 36 mile Manchester Ship Canal which connected to the sea near Liverpool. The canal opened in 1894 for both coastal and ocean going vessels and the docks at Manchester were split into two groups namely the larger Salford docks and the more easterly Pomona docks. Both docks and the nearby large Trafford Park Industrial estate were served by the Manchester Ship Canal Railway and a twin track railway swing bridge connected the industrial estate to the Salford docks. Both pictures date to May 1985 and feature the now disused rail swing bridge which crossed the canal just to the west of the Trafford Road swing bridge. The top picture was taken upstream of the swing bridges with the entrance to No 6 dock on the left in the picture. With the closure of the docks in 1982 the railway bridge was eventually resited across the regenerated No 9 dock as a pedestrian walkway. With increasing traffic levels Trafford Road became a duel carriageway in the late 1990s with an additional bridge being built alongside the former swing bridge.

Manchester - Salford Docks. May 1985

With Paul Wells and I having to run cars up one Saturday to Lex Vehicle Leasings depot in Manchester this proved a golden opportunity to check out Salford Docks. If memory serves, my chum Paul is in the Ford Sierra as I quickly got out to take the picture of the old main entrance along Trafford Road. We were on our way home, but not before a tour around the docks or what was left of them. The above proved to be a lucky shot, closed back in 1982 the last remnants of No 8 docks transit sheds can be viewed framed by the impressive main entrance. But not for long. The Salford Docks comprised of four docks numbered 6 to 9 with No 9 dock being the largest of the group. The more easterly Pomona Docks were located in the upper reaches of the canal east of and on the opposite side to Salford Docks separated by the Trafford Road and railway swing bridges. Salford Docks fell victim to containerisation through the 1970s and the increasing size of ocean going container vessels

Manchester - Salford Docks. May 1985

In these two pictures we take a dockside look of the old Trafford Road main dock entrance. The top picture features the old Trafford Road running behind the entrance with the dock office to the left and disused rail tracks crossing in the foreground. Today (2017) Trafford Road is a fast dual carriageway and the old roadside buildings that are seen in the picture have been long swept away. Taken further back along No 8 dock, lower picture, we get an impressive view of the part demolished transit shed and the impressive 1920s build Dock Office which dwafts the dock main entrance to its right. Both the latter still exist today although our impressive view is now obscured by modern office developments which render the former main dock entrance to little more than an ornament backing onto a car park.

Manchester - Salford Docks. May 1985

Three photographs in and around No 9 Dock. The largest of all four of the Salford Docks the top picture was taken looking towards the back end of the dock. Whilst the housing on the other side of Trafford Road remains and new housing has replaced the dockside transit sheds the dock end itself is now dominated by a massive office development which obscures all else. Looking in the opposite direction towards the Manchester Ship Canal the lower picture reveals transit sheds in the process of being demolished whilst at the docks very end sits the *MV Standfirst* a pump dredger moored alongside Salford Docks only two gantry cranes evidence of an attempt to take on containerisation. The first was commissioned in 1968 with the second in 1972 and they remained at work till the docks closure despite the restricted size of container vessels that could navigate up the Ship Canal. They were both dismantled during the early 1990s. Of our pump dredger we will read more of later. A landside view of No 9 Docks transit sheds feature in the middle picture with that dock's administrative and security offices opposite.

Manchester - Salford Docks. May 1985

End of an era. Dockside transit sheds about to meet their end. The top picture is near to Dock 8 whilst the lower picture is of an unknown location but possibly Dock 9. Three years after closure ours was somewhat melancholy drive around a totally deserted and derelict Salford Docks. Silence ruled. Even the dockside cranes had gone. The closed and neglected Salford Docks had been purchased by Salford City Council in 1984 and within six years redevelopment of the docks had swept away the old infrastructure. With new housing and offices going up Salford Docks had changed out of all recognition and in its regenerated or perhaps even gentrified form is now known as Salford Quays.

Manchester - Salford Docks. May 1985

The Buffer Stops. Top end of No 9 Dock transit shed.

Manchester - Salford Docks, Trafford Wharf May 1985

Commercial shipping along the Manchester Ship Canal did not totally cease with the closure of the Salford and Pomona docks in 1982. On the opposite bank to Salford docks at the Trafford Road swing bridge was Trafford Wharf which stretched along to the dry docks. The canal at this point was wide and the few large sea going vessels still working the MSC could turn here for docking. Whilst Trafford Wharf remained active till the late 1980s the dry docks themselves finally closed in 2007 but remain flooded for the occasional transhipment of bulk commodities. Several other small wharfs in the area continue to trade in bulk liquid and dry cargoes. Following the closure of the docks the MSC changed ownership and the present owners not only maintain its commercial uses but look forward to expanding them. The top photograph was taken along Trafford wharf in 1985 showing some shipping still in evidence. The two lower long focus photographs were taken from Salford Docks the dry docks themselves are all but obscured by a laid up vessel awaiting breaking and the Manchester Ship Canal's steam powered 250ton floating crane. This goliath was built in the Netherlands during 1937 and was non-self moving requiring tugs to tow and position her. Used mainly for lifting lock gates etc she was moved down to Runcorn Docks in the 1990s and has been out of use since around 2000. It is believed she has been recently preserved. The large circular storage tanks of the petrol chemical plant form a backdrop to the three dry docks and these tanks still exist today although some are disused. The lower picture again shows the floating crane which I think is actually moored across one of the three dry dock entrances along with an old MSC barge for company. To the right of the barge the upper structure of a small ship can just be seen just poking above one of the dry docks lock gates.

Manchester - MSC & Salford Docks Barges & Dredgers May 1985

The Barton Road swing bridge, top picture, located on the outskirts of Manchester was always a serious traffic bottleneck especially into the Trafford Park Industrial Estate. Finally replaced by a new high level bridge in 1960 the swing bridge remains in use today although now mostly catering for local traffic. I must have timed my arrival down Barton Road with some precision as a MSC barge the *Mersey Trader* was conveniently passing through working up to one of Manchester's remaining small wharfs with a cargo of either maize or grain. The lower picture shows the only vessel within Salford Docks on our wander around and this was the *WD Tideway* a suction dredger moored up by the disused container gantry cranes at the top of No 9 dock. Built in 1966 she was sold to a Nigerian company in 1989 being renamed *Mowa* only to sink in 2006.

Manchester - Salford Quays March 1988

Come March 1988 I found myself back up in Manchester on a course. And what a waste of time that was. My accommodation was a new luxurious hotel within Salford Quays itself alongside old No 6 dock. The downside was limited free time. The two pictures on this page were taken from my hotel room's balcony, the top picture looking up No 6 dock taking in an early attempt of a marina with the MSC and a sanitised Trafford wharf opposite. The two dockside cranes to the left of the picture were the last to remain within the old docks and were to be shortly relocated to No 8 dock for display. There they remained till removed and scrapped in 2014. Looking across No 6 dock, lower picture, new housing has replaced transit sheds and the background is dominated by the two disused container gantry cranes located at the top end of No 9 dock, standing amid piles of rubble whilst redevelopment gathers pace.

Manchester - Trafford wharf. March 1988

An afternoon wander along Trafford wharf proved interesting with two pictures reproduced here. Once again taking in the disused container gantry cranes of No 9 dock we look up Trafford wharf to the now derelict signal box which once controlled the dockland's railway swing bridge. Walking further along Trafford wharf I came across, lower picture, the main entrance to the dry docks. Surprisingly we meet up again with the Manchester Ship Canals 250ton floating crane but this time occupying the nearest of the three dry docks. Save for the high rise flats in the far distance this picture could easily have been taken from an early picture postcard. The dry docks closed in 2007 and whilst the two cranes were scrapped the docks themselves remain in use with their lock gates permanently open for transhipment of barge carrying bulk cargoes to road haulage.

Lost & Derelict Places - Long Closed Loco Sheds 'Up North'

This business of investigating long closed steam shed sites started with an excursion around London in 1976. Of course the technology that we all now take for granted was not around or even dreamed off in those far off days and each shed bashing trip would be a journey into the unknown. That was part of the fascination. Armed with little more than a tatty copy of Aiden Fuller's 1960s Loco Directory the fate of each old shed would unravel before us. Of course all one has to do these days is poke about on the laptop without so much as leaving ones' chair. Not a lot of fun though.

The three pictures on this page result from different trips. All three sheds were originally of LMSRly origin although Canklow and Mirfield were transferred to the Eastern Region in latter years.

Top picture. Features Canklow a square built roundhouse located near to Rotherham. Closed in March 1966. Photographed in March 1978 the building had been in commercial use but was derelict on our visit. Demolished at some later date, a housing estate now occupies the site.

Middle Picture. Mirfield was an eight road dead-end shed closed in January 1967. The site was sold into commercial use the shed itself being long derelict by our visit in October 1980. At what time its commercial use ceased is unknown but the shed was demolished circa 2007 the site being turned over to housing.

Lower Picture. Mould Junction, near Chester. An eight road dead-end shed that closed in April 1966 the site becoming a scrap yard. Photographed in August 1979 amazingly this view, taken from a nearby road, is still possible today as the site is still in use as a scrap yard whilst the shed building remains intact but in a ruinous condition.

Canklow

Mirfield

Mold Junction

Aintree

Widnes

One of our latter day excursions that Paul and I made was to Liverpool in August 1979. One steam shed that remained standing like a skeleton in a sea of emptiness was, top picture, Aintree. This shed, a typical 1930s LMSRly dead - end eight road affair, had closed in June 1967 and continued to remain standing in this somewhat forlorn state for nearly thirty years. Things haven't improved that much as the area is now a total wilderness although the inevitable housing estate seems to be edging ever nearer. Edge Hill was 'the big one' a large sprawling 19 road affair being in part a dead-end and through shed. Closed in May 1968 on our visit other than the now derelict offices the area was reduced to large coal yard. My photograph is taken from the shed's western end with the dead-end section of the shed's rear wall and offices in the distance. Shortly after our visit the whole site was razed to the ground and remained a wilderness till the 1990s when the site was redeveloped becoming part of the Wavertree Technology Park. Brunswick shed, closed early in September 1961, was a small four road dead-end effort situated alongside running lines with a pair of gas holders tucked in behind. Set low down from the main road the shed was approached by a girder walkway and steps. This was long gone on our visit and we were unable to get down to ground level but as can be seen from my long focus picture the outer wall and a small part of the inner wall remained. Why this was we couldn't fathom. Things haven't changed much on this tight site today and although the gas holders have gone the shed walls remain standing although part buried in heavy foliage. The lower picture on this page is Widnes a six road affair that closed in April 1964. The shed then remained intact but derelict till sold to a scrap merchant in the mid 1970s who demolished the shed just leaving the rear and southern retaining walls in which state it was in on our visit. The scrapyard departed sometime in the 1990s and today the site remains vacant whilst the two walls remain standing despite a new road running alongside.

Lost and Derelict Places - Sheffield's Cooling Towers, March 1985

Sheffield's Tinsley viaduct features in the above picture which opened in 1968 crossing the lower Don valley, the photograph being taken in March 1985. The viaduct itself carries the M1 on its top tier with the A631 underneath. Overlooking the viaduct are the two cooling towers of the coal fired Blackburn Meadows power station which had closed back in 1980 whilst to the left of the picture can be seen waste ground and derelict buildings of Sheffield's once major steel industry which contracted during the 1970/80s. The cooling towers remained a major feature to passing traffic on the M1 till demolition in 2008. The railway interest is of a Class 37 No.37010 on a passing permanent way train.

Lost and Derelict Places - The end of Corby Steelworks, February 1982

An imposing shot of Corby steelworks former four blast furnaces. Commencing working in 1935 they had been demolished three months earlier leaving only their bases which can be seen to the left of the picture whilst much of their ancillary plant still remained. With rationalisation of the steel industry Corby closed in 1980. Whilst tubemaking still continues the old steelmaking site was cleared within four years of closure and has been redeveloped into commercial and retail outlets.

Docks, Diesels and an odd bit of Steam

Immingham Docks
March 1985

Immingham Docks opened in 1912 for the export of coal. Taking the name 'Kings' the dock itself was of a single large configuration taking the shape of two parallel docks connected together at its southern end by another dock. By the mid twentieth century the coal hoists had been swept away and Immingham was concentrating on bulk cargoes and liquid petroleum gas etc. The lower picture features a Class 08 shunter No.08784 alongside the then year old Japanese build bulk carrier *Pacific Defender*. The mix of dockside cranes, *Pacific Defender's* derricks and the solitary old yard lamp make for an interesting picture. During the mid 1980s Immingham docks would require up to four Class 08 shunters for working the transit sheds, mineral quay, reception sidings and pilot duties when required. The top picture features the *Antxon Mari* a general cargo boat berthed alongside what I believe to be the then bulk fertilizer berth whilst a container gantry crane can be observed further along the dock.

Grimsby Docks March 1985

This single picture taken at Grimsby Docks features the *GD Cave Sand* a twin grab dredger moored in the Royal Dock's long disused dry dock located alongside the docks main lock gates. She was built in 1968 for the British Transport Docks Board and was scrapped in 2004. The large building in the far distance to the left of *Cave Sand* is the 1890s Spillers flour mill which is now a listed building and is undergoing redevelopment into up market apartments. Well that's the plan. Unlike Immingham's large single dock Grimsby Docks consisted of commercial docks and an adjacent but separate fish dock. The first commercial dock opened in 1852 being the Royal dock followed by the Alexandra dock in 1880 while the first fish dock opened in 1857 expanded in 1878 and then again in 1934. The Royal and Alexandra docks handled bulk commodities such as coal, timber and steel and with these in decline through the 1960s the Alexandra dock opened its first car import/export terminal in the mid 1970s something which has expanded ever since. But the heart and soul of Grimsby had been its fishing fleet which once numbered some 700 trawlers. Grimsby was once a major fishing port but having suffered from political interference fishing had collapsed by the 1980s. Whilst the fishing fleet has diminished to a pale shadow of its former self the fish docks still survive although a marina now occupies a part of these docks.

Harwich Rail Ferry May 1985

Train ferries commenced during the Great War for military purposes, with the first commercial freight train ferry service being introduced from Harwich to the continent in 1924. With one notable break this service remained in operation till January 1987 when all train ferry traffic was transferred to Dover. The top picture features Class 31 No.31223 disembarking the *MV Cambridge Ferry* of its train load of cargo waggons over the ferry piers link span. This ferry pier and link span still remain today but now long disconnected from the national railway system. The *Cambridge Ferry* was built in 1963 and could carry up to 38 railway wagons. She worked a variety of ferry routes till withdrawn and sold in 1992 to a Maltese company. Renamed the *Ita Uno* she was eventually broken up in Turkey in 2003.

Harwich Parkeston Quay May 1985

Constant difficulties experienced by the GERly at Harwich caused the company to move its passenger & cargo shipping operations a few miles along the coast to Parkeston Quay. Here a long deep water quay was opened in the early 1880s. By the mid 1920s Parkeston Quay became famous for its luxurious boat trains and continental ferries but, unlike Dover, never operated 'on train' passenger ferries. By the 1970s the Parkeston Quay boat trains had become a pale shadow of their former selves and with the introduction of RO - RO services they ceased altogether in 1987. In the top picture we have the front end of Class 31 No.31426 set against the *MV St Nicholas*, the largest ferry boat working at that time whilst the lower picture features a eastern looking view of Parkeston Quay station with Class 47 No.47573 waiting with a Liverpool Street express while we get another glimpse of Class 31 No.31223 rumbling past with its train of ex-continental cargo waggons.

Tilbury Docks February 1985

A single picture of Tilbury docks taken one misty February day in 1985 showing much of the old order of docks. From the cargo boats to the dockside cranes and once numerous lighters all have now long gone. The general cargo boat nearest the camera is the Japanese built *Mergui*. Being located on the River Thames some twenty miles upstream of the London City docks Tilbury deep water docks opened in 1886 consisting of a main dock with three branch docks the East, Central & West leading off from it. By the 1960s London's town docks were in decline but Tilbury had been rapidly adapting to the containerisation of cargo shipping. A new extensive container dock opened in 1967 and by the late 1970s there was further expansion with an additional long riverside berths along the Thames. Tilbury today handles all manner of bulk cargoes and is the UKs third largest container port.

Avonmouth Docks May 1985

Bristol City and its docks were located some six miles inland from the Severn Estuary on the twisty River Avon. By the mid nineteenth century larger vessels were finding the Avon difficult to navigate and a new dock on the Severn Estuary by the mouth of the River Avon proved an ideal alternative. Avonmouth Dock opened in 1877 and following some initial trading difficulties a second dock, the Royal Edward opened in 1908. This dock was then extended in the 1920s with two dock 'arms'. These were known as the Western and Eastern arms although the Western arm would quickly concentrate on the oil trade and become known as the Oil Basin while the Eastern Arm would be further extended during the early 1940s. Containerisation came late to Avonmouth docks and by the 1980s cargo traffic was in general decline while the City Docks had closed in 1974. The docks were privatised in 1991 since when they have prospered and have now changed out of all recognition from my photographs taken over thirty years ago. Avonmouth Docks now handle all manner of bulk goods and as such I have done my best to work out my original photographic locations. The main picture features the Kings Road dock entrance with the local Bristol railway line crossing directly in front. Two large reinforced concrete buildings dominate the picture, the one just glimpsed to the extreme left of the picture is the No 1 CWS granary silos which by the time of my visit had recently closed and were demolished in 2013/14. The other large building, centre, which dwafts a row of single storey warehouses was No 3 granary a pair of massive reinforced concrete buildings which have also since been demolished. From the late 19th century through to the inter war years Avonmouth docks concentrated on the granary trade and several large reinforced concrete mills, silos and warehouses were built for the grinding, milling, and storage of grain. These processes would generate heat and combined with the fine dust in a closed atmosphere could become a fire risk hence the building's reinforced concrete construction. Three of these gigantic buildings still survive around the docks today as does the Kings Road dock entrance although only the passing railway and warehouses remain.

Avonmouth Docks May 1985

This page features the original 1877 Avonmouth Dock. Viewed towards the rear of the dock the top picture is dominated by the large Hosegoods granary with in the far distance the M5 motorway bridge crossing the River Avon. For reasons still unclear the now withdrawn *RMS Manx Maid* has found her way to Avonmouth Docks, she entered service in 1962 with the Isle of Man Steam Packet Service being their first side loading car ferry. With the introduction of RO - RO ferries she was withdrawn in September 1984 and was broken up, location unknown, in 1986. The lower picture is of the disused original Avonmouth Dock lock entrance. This lock was certainly in use following WW2 but when it went out of use is not known. Now relegated to a quiet corner at the top end of the dock it holds a barge and two lighters with the tug *Matthew* and a dredger alongside. The former dock entrance remains flooded to this day, but all the buildings both old and new have been demolished and the site cleared.

Avonmouth Docks May 1985

The bulk carrier *MV Ocean Wind* is berthed in the Royal Edward Dock in the top picture. An interesting shot with the dry dock lock gates in the foreground and a mix of dockside cranes with the *Ocean Winds* four derricks. In the far left hand side of the picture we have the Spillers and Hosegoods granaries of the nearby 1877 Avonmouth Dock. The lower picture was taken along the East Arm Dock and features a Morris Minor car and in the distance a docker assisting in the crane loading of a lorry from a platform mounted static railway wagon. Taken on the docks outer or Severn Estuary side several old static railway wagons can be seen and the absence of any dockside sheds.

Avonmouth Docks. May 1985

The following two pages also feature the Eastern Arm of the Royal Edward Dock. This dock was on the landside of the Western Arm or the Oil Basin and was characterised with transit sheds, warehouses and two huge granary buildings on its inner dock side only. The top picture was taken from the docks end looking across to the outer side of the dock. In the lower picture we have a closer view of the smallest of the three cargo boats, the diminutive *MV Jana*. Of interest in this lower picture is the landside or inner dock backdrop of substantial buildings including transit sheds, warehouses and the huge cathedral like No 3 reinforced concrete granary. In more recent times with the move to bulk cargos this traditional dockside backdrop has gone completely, indeed nothing now remains of the dockside infrastructure in this picture.

Avonmouth Docks May 1985

The second page covering the Eastern Arm of the Royal Edward Dock features the 1966-built suction dredger the *S D Severn* which is, top picture, moored along the Eastern Arms inner dock wall. Berthed along the opposite outer dock wall the tiny *MV Jana* is just about visible whilst of the other two larger cargo boats one sits high in the water obviously empty whilst the other lies at a awkward angle presumably being unloaded or loaded. Whilst the oil basin might be off camera a number of large circular oil/fuel storage tanks are apparent. A better view of the *S D Severn* can be seen in the lower picture and although she still works today, she dredges in Bahrain. Part of the dock's granary complex becomes clear in this picture with No 4 granary and its inter connecting conveyer belts and in the far right distance are both the Spillers No2 and Hosegoods granaries of the 1877 Avonmouth dock.

Avonmouth Docks May 1985

Three of Avonmouth Docks several imposing reinforced concrete granary buildings. A landside view of the Spillers No 2 granary showing the silos, top picture, built in the mid 1930s along with a large mill and warehouse. Built along the inner wall of the 1877 Avonmouth dock this huge granary complex closed in the late 1990s and whilst the derelict silos still stand the mill and warehouse, just out of view, were demolished shortly after. No 3 granary which dates to the 1920s features in the middle picture and comprised of two separate long reinforced concrete buildings and were located along the inner bank of the Royal Edward and East Arm docks. They have since been demolished, date unknown. The lower picture is of the disused 1950s No 5 granary located behind the East Arm Docks transit sheds and warehouses which feature to the right of the photograph. The photograph looks towards the Royal Edward dock, the warehouse nearest the camera dates to the 1940s when the East Arm was extended. Only the now derelict granary building survives all other buildings having been replaced with new structures.

Avonmouth Docks May 1985

Just two pictures of detail and debris that can be found around docks. The top picture shows two discharge hopper systems photographed, I think, near to the junction cut which connected the Royal Edward Dock to the 1877 Avonmouth Dock. In the lower picture we have a less than interesting collection of discarded parts thrown together and now of no possible use other than for spare parts. We seem to have a portable conveyer system, a pair of old trailers some conveyer belt rollers and a portable pump which at least seems to be pumping water. The backdrop holds more interest showing again the once extensive complex of granary buildings including to the left the pre Great War No 1 CWS granary mill. Whilst this building was demolished within a few years the CWS silos situated by the docks main entrance lasted till circa 2013.

Avonmouth Docks May 1985

Three photographs relating to the former internal dock railway system. At its height it held a large steam locomotive fleet which were replaced by diesels in the mid 1960s. The railway system closed in 1983. The top two pictures are internal user wagons which are, I think, of GWRly origin. Both wagons have been modified to hold a wooden platform with a metal safety rail and were used by dockworkers to assist in craning bulk loads directly from ships to lorries. Both pictures were taken looking across the East Arm Dock with the top picture being framed by the huge No 5 granary whilst the middle picture taken further up the East Arm features the back end of No 3 granary building. Along the dockside we have several electrically operated travelling intake plants each one fitted with two suction pipes for sucking up grain from a ship's hold. The tug *Pengarth* puts in an appearance in the middle picture, she dates to 1962 being sold on in 1991 and is believed to be still working down South Africa way. Although much still remained of the old railway system where possible track was being lifted and a stack of concrete railway sleepers form the subject in the lower picture. Whatever, all the buildings that form the backdrop to this picture have been demolished and the site cleared. Taking a modern day view of the docks using computer mapping, ghosts of the old docks railway system remain along the quays with stretches of track coming and going to nowhere.

Southampton Eastern Docks July 1995

Over time you must have come across one or two famous paintings or even photographs of Southern Bulleid Pacifics or Lord Nelsons with their train of Pullman cars standing proud along Southampton's Ocean dock with a Cunard 'Queen' towering in the background. Sometimes even the art deco frontage of the Ocean Terminal gets in on the scene. Well I couldn't quite manage all that but I do submit my photograph of our Class 47 again No.47780 poking out of Berth 41's warehouse, the Queen Elizabeth II terminal and the *QE2* itself. Southampton docks today takes in something of a headland or a spit between the River Itchen to the east and the River Test to the west. This wasn't the case back in 1841 when the first dock opened on what were mudflats to be followed ten years later by a second these being known as the Closed and Open docks. Access was from the River Itchen. With trade flourishing a massive land extension seaward along the River Itchen opened up several berths with a third the Empress Dock opening in 1890. Such was the prominence of this headland that berths were not only available along the River Itchen but also on its western, River Test, side. But even this was not sufficient with the White Star dock opening in 1911 running parallel to and taking in the berths along the west side of the docks. This dock was later renamed the Ocean dock and it was from this dock that for six decades the world's most famous ocean liners docked and sailed from, culminating in 1950 with the opening of the Ocean terminal with its art deco frontage. With the opening in 1932 of the New or Western Docks along the River Test the existing docks then became known as the Old or Eastern Docks. Over the years the commercial traffic through Southampton's Old or Eastern Docks has changed considerably along with a dramatic rise in cargo tonnages. The old Ocean Terminal and many of the transit sheds and warehouses have gone as the docks concentrated on bulk commodities catering for ever larger ships. At times the Eastern docks look more like a car park such is the volume of vehicles passing through the port. Of the docks and berths much remains as before, however the two original docks the 1841 Closed Dock has long been infilled whilst the 1851 Open dock is now known as the Princess Alexandra Dock and has become the Ocean Village marina.

Southampton Eastern Docks July 1995 & March 1985

Two pictures of ships that have survived. Berthed along the Queen Elizabeth II passenger/freight terminal during July 1995 is the *Queen Elizabeth II* herself. Clydebank built for Cunard she remained in service from 1969 to 2008 including taking in the 1982 Falklands War. Converted to diesel power during 1986/87 she worked more latterly as a cruise liner till sold by Cunard. She still remains laid up in Dubai waiting for conversion into a floating hotel. One ship that has made it as a hotel albeit on land is the *MV Doulos* pictured in March 1985 moored alongside the former Ocean Terminal berth. Built in 1914 as the *SS Medina* a steam powered cargo boat she served the US Navy in both wars before being sold on in 1948 and converted to a passenger ship. By 1977 she had been fitted with diesel engines and was sold again becoming the *MV Doulos* a missionary bookshop ship in which role she served till 2009. Escaping the scrapman she now lives on as a land-based hotel in Bantin, Indonesia.

Southampton Eastern Docks July 1995 & March 1985

Two interesting vessels photographed in Southampton's Eastern Dock's Empress Dock were, top picture, the cable laying *C S Nexus* in July 1995 and the *S.H.B. Seahorse* a salvage and buoy laying vessel as seen in March 1985. The *C.S. Nexus* was built in the Netherlands in 1972 as an offshore drilling vessel being named *Pelican*. Converted to a cable layer in 1995 she was sold for scrap in 2004. The *QE2* can be seen in the far background but of more interest are the two tugs the 1977 built *Sun Essex* (left) and the 1985 built *Brightwell*. Both are still working tugs, the *Sun Essex* in Belize whilst the more modern *Brightwell* sailed away to Lisboa, Portugal in 2010. The *S H B Seahorse* was built in 1958 for Southampton Harbour Board and worked in the docks until being sold in 2000, thirteen years later she was laid up in a derelict state at Maldon, Essex. The 1980s silos of the Ocean docks grain terminal can be seen to the left of the picture along with dockside buildings which have all since been replaced by the Ocean Cruise terminal which opened in 2009.

Southampton Eastern Docks April 1995

On a steam special back in April 1995 we had King Arthur Class No.30777 *Sir Lamiel* working from Waterloo down to Southamptons Eastern Docks, from there round to Portsmouth with S15 No. 30828 as Southern Railway No.828 then double headed back to Victoria. Long forgotten who organised the day but it was good fun. The crew of *Sir Lamiel*, top picture, take a break having just arrived at the Queen Elizabeth II terminal whilst, lower picture, No.828 waits to take us forward to Portsmouth. Somehow the magic of seeing a steam train in the Docks rubbed off prompting a return a few months later to photograph a boat train. Sadly it was diesel hauled but you can't have everything

Southampton Eastern Docks July 1995

Two pictures of our Class 47 No. 47780 with its boat train at Southampton Docks Queen Elizabeth II Terminal. The photographs are somewhat out of time with this book, the giveaway being the livery of our Class 47 in a somewhat uninspiring Rail Express Services livery. The train itself consisted of graceful period Pullman coaches whose passengers would be shortly embarking on the *QE2*. The Queen Elizabeth II terminal itself opened in 1966 designed for combined passenger/freight working, the passenger side of operations being restricted to the upper floor. The top picture features the footbridge which crosses over the railway giving access to the terminal's public gallery with the silos of the export grain terminal featuring in the left background. The lower picture has some atmosphere of a maritime railway station not least by the stylish port signal and radar station located adjacent to the Queen Elizabeth II terminal itself.

Southampton Eastern Docks July 1995

Continuing on our boat train theme whilst Class 47 No.47780 has bought the train in, another Class 47 No.47710 named *Lady Godiva* turned out in black 'Waterman' Railway livery has run in light engine to pull the empty Pullman stock out and onto Eastleigh carriage sidings for servicing and cleaning etc. The top picture gives us a good view of the Queen Elizabeth II terminal's railway facilities which do not seem to include to a run round loop. The access to the public gallery footbridge can be seen to the left of the railway tracks with the grain silo terminal, opened in 1983, dominating the background. After an hour or so No.47710 *Lady Godiva*, middle picture, has pulled off the terminal and pauses temporarily just outside Berth 41 transit shed. The terminal and grain silos can be seen in the far distance down Ocean Road which is from where No.47780, lower picture, stands light engine idling with Berth 41's transit shed in the background. Whilst the Queen Elizabeth II terminal remains today as do the grain silos, all other buildings including Berth 41 transit sheds have been demolished and the sites cleared. Both Class 47s have also long gone, No.47780 being withdrawn in August 2003 and No.47710 in December 1999, both locomotives lingering on till being scrapped in 2007. Interestingly No.47710 *Lady Godiva* carried three other names in eighteen years, perhaps someone somewhere had an eye to the future and the value of nameplates. The period in which the locomotives were photographed was interesting for at that time many companies were springing up attempting to lease or hire out refurbished locomotives to the private business sectors. No.47780 and its Pullman train would have been hired by the cruise company, the locomotive from RES. Whilst No.47710 *Lady Godiva* was on the day still in Watermans livery she had already been sold on to a company called Fragonset who in turn hired her out to the cruise company. An accountants dream, but no wonder I gave up trainspotting.

Southampton Western Docks July 1995

The L&SWRly bought out the dock company during the 1890s and following the 1923 grouping the Southern Railway undertook a huge expansion of Southampton Docks. To the west of the existing docks along the River Test lay a large bay of marshlands which were eventually reclaimed to become the New or Western Docks which opened in 1932. The largest building within the New Docks was the Hovis, later Solent, flour mills which opened in 1934. The top picture features the Southern Road dock entrance and the now preserved Solent flour mills building. The New dock consisted of a single deep water quay incorporating four large distinctive single storey transit sheds and at its western end a 1200ft. long dry or graving dock as seen in the lower picture. Known as the King George V dry dock it was at one time the largest in the world but ceased to be used from 2005 and is now permanently flooded in use as a working quay.

Southampton Western Docks January 1984 & July 1995

The Western Docks single long deep water quay incorporated four large brick built double ended art deco styled transit sheds numbered from 101 to 108. Once served by an intensive railway system track rationalisation occurred during the 1970/80s due the contraction of rail freight. By the 1990s much of former railway land had been turned over to commercial use including the then derelict carriage sheds, top picture, photographed in January 1984. With the Solent flour mill in the background the carriage sheds were demolished within months of this photograph being taken. With a move to bulk cargoes rail traffic still thrived as is evident in the lower picture taken in July 1995 of No.106 shed The Mayflower Cruise terminal. Whilst the trackwork is undergoing rationalisathion a car train can be seen alongside the terminal which, surprisingly, remains in original condition. In recent years the Mayflower Terminal has been considerably refurbished following the increase in cruising from Southampton Docks.

Southampton Western Docks July 1995

The Western Docks' four distinctive transit sheds remained mostly intact until the 1980s. By 2017 only Shed Nos.105/106 survived having become the Mayflower Cruise terminal. Sheds Nos.101/2 and 103/4 have long gone with new cargo terminals constructed during the 1990s on the sites of Sheds Nos.101 and 104. Likewise Shed Nos.107/8 were demolished during the 1990s with a new cargo terminal being built on the site of No.107 while the site of No.108 was turned over to bulk aggregates. The *MV Arklow River* features, top picture, berthed alongside Shed No.108 which itself had been considerably enlarged at some time. Meanwhile the lower picture is a landside view of the original joint side entrance to Sheds Nos.107/8 with to the left Shed 107 in the process of demolition. Southampton Docks expanded into container traffic from the 1960s onwards with quays being built to the west of the New Docks but these play no part in this book

Weymouth Quay branch. July 1979 & September 1981

The Weymouth Quay branch was opened by the GWRly in 1865 for goods traffic only with the London Paddington - Channel Islands boat trains commencing in 1889. These ran until 1959 when the service was transferred to Waterloo. Diesels replaced steam on the branch in 1964 and from 1972 onwards Class 33/1s monopolised the boat trains as a warning bell and flashing light could be attached to their 'buckeye' coupling plate. Class 33 No.33109, top picture, sees a Up boat train running past Westham crossing along Commercial Road in July 1979. The New Bridge pub is now an estate agent whilst the building opposite has long gone. Two years later during September 1981 the same locomotive with its boat train, including a Buffet Car at the front, appear in the lower picture running along Custom House Quay being photographed from the Town Bridge. Fishing boats predominate along the quay and whilst the Ship Inn remains it is now graced with a coat of seaside whitewash.

Weymouth Quay branch. August 1993

Through the inter-war years both passenger and cargo traffic increased rapidly resulting in the harbour pier being considerably lengthened during the early 1930s including a fuel oil berth and a second platform being added. Further improvements in the 1960s included the replacement of the Victorian station buildings and an additional track added to the second platform. However dwindling traffic levels throughout the 1970s saw the cessation of goods traffic in 1972 then closure of the pier's oil berth and removal of the second platform in the early 1980s. Total closure came in 1987 although some once weekly Bristol holiday specials ran in 1993 from July to September. One of these specials features on this page with Class 37 No.37425 having run round its train. In the lower picture the full length of the pier can be seen, the site of the former second platform used for additional car parking.

Weymouth Quay branch. April & August 1995

When the railway came to Weymouth it brought with it prosperity. Channel Packets delivering the mails and carrying passengers had been sailing to the Channel Islands from Weymouth since the late 18th century. Prior to that anyone wishing to travel had to make their own arrangements with the ship's owners or captains. Through the 19th century docking facilities remained primitive, boats unreliable, some sinking on the way, and sailing companies came and went. With the advent of the railways and their involvement matters dramatically improved and the harbour line remained extremely busy with both passengers and cargo traffic until the decline of rail transport following the Second World War.

With the increase in road traffic through the 1960s rail went into decline, at Weymouth the land end of the pier was widened during the 1970s for car parking and servicing the newly introduced RO - RO ferries. During 1987 the Condor company introduced the high speed catamaran service and in the top picture taken in April 1995 we glimpse the *Condor 11* berthed alongside the quay. Proving unsatisfactory she only worked for one season before being sold on. Whilst the harbour branch officially closed in 1987 occasional railtours still ran till 1999. The harbour station building remained in use by the ferry companies although by 1995 a wire gate, seen in the top picture, had been installed across the railway tracks near the platform end although this did not impede the occasional trains. The picture also shows the station area suffering further contraction with the severing of the platform and rail tracks with the insertion of a high metal barrier. The two lower pictures both taken in August 1995 feature the car ferry *MV Havelet*, this boat, I was reliably informed, was known locally as the 'Rustbucket'. Norwegian built in 1976 and named the *Cornougilles* she worked Brittany ferries out of Plymouth till sold to Condor Ferries for theWeymouth to Channel Islands service. Renamed the *Havelet* she worked the route for ten years from 1989. Sold on she became the *Sveti Stefan* and worked from Bari to Bar till broken up during 2013 in Turkey.

Those Magnificent Men in their Flying Machines . . .

RNAS Yeovilton, Somerset March 1982

Iris and I first visited the FAA museum at Yeovilton back in 1976. Then we had no children and the museum was little more than a hangar with some long retired aircraft dotted around outside. By March 1982 we had acquired three children and following a visit round the museum I went in search of something else. The Falklands conflict was fast approaching and both Royal Navy Sea Harriers and RAF GR3 Harriers were out and about practising on the RNAS airfield. Yeoviltons history goes back to the early days of WW2 becoming the home base for the Royal Navies Fleet Air Arm. Located in open countryside even by the 1980s little had changed and driving down one of many pretty country lanes I finally came across Yeovilton village and then a long lane which terminated at a large wooden gate with a equally large MOD 'No Entrance' sign attached. So from there we spent a happy hour or so watching Harriers take off, land and do their magical hovering tricks. And that's what's occurring in the picture above as a RAF Harrier GR3 is put through its paces providing a private air show for Mum, Dad and three children.

RNAS Yeovilton, Somerset March 1982

Two Harriers, one a RAF 1 Squadron GR3 the other a Royal Navy 800 Squadron Sea Harrier as photographed from our vantage point with a long focus lens. Both aircraft remain unknown however the Sea Harrier fuselage bears the markings '002'. The British Aerospace Harrier entered service with the RAF in 1969 and the Royal Navy in 1980 as the Sea Harrier. Two squadrons 800 and 801 were so equipped and during the Falklands conflict they operated from the aircraft carriers *HMS Hermes* and *HMS Invincible.* An additional squadron 809 was formed with 899 squadron having been set up for Sea Harrier aircrew training located at the 'home' base of Yeovilton. A total of 28 Sea Harriers and 10 RAF GR3's were involved in the Falklands the Sea Harriers role being primarily combat air patrol whilst the GR3 undertook ground attack although I believe the Sea Harriers were involved in both.

RNAS Yeovilton, Somerset

Three photographs of Yeovilton's Sea Harriers. Whilst the top and lower pictures were taken in March 1982 the middle picture dates to September 1981. The top picture was, I think, at or near the top end of a runway hence the bank of ground lights. The Sea Harrier shows no tail markings and has some connection to the mobile hut behind but for what purpose was unclear. And still is. The middle picture features four Sea Harriers carrying the tail fin markings of 899 training squadron, several of their Harriers being used operationally in the Falklands War. In the lower picture we have three Sea Harriers outside No 4 hangar. Of the three examples the Sea Harrier to the left belongs to 899 squadron, the middle example to 801 squadron whilst the third Sea Harrier remains unknown as she displays no tail markings. Of the two aircraft carriers and the Harriers involved in the Falklands War *HMS Hermes* was decommissioned in 1985 and *HMS Invincible* in 2005. Two years after the Falklands the Royal Navy's then latest aircraft carrier *HMS Ark Royal* was commissioned. The Sea Harriers were retired in 2006 being replaced by former RAF Harrier GR7 & 9's but these were in turn retired, somewhat prematurely, in 2010 with the decommissioning of the *Ark Royal*. RNAS Yeovilton remains an active base but other than a handful of fixed wing trainers now predominantly operates helicopters.

RNAS Yeovilton, Somerset   April 1982 & Setember 1984

Whilst better known for its Sea Harriers Yeovilton also operated fixed wing Hawker Hunters and English Electric Canberras. The Hunter entered RAF service as a fighter in 1954 being withdrawn in the early 1990s. The top picture taken in April 1982 features a line up of Hunter GA11s converted from RAF F4s for weapons training within the Royal Navy and served at Yeovilton from 1972 till 1995. The English Electric Canberra entered service with the RAF as a bomber in 1951 with the last examples being withdrawn during 2006 operating in the photo reconnaissance role. The Canberra entered Royal Navy service during the early 1970s in two training versions, the T4 and T22 and as a target tug, TT18. The training versions were withdrawn in the mid 1980s whilst the target tug version remained at Yeovilton till 1992. The lower picture dating to September 1984 shows three Canberras outside No 4 hangar they being, I think, from left to right a TT18, a T22, and another TT18.

RAF Waddington, Norfolk October 1982

Continuing on the theme of the Falklands War whilst Yeoviltons Sea Harriers still had years to run Waddingtons Avro Vulcan's were time spent. By the end of the Falklands in June 1982 the last remaining operational Vulcan squadrons were due to be disbanded. So come October 1982 Peter Askey and myself took ourselves on a wander up Lincolnshire way to have a gander. Paul Wells must have been wandering elsewhere. With RAF Waddington being the last base operating Vulcans we came across a dozen or so disposed off along the airfields northern perimeter fence. So we parked up along the A15 and went exploring. Despite Lincolnshire's heavy clay soil we struggled alongside a variety of assorted wire fencing to eventually take our photographs. If memory serves the Vulcans pictured above and on the next page were still just operational, 44 Rhodesia Squadron being disbanded two months later. Vulcan XM607 would alone remain at Waddington and still does as the Gate Guardian. However for us trudging back to the road became a nightmare as our shoes took on more clay reducing our progress to something more akin to a pair of deep sea divers. More worrying the police were waiting for us on our return. Explanations given our friendly officers drove off to enquire on our behalf if anything was flying that day. Sadly not, for on his return he explained that the Royal Air Force simply didn't fly at the weekends. Today RAF Waddington remains an active base operating in the fields of surveillance, reconnaissance and intelligence.

RAF Waddington, Norfolk, October 1982

Deliveries of the Avro Vulcan to the RAF commenced during the Cold War taking on a high level nuclear strike capacity. This would change over the years. Waddington became the first base to receive Vulcans with 83 Squadron in 1957. These moved out in 1960 being replaced by the Vulcans of 44, 50 & 101 Squadrons followed by 9 Squadron in 1975 which moved on again in early 1982. With the Falklands War in April 1982 Waddingtons Vulcans from all three Squadrons made seven raids on Port Stanley airfield and associated targets. Following the Falklands War 101 Squadron was disbanded in August 1982 followed by 44 Squadron four months later whilst 50 Squadron remained operational till March 1984 flying six hastily modified Vulcan bombers to air tanker configuration.

RAF Waddington, Norfolk, October 1982

An Avro Vulcan, top picture, photographed against a setting sun. Two close up views, lower right, of 44 Squadrons Avro Vulcans XM575 and XM594. Both would be struck off charge by year's end with the Squadron's disbandment. Whether any of the Vulcans that we saw that day ever flew operationally again I doubt as they all appeared to have been cast aside, however both XM575 & XM594 would fly out of Waddington into preservation during early 1983. The RAF was not quite done with the Avro Vulcan as the RAF Display Flight was formed in 1984 with XL426 and XH558 and whilst the former was retired in 1986 XH558 continued flying till the Display Flight was disbanded at the end of 1992.

RAF Scampton, Norfolk, October 1982

Scampton was to me the most famous of the WW2 RAF bomber bases being home to 617 Squadron, the Dam Busters. Fittingly Scampton's Gate Guardian was Lancaster NX611 and a friendly airman at the gatehouse allowed us to come on site to take our pictures. Avro Vulcans had arrived at Scampton with 83 squadron in 1960 followed in quick succession by 617 and 27 squadrons. Whilst 83 squadron was disbanded early in 1969 35 squadron arrived in January 1975 from Cyrus. By the 1980s time was up for the Vulcans with 617 squadron being disbanded in December 1981 to be followed two months later by 27 squadron. This left 35 squadron which on being disbanded in March 1982 brought Scampton's association with the Vulcan to an end. However seven months on we were still to find two of 35 squadrons Vulcans XL446 & XL359 dumped 'round the back' still waiting to be disposed of.

East Kirkby, Norfolk, September 2001

Avro Lancaster NX611 outside its hanger one evening in September 2001 when I and a chum went up to participate in a motorcycle sprint meeting at the former RAF airfield of East Kirkby. The Lancaster is owned by the Lincolnshire Heritage Centre which takes in a part of the former airfield cantered around the old watch, or control, tower. As regards the picture I'm attempting a bit of atmosphere something which I fancy would now be a lot easier with a digital camera. East Kirby opened in August 1943 as a bomber airfield operating Lancaster bombers till war's end when it fell out of use till the USAF arrived during the 1950s. On their departure in 1958 the airfield returned to 'care and maintenance' basis till 1964 when it was purchased by the Pantons, a local farming family. With the site put over to farming the Pantons also instigated the Heritage Centre which opened in 1988. The Lancaster itself was built too late for war service and went straight into storage till sold to the French Airforce in 1952 initially for marine patrol duties followed by air sea rescue. On retirement in 1964 she was donated to the Historic Aircraft Preservation Society undergoing overhaul in Sydney, Australia. Upon flying back to the UK in 1965 she had many adventures including being put up for auction. Purchased privately she was placed as Gate Guardian at RAF Scampton in 1974 and here she served till sold to the Panton's for display within the Heritage Centre. The RAF delivered NX611 to her new home in 1987

RAF Coningsby, Norfolk, July 1990

Opened in 1940 as a Bomber Command airfield Coningsby operated Hampdens, Avro Manchesters and Lancasters throughout WW2 to be followed post war with Lincolns, D/H Mosquitos and Boeing Washingtons. Jets arrived in 1953 with Canberras and then Vulcans during the middle 1960s. Becoming a fighter base in the 1970s McDonnell Douglas Phantoms arrived in 1974 with Panavia Tornados in 1983. The Phantoms departed five years later. The Battle of Britain Memorial Flight arrived from RAF Coltishall in 1976 its origins dating back to the Historic Flight formed in 1957 at Biggin Hill. Our Lancaster pictured above PA474 joined the Memorial Flight in 1973 and sits alongside two operational Tornados. Built too late for the war service she went into storage and stripped of her armaments was taken up by 83 squadron from 1948 to 1952 for photographic reconnaissance. Transferred to the Royal College of Aeronautics, Cranfield, she was employed on testing aerofoil wing sections till 1964 when transferred to the Air Historical Branch for eventual museum display. But the then Commanding Officer of 44 squadron at Waddington had other ideas thinking the Lancaster more suitable as their Gate Guardian. Flying in during 1965 a lengthy restoration began but within a few years she was, surprise, surprise, up in the air once more.

RAF Coningsby, Norfolk, July 1990

On the family's arrival at Coningsby we just caught two aeroplanes of the Memorial Flight, a Hawker Hurricane and a Supermarine Spitfire, top picture, preparing to take off for a display somewhere. The Hurricane was a Mk IIC PZ865 and was delivered to the RAF in July 1944. Being the last one delivered to the RAF Hawkers repurchased the Hurricane and retained it till donating her to the Flight in 1972. The Spitfire a Griffon engined Mk XIX PS853 was delivered to the RAF in January 1945 for unarmed photo reconnaissance duties. She saw active service with 16 squadron before being placed in storage in 1946. During the early 1950s she saw use doing meteorological research before becoming one of the original aeroplanes joining the Historic Flight in 1957. Sold on to Rolls Royce in 1995 she remains active on the display circuit. The lower picture features one of the two Memorial Flights De Havilland Chipmunks. Rarely seen at airshows etc they are used for, amongst other things, pilot conversion to aircraft with a tailwheel configuration something long gone from the modern day RAF.

RAF St. Mawgan, Cornwall & RAF Abingdon Air Tattoo.

A distant shot of 42 Squadron's Nimrods photographed in September 1979 up on the high ground of RAF St. Mawgan near Newquay. The Nimrods commenced replacing Shackletons in 1969 in the maritime patrol role taking on other duties in later years. 42 Squadron's Nimrods departed St. Mawgan for Kinloss in 1992 with the last Nimrod being withdrawn from RAF service in 2011. Opened during WW2 military flying ceased at St. Mawgan in 2008 to become Cornwall Airport.

Commencing with a 168 aircraft fly past, the September 1990 Abingdon Air Tattoo later witnessed a lone Avro Shackleton WL757 of 8 Squadron flying over during the following display. And that's all it did do. The Shackleton entered service with Coastal Command in 1951 as a maritime patrol aircraft till replaced in this role by the Nimrod. During 1973 a dozen Shackletons, including WL 757, were converted to the Airborne Early Warning role till retired in 1991. Sold on, WL757 still survives in a derelict state on the isand of Cyprus.

RNAS Culdrose, Cornwall, September 1979

Opened in 1947 RNAS Culdrose covered many roles including being the home base for Royal Navy carrier aircraft. Culdrose operated Fireflys, Sea Furys, Skyraiders and Gannets with jet Sea Vixens and Sea Hawks arriving during the 1960s. Helicopters made their first appearance in the late 1950s Culdrose becoming the Royal Navy's main training base with helicopters such as the Westland Wessex, Sea King and today's Merlin. The Sea King entered service in 1969 with two examples featuring on this page, the top picture being XZ587 a RAF search and rescue machine in characteristic all over yellow. The Sea King was phased out of RAF service during 2015 however XZ587 has been preserved and now lives on at RAF St. Mawgan. The lower picture features a Royal Navy Sea King in, I think, the airborne early warning role in which a few Sea King's still serve while their more distinctive gray and red search and rescue Sea Kings were withdrawn at the end of 2015.

Supermarine Spitfire Gate Guardians, West London May 1977

Being a West London lad we were accustomed to our Spitfire gate guardians at both RAF Northolt and RAF Uxbridge - top and lower pictures. Both establishments had an intimate association with the Battle of Britain itself. Spitfire LFXVIe TE476, top picture, sits outside the now demolished Northolt airports civilian entrance just off the main A40 road. Delivered in 1945 and following some use with anti-aircraft co-operation units she joined the historic flight in 1958 for two years. Taking up gate guardian duties in 1960 she resided at Northolt from 1970 to 1988 from where she was sold privately to a purchaser in the USA becoming airworthy in 1995. Likewise Spitfire LFXVIe RW382, lower picture, became an instructional airframe in 1954 taking up gate guardian duties in 1959. Residing at Uxbridge from 1973 to 1988 she was likewise sold privately to a purchaser in the USA. Restored to flying condition in 1991 RW382 sadly crashed in 1998 killing the pilot.

Airshows - No.1 Bombers, Lancaster to Vulcan,

The two pictures depict the first and last but one airshows that we went to. The Battle of Britain Memorial Flights Avro Lancaster flies low at Old Warden during a July 1977 Shuttleworth Collection airshow. The Lancaster joined the Memorial Flight in 1973 the mid upper turret being fitted two years later. My recollections of airshows during this period were that 1940s 'warbirds' were not so common unlike those of later years when more second world war aircraft were in the air than you could shake a stick at. Even dog fights were reinacted with vintage jets eventually putting in an appearance. The lower photograph is of the RAF's Vulcan Display Flights Avro Vulcan XH558 being taken at the Science Museums Wroughton airshow in September 1992 shortly before the Flight was disbanded. However XH558 was to fly another day...

Airshows - No.2 Old Adversaries

Supermarine Spitfire Mk Vc EE606 & Messerschmitt Bf 109G-2 Black 6. Both photographed at Duxford the Spitfire in June 1989 and the Messerschmitt in early 1993.The Spitfire was a new machine incorporating parts recovered from the original 1942 build EE606 which on being shipped out to Australia suffered two landing accidents before being placed into storage and disposed of in 1946. The new build EE606 first flew in 1988 but crashed the following year due to engine failure sadly killing the pilot. The Messerschmitt 109 was delivered to the Luftwaffe in 1942 taking part in the North African campaign. Suffering combat damage she eventually fell into Allied hands finally arriving in the UK during late 1943 for professional flight evaluation. Placed into store in 1946 she was displayed on a few occasions till finally restored to flying condition in 1991. Following a crash landing at Duxford during 1997 she now remains as a static museum exhibit.

Southend Historic Aircraft Museum, Essex July 1977

The SHAM museum opened to the public in 1972 and closed some eleven years later. Its origins centred around a collection of historic aircraft that had been gathering at the nearby Southend airport since the mid 1960s. The top picture features a 1951 build Spanish Air Force CASA 2111, a German Heinkel 111 in all but name and Rolls Royce engines. Purchased following the 1967 film 'Battle of Britain' the SHAM acquired her in 1972 and on closure she was dismantled and placed into storage at North Weald. Restored c1990s she now resides at Duxford waiting possible sale to the USA. Delivered to the RAF in late 1945 Avro Lincoln B2 RF342 went straight into storage before spending many years as a flying test bed for Napiers Ltd having acquired a Lancaster front end. Eventually flying into Southend during 1967 she was dismantled on the museum's closure spending many years stored at numerous locations before moving on to Australia in 2006 for complete restoration and eventual display.

Blackbushe, Hampshire July 1978

Opened as RAF Blackbushe in 1942 undertaking reconnaissance and strike roles operating Spitfires and Mosquitos amongst other types. Closed in 1946 but reopened the following year as an airport it became a major centre for cargo movements till closed again in 1960. Now reduced in size Blackbushe reopened again in 1962 as a private general aviation field. Through the late 1970s/early 1980s Blackbushe became a holding point for former Spanish Air Force and WW2 warbirds passing through to the USA and elsewhere. Both the above photographs were taken during July 1978 of several ex Spanish Air Force Douglas C-47's (DC-3) and Spanish built CASA 352's (Junkers Ju 52). At least eight C-47s and four CASA 352s passed through Blackbushe and whilst many of the former were sold on for further commercial use the CASA 352's escaped into preservation.

Blackbushe, Hampshire July 1977 & August 1984

Two former bomber types photographed at Blackbushe, a CASA 2-111 Spanish built Rolls Royce engined Heinkel He 111 photographed during July 1977 and a Boeing Flying Fortress B-17G seen there in August 1984. I was lucky enough to photograph the CASA from the control tower. She arrived a year earlier and was eventually sold to an American buyer but was sadly destroyed in a fatal flying crash during July 2003. It is believed the Flying Fortress saw no war service being sold in 1947 to the French Institute Geographic which operated her till 1977. Sold to a UK buyer she resided at Blackbushe from 1984 to 1986 before being sold on to an American buyer in 1987 refurbished and remains on the US airshow circus to this day.

Heathrow Airport October 1977 & June 1981

Heathrow, formerly London Airport, opened in 1946. A small grass airfield in the 1930s the site was developed during the latter part of WW2 for military transport. It was once possible to take a short cut through the airport's maintenance area, strictly speaking a private road for airport staff but back in those care free days of yesteryear nobody bothered with such things. Back in the 1980s I remember witnessing the last of London Airport's original hangars being demolished. The two photographs were taken from within the maintenance area, the top picture taken in October 1977 featuring De Havilland Comet G-APDT in use for apprentice training. She fulfilled this role for ten years from 1970 till being moved on as a fire practise training airframe. She was scrapped c1990. The lower picture taken in 1981 features an H S Trident 2 in the process of being broken up. Entering service with BEA in 1964 the Trident eventually fell foul of 1980s noise regulations and the final variation, Trident 3, were all withdrawn in 1986.

Mostly Scrap

North American B-25 Mitchell

For the 1979 film 'Hanover Street' five B-25 Mitchells were acquired and flown over from the USA. The frontispiece picture shows all five Mitchells in 1978 at Blackbushe airfield shortly after their arrival. Suitably repainted filming took place at former RAF Bovingdon and on completion they were sold on. For the film our Mitchell became Gorgeous George-Ann and by September 1984 was in a perilous state in open store back at Blackbushe. She remained in store around the UK for many years till finally securing a permanent home in Belgium.

Armstrong Whitworth Argosy

The Argosy served as a cargo/transport aircraft with the RAF from 1962 to 1978 when our particular Argosy XR137 found its way to RAF Northolt fire section and was photographed there in August 1980. She perished there in 1987 but not before starring in the James Bond film 'Octopussy'.

Hawker Hunter F2

Reduced to a fuselage this Hunter resides at the Ascot, Berkshire yard of Staravia in February 1982. This Hunter could possibly be WN907 supplied to the RAF in 1954 or possibly a former Danish Air Force example. If WN907 she had an undistinguished RAF career being sold to Starvia in 1976. The yard itself was believed to have commenced breaking up military aircraft some time after WW2 and closed during the late 1980s.

Canberra TT18

Former Canberra B2 WJ635 looks to be in a desperate situation dumped at the rear of RAF St. Mawgan. Delivered to the RAF in 1954 as a bomber she was by the 1970s converted for target tug duties and was struck off charge in 1975 then finding herself on the St. Mawgan fire dump and photographed there in September 1979. The nose section moved on to Chivenor fire dump in 1981 and scrapped there by 1989. St. Mawgan's association with Canberras lasted from 1970 to 1982 operating former B2's as TT18's on target tugs duties.

Rusty Cars and Dodgy MOTs. Moments of humour

Dad's Ford Prefect, 1963

Peter's £5 Ford Popular, 1965

The RT Hon. Lord Wells poses in the 1931 Morgan Aero with his trusted mechanic Durrant.1966

Dad and his Vauxhall PA Velox, 1967

My first vehicle was an elderly blue Austin A55 half ton van in which to cart my motorbike to race meetings. This was 1966 and its presence immediately caused a problem as it joined dad's and elder brother's cars down our drive. On reflection dad was a man before his time restoring an elderly side valve four door Ford Prefect long before anyone thought that such mass produced cars warranted such treatment. Meanwhile elder brother Reg had a proper car, a 2.6 litre Austin A105 Westminster equipped with thick leather seats, twin carburettors and an impressive turn of speed. We were now a three car family and as the 1960s slipped by we were to be not alone in this. A decade earlier would have found only three cars down the whole road. Considering dad always thought that cars should have a chassis with body attached, his next car came as something of a surprise buying a late 1950s 'pressed tin' Vauxhall PA Velox. American styled rust with a six cylinder 2.2 litre engine and fitted out with bench seats and three speed column gearchange, a car that also did wonders for my love life. Until the night I missed a set of traffic lights with disastrous results. Hospital job for Iris.

As the 1960s gathered pace all us young lads abandoned the motor bike for the car. Peter Askey acquired a 'sit up and beg' side valve two door Ford Popular for a five pound note which one evening whilst heading home suffered a seized rear differential. His dad eventually came to the rescue with some work mates but having failed to locate a diff from any of the local scrap yards arrived with a rear axle assembly complete with wheels. This was promptly fitted on the busy road side, the old one being temporarily dumped into some bushes. On Peter's return the next day to sort out the old axle assembly he beat a hasty retreat as the wretched thing had seemingly rolled down out of the bushes and was now residing on one of the local golf club greens surrounded by a crowd of rather angry golfers. With tyres down to the canvas the old Pop eventually succumbed to a 1.5 litre twin carb Riley sports saloon. On driving it home his father immediately pointed out that the front and back number plates didn't quite match up. This was something we had all failed to notice at the dealers and led to the discovery that Peter's Riley was in fact two different Rileys welded together in the middle.

Paul Wells like me would 'borrow' his dad's car on occasions which led to dire results one night by ramming another car then departing the scene at a rapid rate of knots. Despite the growing of a Fu Manchu moustache this disguise was not to fool anyone especially when a pair of detectives came knocking at the front door, so once again Paul found himself banned. To curtail any possible illegal excursions his father cut the car up in the front garden. His dad could be a bit extreme at times.

With Paul eventually back on the road the excitements continued. Now driving an Austin Minivan along with myself he unknowingly? managed an excursion across a snow bound housing estate's open front gardens before finishing up in a snow-filled ditch. Some months later with Iris in the passenger seat and myself in the back he managed to drift the poor thing into a high kerb whilst attempting the racing line round a fast bend. For ever more its rear wheels never followed the same track as the front so it went on its way.

Mention must be made of the fate of our 1600cc Ford Corsair GT* that we then sold to Paul. A car with performance. This would be 1976. No doubt its performance was a factor in the car then being nicked as 'the wheels' for a bank job but it later met its fate when Paul sank the car in one of Greenford's many winter floods. I think after that the engine gave up in disgust. Deem's young driving days were also what you could call eventful. He also fell for the charms of big rusty six cylinder two litre plus jobs. On one cold frosty night travelling in his Vauxhall PA Cresta we picked up a couple of girl hitch hikers wanting a lift into London. Sadly they didn't get as far as Uxbridge as Deem managed to complete a few 360 degree spins coming out of a roundabout landing up like Paul deep in a ditch but unlike Paul inflicting grievous damage to the off side front wing. The ladies never even said goodbye. Short of the necessaries Deem struggled on with the battered PA but more indignities were to be heaped upon it whilst racing another car down the A40 Western Avenue one night. The bonnet catch failed, the bonnet then rolling back like an opened sardine can lid. Deem it has to be said was good in a crisis and with our heads hanging out of the near side windows he got us safely stopped by the kerb. Our fellow competitor in all this fun pulled up behind us full of enthusiasm for our little escapade and somehow failing to take in the bonnet's demise wanted to know if we might be back the following weekend. Eventually the law requested that he took the wreck off the road. The replacement Ford Zephyr Mk2 then kindly threw a con rod through its crankcase in the early hours of one morning resulting in a long walk home. Deem decided a second hand engine was just the ticket so purchased one from the local scrappy, these being the days when you stripped scrap cars yourself. The exercise was performed in the road outside the parental home. A hoist was acquired, the bonnet off and all hands to the job. It would have gone off well save someone forgot to drain out the old engine oil which resulted a miniature *Torrey Canyon* like oil spill once the engine tipped over as it parted company from the chassis. That wouldn't have been so bad save we trod the mucky black slick all over the pavement. The sand didn't improve matters either spreading the oil even further. His mum and dad never lived it down with the resulting mess taking many months to weather away.

Shortly after this excitement the near side front wing took a hit so that old wreck went for our elderly 2.0 litre Vauxhall Velox a big black battleship of a car. Despite being a four cylinder job she had the speed of its later day six cylinder PA models. Other than the rear wheel falling off up Ruislip way it lead a charmed life.

Another battleship was 'Ginger' Baker's American job, a convertible. A Packard or a Pontiac. We went parading around West London in this monster before the parading of cars had been invented. It didn't last as with a petrol consumption of about five miles to the gallon he needed six of us to keep it running. Good fun though. By comparison John Durrant's early motoring days were relatively quiet but he did take to an interesting pre-war open top

Peter & John, Triumph Herald 1968

Deem's Troubled Vauxhall Cresta with author on the roof. 1969

'Get me to the church on time'. Deem with his Ford Zephyr about to pick up the author on his wedding day - well he could have cleaned it!, 1970

'The Battleship' Vauxhall Velox, 1970

More rust than van, Austin A55 half-tonner, 1970

sports Morgan three wheeler paying seventy quid for it. Today they sell for £30,000 plus. Powered by a 998cc V twin ohv JAP engine she had white bodywork with a red stripe so it looked the part. John fell in love with this temperamental old beauty but eventually she went as a non-runner for a more reliable but mundane Italian styled Triumph Herald. Selling the Herald for a red Ford Cortina Mk 1 GT had its moments when the new owner quickly returned threatening legal action having found the box chassis to consist more of rust than actual metal. It has to be said that fibre glass, filler and chicken wire were much in demand back in the 1960s. Peter Askey had meanwhile acquired a two litre Triumph Vitesse convertible and took us all down to Brighton one day failing to notice a little red light winking at him. It was to be a painfully long drive home on sidelights. On another occasion the Vitesse became a true convertible when one rainy day the fabric hood parted company from its fixings flapping away behind us like a bloody great flag.

Whilst John acquired a small racing steering wheel and matching string gloves for the Cortina GT it couldn't hold Peter's next car a Volvo P1800S down the Western Avenue. Our smoking Ford Zephers and Vauxhall Crestas were left in their wake. The Volvo's only problem was reliability, it didn't have any. Simon Templar 'The Saint' never seemed to have this problem on the TV programmes so despite its attractive looks and stylish design it got the chop. Meanwhile my old blue Austin van had long gone when it decided to lose all its brake fluid in one long desperate pump on the brakes. So it went its way for a white Bedford van* purchased by Iris, my new girl friend. This was a van which later met its own sad end.

As the 1970s dawned Iris and Teddy got married so especially for the occasion we purchased that old battleship of a Vauxhall Velox which went its way to 'Deem', later replacing it with another half ton Austin van*. This was a van you could see the road pass beneath your feet and passenger seats fitted with now worn spring clips which on acceleration could tip your passengers into the back. Fun that. This then went for a three speed Ford Thames van* fitted with column gear change. With the engine set in between the front seats its cowling served as a third seat and much chosen in cold weather as the passenger could sit on it thus warming up their bum. Heaters were extras in those days.

Finally retiring from the bike racing in 1975 the Thames van went for that 1965 Corsair GT* only to be sold to Paul as a 'hand me down' large white 1968 two litre Vauxhall Victor 2000* came via brother Reg. Following Vauxhall's tradition the front wings were already rusting away. It was in this car the following year that I took Iris to hospital to have child number one. That was 1977. Over the preceding ten years we'd owned nine vehicles varying from a few months to a few years and sometimes several at the same time. We had even owned two little Morris's for a while, a little black split screen Minor saloon and a former Post Office van. As we drifted into the 1980s John went the way of company cars, Peter continued his taste for exotic sports models, Paul remained faithful to the 'Dagenham Dustbins'* and we settled for a lifetime of family cars. As for Deem he was last seen driving a rather large red London Bus down Greenford Broadway. The bugger cut me up.

* Vehicle as mentioned pictured in the book.

Peter takes two birds for a spin, 1970

The Honeymoon car.
Peter and Pat Volvo P1800S, 1971

Paul's Minivan, 1971

Ford Thames, Cornwall, 1973

Morris 1800, 1981.
Boring but practical!

The British Bath Works April 1976

An apprenticeship for redundancy

On winding this book up the last few pictures were taken in April 1976 and are devoted to my old apprentice stamping grounds at the former Allied Ironfounders, British Bath Works plant in Greenford, West London. Redundancy came to the 500 odd employees in April 1975 when the factory closed. It took about four years to clear the site but for those who had worked a lifetime there I doubt it ever closed. For me I thought I had a job for life, we used to think like that in those days. The top picture takes in the foundry and in the far distance the bath enamelling plant, note the large Great Western styled water tank. The rail connection to the former GWR Birmingham main line is behind me, the tracks leading to the Bath Works have been cut whilst the short industrial branch to the left was lifted a few years previously. Whilst the majority of the foundry buildings are still standing the melting plant area, lower picture, has been demolished leaving just the old cupola control room from where a young Teddy spent much of his time hiding away reading the weekly motorcycle magazines.

This last picture looks across the former melting plant area which held two modern water cooled twelve tons per hour hot blast cupolas. They were installed in the late 1950s along with the 'Herman' a gigantic high capacity fully automatic bath moulding plant. Suburbia never got over it, the vibrations from which were enough to waken the dead let alone the living. The picture takes in the foundry laboratory block with the rusting remains of the large covered shed which housed the two overhead gantry cranes. One year on from closure the seventy foot high gantry along with the cupolas which once had a vociferous appetite for metal scrap have been scrapped themselves Today (2018) nothing remains of the Bath Works modern industrial units occupying the site.

THE END